DEBATING THE OBAMA PRESIDENCY

Edited by Steven E. Schier

ROWMAN & LITTLEFIELD
Lanham • Boulder • New York • London

Published by Rowman & Littlefield
A wholly owned subsidiary of The Rowman & Littlefield Publishing Group, Inc.
4501 Forbes Boulevard, Suite 200, Lanham, Maryland 20706
www.rowman.com

Unit A, Whitacre Mews, 26-34 Stannary Street, London SE11 4AB

British Library Cataloguing in Publication Information Available

Library of Congress Cataloging-in-Publication Data

Names: Schier, Steven E.
Title: Debating the Obama presidency / Steven E. Schier.
Description: Lanham, MD : Rowman & Littlefield, 2016. | Includes bibliographical references and index.
ISBN 9781442261242 (cloth : alkaline paper) | ISBN 9781442261518 (paper : alkaline paper) | 9781442261259 (electronic)
Subjects: LCSH: Schier, Steven E., 1952-

∞ ™ The paper used in this publication meets the minimum requirements of American National Standard for Information Sciences Permanence of Paper for Printed Library Materials, ANSI/NISO Z39.48-1992.

Printed in the United States of America

DEBATING THE OBAMA PRESIDENCY

CONTENTS

INTRODUCTION

A Controversial Presidency

Steven E. Schier, Carleton College

Many presidents initially enter office with grand ambitions, but no recent president has matched the scale of Barack Obama's transformative plans. Domestically, they included a government restructuring of a health-care system comprising one-sixth of the nation's economy, the largest public investment program for economic stimulus in America's history, a new focus on climate change as the major national security threat of our time, a thorough reshaping of governmental regulation of the financial sector, comprehensive immigration reform, and both revoking the Don't Ask, Don't Tell policy for gays in the military and, eventually, legalizing gay marriage. In foreign policy, Obama promised to "reset" America's relations with many nations and regions of the world. He favored greater accommodation with Russia and Europe, a "pivot" of diplomatic focus to Asia, new overtures of friendship with the Muslim world, a stronger focus on nuclear proliferation, and reduction of America's military involvement in Iraq and Afghanistan.

Obama's ambitions inevitably made him a highly polarizing figure for Americans, just as his predecessor George W. Bush, also a person of grand ambitions, had been. Like Bush, Obama led by acting as a national "clarifier" of differences between him and his partisan opponents. John F. Harris's description of Bush's leadership style fits Obama rather well: "Rather than blurring lines, illuminate and even exaggerate them. Rather than try to reassure opponents, antagonize them—at least on issues in which he believed he could excite his own supporters in even greater measure" (Harris 2009, 67–68). Obama's approach yielded sharply differing evaluations of his presidency, as are contained in this volume.

A DIRECTIVE PRESIDENCY

This "clarifying" style is a characteristic of a "directive" presidency, defined by political scientists George C. Edwards III and Stephen Wayne: "The president is the director of change, who creates opportunities to move in new directions and leads others where they otherwise would not go. In this view, the president is out front, establishing goals and encouraging others inside and outside of government to follow. Accordingly, the president is the moving force of the system and the initiator of change" (Edwards and Wayne 2009, 19). This approach, again similar to that of his immediate predecessor, held the possibility of big changes, which Barack Obama ardently pursued in the White House, but also entailed large political risks.

A safer course, according to Edwards and Wayne, is for a president to act as a "facilitator" who builds coalitions, "exploiting opportunities to help others go where they want to go anyway or at least do not object to going" (2009, 20). Bill Clinton, who hugged the political center during much of his presidency and worked productively with Republican Congresses, was the archetypical facilitator, willing to settle for limited policy changes. A facilitator settles for narrower influence, but Obama, given his large Democratic majorities in Congress in 2009, had bigger goals in mind.

No "small ball" for Obama. Obama sought a political "reconstruction" that would create a lasting Democratic regime in the same fashion that Ronald Reagan revived GOP fortunes in the 1980s. That accomplishment proved unattainable. Though Obama won a close reelection contest over Republican Mitt Romney in 2012, GOP successes in congressional and state elections in 2014 reduced Democratic officeholders in states and the US House to their lowest numbers since the 1920s. Obama's transformative successes were limited largely to his first two years in office.

What led Obama to pursue a directive, clarifying presidency? The sweeping Democratic electoral victories in 2008 no doubt emboldened him, but certain personal qualities also fueled his big ambitions. Obama's public career consistently involved advocacy of strongly liberal principles, an approach that he carried with him into the White House. By 2010 the American public identified him as on the left of the political spectrum. One survey by the Democracy Corps, a Democratic polling firm, found that 55 percent of registered voters thought the term "socialist" accurately described his ideological orientation (Greenberg Quinlan Rosner 2010). In 2012 YouGov surveys throughout the year revealed that respondents viewed Obama as a liberal. By the end of his reelection campaign, respondents rated him on a scale of 0 (very liberal) to 100 (very conservative) at 21. Respondents on average rated themselves at 55 or slightly right of center. In November 2012, 52 percent placed themselves closer to GOP nominee Romney ideologically while only 38 percent saw themselves as closer to Obama. The president's 2012 reelection victory resulted from voters weighing other considerations—the president's record, character, and positions on particular salient issues—more heavily than their ideological distance from him (Sides and Vavreck 2013, 203–5).

Given his confident possession of liberal ideological convictions, a directive, clarifying leadership in their pursuit characterized his presidency. Obama's academic background had given him a critical, analytic temperament, contributing to a policy-making style in which he worked from his ideological principles to specific policy proposals. Obama's management style also encouraged dogged pursuit of his principle-based priorities. His approach contrasted with that of Democratic predecessor Bill Clinton, whose more "horizontal" thinking contemplated a wide range of principles and alternatives and whose White House organization at times suffered from consequent disorganization. Barack Obama would have none of that. Early on in his presidency, he opted for a hierarchical White House organization with a strong chief of staff, a format usually favored by GOP presidents, including his predecessor George W. Bush. This style of organization facilitated the persistent pursuit of the president's goals.

BIG CHANGES

Working with a kindred congressional leadership and large Democratic majorities in Congress in 2009 and 2010, Obama's directive, clarifying leadership racked up a remarkable number of policy accomplishments during the early months of his presidency. That momentum stalled with GOP electoral successes in 2010 that delivered the US House into Republican hands for the remainder of his time in the White House. Despite this, Obama did follow through on much of his agenda. PolitiFact, the award-winning research site of the *Saint Petersburg Times*, charted Obama's success with campaign promises. During his presidency's first seven years, the president had kept 45 percent of them, compromising on 20 percent, breaking 22 percent, with 7 percent "in the works" (PolitiFact 2015). Among those promises kept were major changes in public policy enacted in 2009 and 2010: the first comprehensive health-care reform since 1965, the largest public investment program ever, sweeping reform of financial regulation, a new federal "hate crimes" law, and a nuclear arms reduction pact with Russia.

Three early landmark laws, discussed and debated by several authors in this volume, were the health-care reform, the economic stimulus, and the Dodd-Frank financial reform. The stimulus became law first. On February 17, 2009, in his first month in office, Obama signed the American Recovery and Reinvestment Act of 2009, a $787 billion assemblage of spending increases and tax cuts designed to boost economic growth. Approximately 90 percent of its cost involved spending hikes in a wide variety of programs. Most notable among these were grants to state governments for their budget needs, temporary increases in Medicaid, emergency energy assistance and food-stamp spending for low-income Americans, extension of unemployment insurance, and highway and school construction (*Washington Post* 2009). The economy remained sluggish throughout 2009 and 2010, however, with unemployment rising from 7.7 percent in January 2009 to well above 9 percent by early 2011. Furious debate erupted about the effectiveness of the 2009 stimulus legislation (Biden 2009, Levy 2010). That debate continues in this volume, principally in the dueling chapters by Daniel Ponder and Raymond Tatalovich. The economy gradually recovered in succeeding years, and annual federal budget deficits shrank considerably from their peak earlier in Obama's first term. Unemployment also fell to 5 percent by 2015. Many by then had dropped out of the labor force, however, producing the lowest labor force participation rate since 1977. The debate over the "recovery" rages on throughout the ensuing chapters by Tatalovich, Ponder, John Kenneth White, John J. Pitney, Andrew E. Busch, and Ruth O'Brien.

On July 21, 2009, Obama signed the Dodd-Frank Wall Street Reform and Consumer Protection Act, producing the biggest changes in financial regulation since the Great Depression of the 1930s. The goal of the controversial legislation was to prevent the speculative behavior that led to the financial crisis of 2008. The law created several new agencies, including the Financial Stability Oversight Council, Office of Financial Research, and Consumer Financial Protection Bureau. It included 243 new financial rules and mandated sixty-seven studies and twenty-two periodic reports (Restoring American Financial Stability Act 2010). Supporters of the legislation argue it promotes needed financial stability and consumer protection, but opponents argue the blizzard of new regulations and bureaucracies does little to achieve that goal. The Ponder and Tatalovich chapters debate this issue in depth.

On March 23, 2010, Obama signed into law the Patient Protection and Affordable Care Act and later that month signed companion legislation, the Health Care and Education Reconciliation Act. Together they comprised the most sweeping change in health policy since the passage of Medicare in 1965. The legislation took effect over a four-year period. It prohibited private insurers from denying coverage due to preexisting conditions, subsidized insurance premiums, supported medical research, and expanded eligibility for federal health care for low-income individuals through the Medicaid program. It also established health insurance exchanges to facilitate more choice among insurance plans by consumers. The large cost of the program was offset by taxes on certain medical devices and a $500 billion cut in the Medicare advantage, an optional program for higher-income seniors (Grier 2010). Ruth O'Brien in this volume argues that one of the law's great accomplishments is its expansion of health insurance coverage to millions of the previously uninsured. Opponents, such as Andrew Busch in his chapter here, believe the cost of the reform will eventually bust the federal budget.

The stimulus, financial reform, and health-care laws were the product of a successful "elite governing strategy" employed by the president in the administration's first two years. Obama's rationalistic governing style encouraged him to pursue his policy principles with fellow partisan power-holders, without much consideration for the popular politics of his actions (Alter 2010, 330). John K. White notes in his chapter how Obama's initial approach relied on his congressional party as a resource for presidential leadership. Major domestic initiatives involved working with a heavily Democratic Congress to build partisan coalitions to pass the president's program. Obama cut many particular deals to ensure passage of major legislation with long-lasting impact. Given the controversial and sweeping nature of Obama's main proposals, elite coalition building proved difficult, particularly regarding the health-care reform. Obama could usually rely on the House to take the initiative and help encourage the balkier Senate to pass similar legislation.

This approach resembled that of the George W. Bush administration when it worked with a GOP-majority Congress from 2001 through 2006 (Schier 2008). For the remainder of his presidency, however, Obama encountered great frustration in governing with the arrival of a Republican-controlled House in 2010 and a GOP Congress in 2014. The great policy differences between Hill Republicans and the White House lead to a multiyear path of fiscal brinksmanship from 2011 to the final months of his presidency. Republicans in Congress repeatedly balked at raising the US government's debt limit and funding the government, and in 2013 they precipitated a brief shutdown of the government over budget disputes. The GOP House repeatedly demanded repeal of the Affordable Care Act and at times sought changes in immigration policy and the defunding of the abortion provider Planned Parenthood in return for passing necessary spending bills. The blame for these frequent shutdown battles receives divergent interpretations in this book's chapters.

The president was unable to extricate himself from the "rutted paths" of several long-lasting policy controversies. On "culture war" issues such as abortion, gay rights, and the role of religion in public life, Obama held to culturally liberal positions. Obama's successful 2010 repeal of the Don't Ask, Don't Tell policy concerning gays in the military and 2012 policy switch to support a constitutional right to gay marriage received strong criticism from cultural conservatives. A similar split persisted regarding his federal court nominees. Liberals complained that his choices for the federal bench were not sufficiently activist while conservatives derided their approach to constitutional interpretation. The culture and judicial wars showed no sign of receding.

Internationally, Obama engaged in negotiations with foreign leaders and delivered speeches—notably to the Muslim world in Cairo in 2009—in order to redirect American foreign policy. Obama's international outreach resulted in a warming of international opinion toward the United States and his receipt of the Nobel Peace Prize after only six months in office. He notably forged several diplomatic agreements with Russia, including the congressionally approved 2010 Strategic Arms Reduction Treaty, in order to "reset" relations with that nation. Obama pursued a time-limited military "surge" in Afghanistan while removing all US troops from Iraq by 2012. The administration claimed a major victory against terrorists with the assassination of Osama bin Laden in May 2011.

The president's emphasis on the threat of climate change made it a prominent focus of his foreign policy, with the president often terming it the nation's top national security problem. The administration was a major player in international climate negotiations in Copenhagen in 2009 and Paris in 2015. The 2015 Paris climate change accords committed 196 nations to pursue national policies to limit emission of greenhouse gases, albeit voluntarily. The president hailed the accord as "a turning point for the world" (Warrick and Mooney 2015). Time will tell if that is the case.

Foreign policy controversies and difficulties mounted during Obama's second term. Instability in the Middle East consumed much of the president's attention. The administration's military support for the overthrow of the Muammar Gaddfi dictatorship in Libya produced internal chaos and the rise of Islamic extremism in the country. The turmoil in Libya cost the lives of several Americans in Benghazi—including that of the US Ambassador J. Christopher Stevens—in the midst of the 2012 election campaign. The administration initially claimed the attack on the American compound there was a spontaneous response to an anti-Muslim video originating in the United States, but after the election admitted it was an organized terrorist attack.

The president's varying responses to the onset of civil war in Syria produced problems for the administration during Obama's second term. When dictator Bashar al-Assad resorted to chemical weapons, the president reversed course and failed to act when his previously labeled "red line" prohibiting such weapons use was crossed. He then asked Congress for a vote of support under the War Powers Resolution for military action against Assad. It was not forthcoming from Congress.

Out of the chaos arose a major new threat known as ISIS, the Islamic State of Iraq and Syria, a radical Muslim entity operating in areas outside of the control of the Syrian or Iraqi governments. Though the president initially downplayed them as a "jayvee [junior varsity] team," in late 2015 ISIS staged a major terrorist attack in Paris and ISIS sympathizers killed fourteen Americans at a holiday party in San Bernardino, California. The administration, which had by then undertaken an aerial bombing campaign against ISIS, vowed to continue efforts to contain this growing terrorist threat. As of early 2016 these efforts had not yet "contained" ISIS.

Obama also had to deal with a resurgent, challenging Russia under President Vladimir Putin. Russia invaded and forcibly annexed the Crimea region from neighboring Ukraine and supported guerilla warfare in the ethnically Russian region of eastern Ukraine. The United States and NATO nations placed economic sanctions on Russia in response, but Putin did not retreat. Instead, he increased Russian support to Syria's Assad, a longtime ally, and began bombing anti-Assad guerillas in the region, some of whom had US support.

Obama also attempted far-reaching diplomacy by concluding a nuclear agreement with the Islamic Republic of Iran. The administration argued the pact, which remained "informal" and not subject to congressional approval, would limit Iran's development of a nuclear weapon for ten years. Opponents of the deal doubted this and argued that Iran, a sponsor of terrorism, did not deserve to have economic sanctions lifted as a reward.

In the face of these challenges, public support for Obama's foreign policy performance fell below 50 percent in May 2011 and persisted below 40 percent through 2015 (Gallup 2015a). Obama's foreign policy challenges receive a full discussion via the contrasting perspectives of Lawrence Korb and Danielle Pletka in this volume. Korb argues Obama has artfully led America through a series of challenging international situations, but Pletka contends his foreign policy has promoted the unfortunate decline of America's role in the world.

PROBLEMS WITH THE PUBLIC

The key risk for a directive president lies in taking people "where they otherwise would not want to go." As one persists in office, this tension mounts and the public's approval of a president's job performance can drop. Obama's declining job approval resulted from public resistance to many aspects of his policy leadership. This was particularly evident in his second term. His overall job approval fell below 50 percent in May 2013 (Gallup 2015b). Opinion polls in his second term revealed public disapproval of many of his policies: foreign policy, relations with Russia and Iran, immigration, health care, and economic management (Gallup 2015a). Pursuit of an elite governing agenda without careful cultivation of mass support inevitably produces political problems for a president.

Yet Obama's popularity problems date to the early months of his presidency as well. During Obama's first two years in office, his job approval steadily declined as first Republicans and then political independents took exception to the major policy changes. What prompted this rise in public disaffection? Short-term outcomes of the administration's economic policies were important causes. As Raymond Tatalovich details in his chapter, economic growth remained sluggish. Unemployment, which Obama promised would not rise above 8 percent due to his stimulus spending, instead rose to 10 percent and then hovered above 9 percent through 2010. Many political science models have found that economic conditions strongly affect presidential job approval (for a summary, see Gronke and Newman 2000).

One can point to other contributing factors. As mentioned previously, many in the public came to view Obama as liberal in his political orientation, which inhibited his public support. This was evident in a series of Gallup polls. Already by late 2009, 54 percent of the public termed Obama's policies "mostly liberal" (Saad 2009). By the summer of 2010, 48 percent termed the Democratic Party "too liberal" (Saad 2010). A big ideological distance from much of the public is seldom helpful to presidents. It also spawned a diffuse but effective grassroots opposition in the Tea Party movement of activists pressing for smaller government. Their enthusiastic activism helped propel the GOP to victory in the 2010 elections.

The sweeping Obama agenda proved difficult to explain to the public, and the president, focused on conceptualizing policy and pursuing his elite governing strategy, did not defend or explain his agenda well. The initial Obama agenda included increased deficit spending first, with a promise of later deficit reduction; an expansive stimulus, to produce both green jobs and economic recovery; sweeping financial reform; comprehensive immigration reform; cap-and-trade environmental legislation; and health-care reform, both to reduce health-care spending and simultaneously to broaden coverage. It was not obvious how all these pieces related to each other or added up.

Shortly before the 2010 elections, Obama advisor David Axelrod spoke forebodingly about their likely outcome: "We have [Democrats] in office now whose elections were completely improbable. They got dragged in by a high tide. Now the tide is going out. I think structurally we're set up for a difficult election" (Wolffe 2010, 274). So it proved. The American electorate voiced their concerns over policy and the economy with a large GOP victory. Republicans took control of the House by winning 242 seats, a gain of 63, the largest for the opposition party since the 1938 elections. Republicans won 6 Senate seats, reducing the Democratic majority in that chamber from 59 to 53. Pre-2008 divisions in the electorate reappeared to the GOP's advantage.

A very different electorate, however, appeared in the 2012 elections, producing better results for the Democrats. Obama faced no serious rivals for renomination; the GOP-nominated Mitt Romney, a businessman and ex-Massachusetts governor. That fall the Obama campaign had superior resources and a better get-out-the-vote effort. Romney's effort was organizationally inferior and plagued by the candidate's gaffes. Despite a mediocre economy, the president won reelection by 51.1 percent to Romney's 47.2 percent, amassing 332 electoral votes to his rival's 206. Democrats also gained two Senate and eight House seats, though the GOP remained in control of the US House.

The 2014 elections, however, saw a reversion to 2010 form. Second midterm elections often go badly for a president's party due in part to declining presidential job approval, which afflicted Obama. His ratings during the election season were "underwater," with popular majorities disapproving of his conduct of office (Gallup 2015b). The GOP swept many congressional, gubernatorial, and state legislative races. Republicans gained 14 House seats and 9 Senate seats to take control of Congress with majorities of 247 to 188 in the House and 54 to 44 with two Democratic-leaning independents in the Senate. The GOP took control of sixty-eight state legislative chambers to thirty for the Democrats, and held thirty-one governorships to only seventeen for the Democrats.

Are the 2012 or 2014 elections a harbinger of America's electoral future? The authors here offer contrasting views about that. Alan Abramowitz argues that demographic change favors long-term dominance by Obama's coalition of racial minorities and younger voters. William Mayer disputes this, arguing that negative public evaluations of Obama's governance will have a great impact on the Democratic Party's prospects.

The party's prospects may dim due to Democrats' waning support with white voters, unsolved national security challenges, a mediocre economy, and the decline of the party's vote in many areas of the nation.

OBAMA AND THE DEMOCRATIC PARTY

American political parties have changed greatly over the last one hundred years. Formerly, they were pragmatic organizations that included far-flung coalitions of disparate elements requiring issue compromises for their internal maintenance. At the turn of the twentieth century, parties also were "the primary connection between the average citizen and government" (Burbank, Hrebnar, and Benedict 2008, 20). Now, parties are just one of many players in our "candidate-centered politics," alongside interest groups, political action committees, and the campaign organizations of candidates themselves. The social ingredients of parties are different now as well. As political scientist Morris Fiorina puts it: "Rather than broad coalitions deeply rooted in the American social structure, today's parties are coalitions of minorities who seek to impose their views on the broader public" (Fiorina 2009, 98).

Barack Obama's political career was shaped by these circumstances. His 2008 campaign, an impressive financial and grassroots exercise, was strongly candidate-centered. His consistent liberalism fit the ideological mainstream of his party activists. The Obama presidency has demonstrated greater fealty to liberalism's agenda, particularly in domestic policy, than any president since Lyndon Johnson. Yet Obama has not devoted attention to party building that might entrench his partisan regime as a dominant force in American politics.

The opportunity was there in early 2009. He ended his presidential campaign with a list of two million active volunteers and almost four million small donors, the makings of a grassroots partisan army geared to organize and agitate for liberal causes. But the White House balked at such a suggestion, instead creating an organization called "Organizing for America" as a project of the Democratic Party. OFA was slow to organize and then confined itself to community projects and occasional grassroots exercises in support of the administration's legislation, such as rallies and house parties.

The tepid pace of the organization drew criticism from veteran Democratic organizers Peter Dreier and Marshall Ganz: "Once in office, the president moved quickly, announcing one ambitious legislative objective after another. But instead of launching a parallel strategy to mobilize supporters, most progressive organizations and Organizing for America—the group created to organize Obama's former campaign volunteers—failed to keep up" (Dreier and Ganz 2009). The Obama administration limited Organizing for America to a grassroots lobbying adjunct of marginal utility, instead of employing it to energize new partisan commitments. The president "failed to do what Reagan and Eisenhower did: he asked his supporters to rally around Democratic causes, but he has balked at asking them to become Democrats. He has asked his loyal enthusiasts to take ownership of a presidency, but not of a party" (Homans 2010).

OFA, however, proved to be an able voter-mobilization tool in the 2012 elections. In April 2011 the organization was placed under the direction of the Obama presidential campaign, which launched a very successful voter-outreach effort. The campaign created hundreds of field offices in key 2012 states and claimed to have registered 2.9 million new voters both in person and online. After 2012, Organizing for America was renamed Organizing for Action to engage in issue advocacy for the president's agenda. The group had far less success at these efforts, given GOP strength in Congress, than it did in election-related activities (p2012.org 2012).

Obama's approach to his party fit his times in some ways. The president dutifully raised funds for his party and touted fellow Democratic candidates, as did his predecessors. Sticking to that traditional role meant not devoting much effort to partisan regime building, as his predecessor George W. Bush and Karl Rove attempted, but instead encouraging his grassroots arm to further his specific policy plans. Those plans were ideologically liberal, substantively in tune with the president's activist base. But Obama's party leadership ultimately served the president's specific goals rather than aiming to reshape partisan allegiances in a lasting way. Obama's presidency, both directive and clarifying, became a politically personal project.

OBAMA AND THE INSTITUTIONAL PRESIDENCY

In recent decades presidents have expanded their ability to act unilaterally to achieve results. Recent presidents have found increased executive powers to their liking. This trend grows from long-standing presidential management and appointment powers and, more controversially, presidential use of several unilateral tools. One such tool is the use of the executive order, a legally binding document that sets policy. To be constitutional, these orders must present an argument that the order derives from a congressional law. Given the broad language of many laws, this gives presidents a wide range of discretion. In recent decades presidents have increasingly used these orders to impose their will—George W. Bush issued 290 and Bill Clinton 363 executive orders. As of December 2015 Barack Obama had issued 221 (Archives.gov 2015).

Given his directive approach to the presidency, Barack Obama issued a flurry of executive orders upon taking office. The purpose of many of them was to reverse politics of the previous presidency. By March 2009 Obama had issued orders reversing Bush policies on the use of terrorist interrogation techniques, regarding union organizing, on access to the documents of former presidents, and concerning US governmental support for international family-planning organizations. His early executive order requiring the closing of the Guantanamo Bay detention facility by the end of 2009 eventually was postponed indefinitely as problems of transferring the prisoners arose. An executive order proved vital to the passage of his landmark health-care reform legislation. In order to secure the support of a crucial bloc of antiabortion Democrats, Obama issued an executive order "to ensure that Federal funds are not used for abortion services (except in cases of rape or incest, or when the life of the woman would be endangered)" (Executive Order 13535, 1). Executive orders can be overturned at any time by a current president, causing antiabortion groups to decry the order as inadequate protection for their cause. Obama's agreement to issue the order propelled the bill to passage in the House.

A more controversial tool of unilateral executive power is the signing statement, a public document issued by the White House when a president signs the bill. Traditionally, signing statements have been hortatory, but recent presidents, particularly George W. Bush, used them to impart extensive instructions to executive officials about how to interpret and implement new laws. Bush, in signing statements, challenged nearly twelve hundred provisions of bills over eight years, twice the number challenged by all of his White House predecessors. Most notably, Bush asserted that he could authorize officials to bypass a torture ban and oversight provisions of the antiterrorist USA Patriot Act (Savage 2009). As a candidate, Obama voiced strong criticism of Bush's approach, asserting, "It is a clear abuse of power to use such statements as a license to evade laws that the president does not like or as an end-run around provisions designed to foster accountability. I will not use signing statements to nullify or undermine congressional instructions as enacted into law" (Savage 2007).

But Democrats and Republicans in Congress accused Obama of just that. In a March 2009 signing statement, he declared five provisions of a budget bill to be unconstitutional and nonbinding, including one restricting US troop deployment under UN command overseas and another aimed at halting punishment of bureaucratic whistle-blowers (Weisman 2009). In June 2009 he issued a statement declaring that he would not comply with a spending bill that put conditions on aid to the World Bank and International Monetary Fund (Associated Press 2010). This prompted a bipartisan uproar in Congress, causing four senior House Democrats to draft a letter to the president expressing their disapproval: "During the previous administration, all of us were critical of the president's assertion that he could pick and choose which aspects of congressional statutes he was required to enforce. We were therefore chagrined to see you appear to express a similar attitude" (Savage 2009).

In the wake of the controversy, Obama immediately stopped issuing signing statements and issued relatively few of them during the remainder of his presidency (American Presidency Project 2015). In early 2010 the administration revealed that the president would sign bills containing problematic provisions without issuing signing statements, but the administration would still disregard laws it found to be unconstitutional. This raised obvious questions of accountability. Democratic Representative Barney Frank objected: "Anyone who makes the argument that 'once we have told you we have constitutional concerns and then you pass it anyway, that justifies us ignoring it'—that is a constitutional violation" (Savage 2010). The White House, however, claimed that its previous statements about problems in new laws would suffice as public notice in lieu of signing statements.

A third tool of unilateral power, the presidential memorandum, also can "specify how agencies should implement recently enacted laws" (Devins 2007). Like executive agreements and signing statements, memoranda must have some statutory basis but usually are narrower in scope and receive less public notice. This is because, unlike executive orders and signing statements, they do not have an established process for issuance of publication. Obama's White House issued more presidential memoranda than any of his predecessors, 198 by the end of 2014 (Korte 2014). During his first year, for example, Obama issued memoranda extending scientific reviews regarding possible endangered species, directing the secretary of transportation to formulate higher fuel-efficiency standards for cars and directing the secretary of energy to create new appliance-efficiency standards. This practice continued into his second term. In his 2014 State of the Union Address in January, Obama proposed a new retirement savings account for low-income workers called a MyRA. The next week, he issued a presidential memorandum to the Treasury Department instructing it to develop a pilot program (Korte 2014). In all, Barack Obama has found the use of unilateral powers more desirable than he did as a candidate. The tools of executive orders, signing statements, and presidential memoranda proved quite useful to his directive approach to the presidency.

Another important implement in a president's arsenal is presidential appointments. Federal law gives the chief executive the power to fill several thousand positions at the top levels of cabinet departments and federal agencies, boards, and commissions. By law the Senate must approve 526 of these top-level appointments. Progress in securing appointments initially proved slow for the administration. Just over three hundred secured Senate confirmation during the administration's first twelve months. By January 2011 about one hundred positions remained open or unconfirmed (*Washington Post* 2009). The fractious politics of the highly partisan Senate combined with the administration's lengthy process for vetting appointees contributed to this slow pace. A similar slowdown beset Obama's judicial appointments. By March of 2010 Obama responded to the recalcitrant Senate by announcing fifteen people as his first recess appointments. Federal law allows the president to make recess appointments—allowing those appointed when the Senate is in recess to serve until the end of the next Senate's term. In 2014, however, the Supreme Court ruled against an administration attempt to make recess appointments during a time when the Senate was technically still in session (Slattery 2014).

Two terms in office allowed Obama to have an important impact on governmental personnel via appointments. By late in his second term, Obama's judicial appointments were on track to outnumber those of his predecessor George W. Bush. His Supreme Court appointees, Elena Kagan and Sonia Sotomayor, proved to be reliable liberals but did not change the ideological balance on the court, where a 5–4 conservative majority prevailed on most decisions until Justice Antonin Scalia's death in 2016. His executive branch appointments also featured greater diversity than had those of his immediate predecessors. Fully 53.5 percent of Obama's executive branch appointees were minorities and women, compared to 25.6 percent for George W. Bush and 37.5 percent for Bill Clinton (Eilperin 2015).

Presidential management authority, granted through many federal laws, is another useful implement for chief executives. Political scientist Donald Kettl described Obama's management approach as a "stealth revolution" with four main components. First, the administration increased usage of new media such as social networks to improve bureaucratic coordination and contact with citizens. Second, it created of a group of "policy czars" in the White House—one each, for example, for auto industry reorganization, banking reform, energy, environment, Afghanistan, and the Middle East—to improve bureaucratic response in these areas. None of the "czars" was subject to Senate appointment, and they represented "a revolutionary-in-scale move to maneuver past the permanent bureaucracy" (Kettl 2009, 41). Third, the White House accepted the frustrations involved in accommodating congressional policy concerns, a challenge complicated by 2010 GOP gains on Capitol Hill. Fourth, it enhanced accountability by pushing out "enormous quantities of information about federal programs" and relying on interest groups and the public to digest the data, with information on the economic stimulus an initial example. For Kettl, this amounted to an overall strategy of "transparency and working organically from the bottom up. They want to test their ideas before they latch themselves to a loser" (Kettl 2009, 40).

The administration's experiments with czars and transparency constitute a departure from the management approaches of Obama's predecessors, who focused mainly on getting results without transforming executive bureaucratic operations. In contrast, the Obama approach was to try to shake up ongoing administrative processes with social networks, transparency, and czars in order to, perhaps, improve outcomes. The very complexity of "permanent Washington"—the networks of bureaucratic agencies, interest groups, and congressional committees who have their own, frequently consensual agendas that rival those of the president—makes enduring management transformations engineered by the White House a daunting task.

When a president's political clout is blunted by the slow pace of appointments and by ongoing policy networks that predate a president and will persist after he loses office, chief executives will seek ways to circumvent such impediments. Influence with the Washington establishment is hard for a president to maintain. So why not use unilateral powers like executive orders, signing statements, and memoranda? The risk is that the exercise of unilateral powers courts political danger for a president and risks a lasting loss of political clout. George W. Bush encountered costly political opposition to his embrace of unilateral power in combating terrorism, drawing rebukes from the Supreme Court, Congress, and the public. Barack Obama incurred similar reversals during his time in office as well (Schier and Eberly 2013). The GOP Congress slowed the pace of judicial confirmations. By 2014 the Supreme Court had ruled against Obama's unilateral actions twelve times (Slattery 2014).

This phenomenon is the presidential "power trap" in which use of unilateral powers produces political blowback that mires a president in increasing political difficulties (Schier 2011). Maintaining popular support is hard and frustrating work, and in seeking to maintain it, presidents encounter widespread constraints. The modern presidency grants an incumbent many formal powers over executive branch administration, as well as over foreign and security policy. So why not use the power while you have it, if popular support is so impermanent? The risk is that by using such powers, a president effectively weakens his popular support—the presidential power trap. That has been Obama's fate as his presidency progressed.

ON TO THE DEBATE

Obama's "directive" presidency produced sharply different assessments among the public and scholars alike. The following chapters present opposing perspectives on various aspects of Obama's presidency. John K. White argues that Barack Obama's presidency is "consequential" and amounts to "sound work in a tough environment." In contrast, John J. Pitney argues that the president's actions have been quite inconsistent with his professed rhetoric. Alan Abramowitz holds that despite electoral setbacks in 2010 and 2014, Obama's presidency heralds the onset of a new Democratic electoral dominance rooted in the votes of African Americans, Latinos, and today's young voters. William Mayer disagrees, contending that Obama's liberalism and poor leadership has resulted in GOP electoral dominance in Congress, state legislatures, and governorships and has compromised the Democratic Party's electoral future.

Lawrence Korb argues that Obama's foreign policy, based on restraint, multilateralism, and diplomacy, has carried the nation successfully through many severe international challenges. Obama's overtures to Iran and China promise constructively to engage these emerging world powers. Danielle Pletka, in contrast, contends that Obama has not kept the nation safe because he has failed to acknowledge and respond adequately to ongoing chaos in the Middle East and the terrorism it spawns, growing Russian aggression, and increased Chinese assertiveness. Ruth O'Brien notes how Obama in domestic policy pursued his vision of "interactive, multilateral, participatory government" that produced major, constructive changes in the country regarding health care, education, and multicultural tolerance that will be difficult to reverse. Andrew Busch, in contrast, labels Obama's domestic agenda as extreme and polarizing. His health-care reform failed to control health-care costs and placed great burden on small businesses, and his positions on abortion and gay marriage have created deep divisions among the public. Daniel Ponder contends that Obama's economic policies brought America back from the brink of a disastrous economic depression and helped the economy reinstate a constructive cycle of job creation, economic growth, and shrinking federal budget deficits. Raymond Tatalovich sees Obama's economic record as producing inadequate recovery while ballooning the national debt and burdening future generations with lower living standards.

In all, there is much to dispute about the Obama presidency. That is one significant measure of its importance and consequence. Let the debate begin.

WORKS CITED

Alter, Jonathan. 2010. *The Promise: President Obama, Year One*. New York: Simon & Schuster.

American Presidency Project. 2015. University of California–Santa Barbara. "Written: Statements—Signing Statements." http://www.presidency.ucsb.edu/signingstatements.php. Accessed December 6, 2015.

Archives.gov. 2015. "Executive Orders Disposition Tables Index." www.archives.gov/federal-register/executive-orders/disposition.html. Accessed December 6, 2015.

Associated Press. 2009. "Obama's Signing Statements Draw Fire for Mimicking Bush." http://www.startribune.com/politics/S1359172.html. Accessed December 9, 2010.

Baker, Peter. 2010. "Obama Making Plans to Use Executive Power." *New York Times*. February 13.

Biden, Joe. 2009. "What You Might Not Know About the Recovery." *New York Times*, July 26.

Burbank, Matthew J., Ronald J. Hrebnar, and Robert C. Benedict. 2008. *Parties, Interest Groups and Political Campaigns*. Boulder, Colorado: Paradigm Publishers.

Davis, Steven J., Gary S. Becker, and Kevin M. Murphy. 2010. "Uncertainty and the Slow Recovery." *Wall Street Journal*. January 4. www.aei.org/ article/101501. Accessed July 22, 2010.

Devins, Neal. 2007. "Signing Statements and Divided Government." *William and Mary Bill of Rights Journal* 16 (1): 63–79.

Dreier, Peter, and Marshall Ganz. 2009. "We Have the Hope. Now Where's the Audacity?" *Washington Post*. August 30.

Edwards, George C. III, and Steven J. Wayne. 2009. *Presidential Leadership: Politics and Policymaking*. Florence, KY: Wadsworth.

Eilperin, Juliet. 2015. "Obama Has Vastly Changed the Face of the Federal Bureaucracy." *Washington Post*. September 20. https://www.washingtonpost.com/politics/obama-has-vastly-changed-the-face-of-the-federal-bureaucracy/2015/09/20/73ef803a-5631-11e5-abe9-27d53f250b11_story.html. Accessed December 6, 2015.

Executive Order 13535. 2010. "Ensuring Enforcement and Implementation of Abortion Restrictions in the Patient Protection and Affordable Care Act." March 24. www.presidency.ucsb.edu/ws/index.php?pid=87661. Accessed December 9, 2010.

Fiorina, Morris P. 2009. *Disconnect: The Breakdown of Representation in American Politics*. Norman: University of Oklahoma Press.

Gallup.com. 2015a. "Presidential Ratings—Issues Approval." www.gallup.com/poll/1726/presidential-ratings-issues-approval.aspx. Accessed December 6, 2015.

Gallup.com. 2015b. "Presidential Approval Ratings— Barack Obama." www.gallup.com/poll/116479/barack-obama-presidential-job-approval.aspx. Accessed December 6, 2015.

Greenberg Quinlan Rosner Research. 2010. "Democracy Corps June Survey: Grim Stability Will Require Race-by-Race Fight." July 8. www.democracycorps.com/wpcontent/files/DC1006292010.political.FINAL_.pdf. Accessed July 22, 2010.

Grier, Peter. 2010. "Health Care Reform 101." *Christian Science Monitor*. www.csmonitor.com/USA/Politics/2010/0322/Health-care-reform-bill-101-what-the-bill-means-to-you. Accessed December 16, 2010.

Gronke, Paul, and Brian Newman. 2000. "FDR to Clinton, Mueller to ??: A State of the Discipline Review of Presidential Approval." Paper presented at the Annual Meeting of the American Political Science Association. http://people.reed.edu/~gronkep/docs/apsa2000-gronkeandnewman.pdf. Accessed July 22, 2010.

Harris, John F. 2009. "Bush and Clinton: Contrasting Styles of Popular Leadership," pp. 62–74 in *Ambition and Division: Legacies of the George W. Bush Presidency*, ed. Steven E. Schier. Pittsburgh: University of Pittsburgh Press.
Homans, Charles. 2010. "The Party of Obama: What Are the President's Grass Roots Good For?" *Washington Monthly*. January/February. www.washingtonmonthly.com/features/2010/1001.homans.html. Accessed July 22, 2010.
Kettl, Donald F. 2009. "Obama's Stealth Revolution: Quietly Reshaping the Way Government Works." *The Public Manager*. Winter 2009–2010: 39–42.
Korte, Gregory. 2014. "Obama Issues 'Executive Orders by Another Name.'" *USA Today*. December 17. www.usatoday.com/story/news/politics/2014/12/16/obama-presidential-memoranda-executive-orders/20191805/. Accessed December 6, 2015.
Levy, Phillip I. 2010. "The Straw Stimulus." *The American*, February 18. www.american.com/archive/2010/february/the-straw-stimulus. Accessed December 16, 2010.
McCormick, John, and Carol Dodge. 2010. "Americans Disapproving Obama May Enable Republican Gains." www.bloomberg.com/news/2010-07-14/americans-disappoving-of-obama-policies-poised-to-enable-republican-gains.html. Accessed July 22, 2010.
P2012 Democracy in Action: Race for the White House. 2012. "Key People—Barack Obama, Obama for America." www.p2012.org/candidates/obamaorg.html. Accessed December 6, 2015.
PolitiFact.com. 2015. "Tracking Obama's Campaign Promises." www.politifact.com/truth-o-meter/promises/obameter. Accessed December 6, 2015.
"Restoring American Financial Stability Act of 2010—Summary." PDF. 11th Congress, Washington, D.C.
Saad, Lydia. 2009. "In U.S., Majority Now Says Obama's Policies Mostly Liberal." Gallup.com. November 4. www.gallup.com/poll/124094/majority-say-obama-policies-mostly-liberal.aspx. Accessed July 22, 2010.
Saad, Lydia. 2010. "Conservatives Finish 2009 as No. 1 Ideological Group." Gallup.com. January 7. www.gallup.com/poll/124958/Conservatives-Finish-2009-No-1-Ideological-Group.aspx. Accessed July 22, 2010.
Savage, Charlie. 2007. "Barack Obama's Q and A." *Boston Globe*, December 20.
Savage, Charlie. 2009. "Obama Says He Can Ignore Some Parts of Spending Bill." *New York Times*, March 12.
Savage, Charlie. 2010. "Obama Takes New Route to Opposing Parts of Laws." *New York Times*, January 9.
Schier, Steven E. 2008. *Panorama of a Presidency: How George W. Bush Acquired and Spent His Political Capital*. New York: Routledge.
Schier, Steven E. 2011. "The Presidential Authority Problem and the Political Power Trap." *Presidential Studies Quarterly* 41 (4): 793–808.
Schier, Steven E., and Todd E. Eberly. 2013. *American Government and Popular Discontent: Stability without Success*. New York: Routledge.
Seltzer, Irwin M. 2010. "Obama Rattles Business." *Weekly Standard*. June 26. www.weeklystandard.com/blogs/obama-rattles-business. Accessed July 22, 2010.
Sides, John, and Lynn Vavreck. 2013. *The Gamble: Choice and Chance in the 2012 Presidential Election*. Princeton, NJ: Princeton University Press.
Sides, John, and Lynn Vavreck. 2013. *The Gamble: Choice and Chance in the 2012 Presidential Election*. Princeton, NJ: Princeton University Press.
Slattery, Elizabeth. 2014. "Supreme Court Rules Obama's Recess Appointments Violated the Constitution." *Daily Signal*. June 26. Washington, DC: Heritage Foundation. http://dailysignal.com//2014/06/26/supreme-court-rules-obamas-recess-appointments-violated-constitution/. Accessed December 9, 2015.
Warrick, Joby, and Chris Mooney. 2015. "196 Counties Approve Historic Climate Agreement." *Washington Post*, December 12. https://www.washingtonpost.com/news/energy-environment/wp/2015/12/12/proposed-historic-climate-pact-nears-final-vote/. Accessed January 15, 2016.
Washington Post. 2009. "Head Count: Tracking Obama's Appointments." http://projects.washingtonpost.com/2009/federal-appointments/. Accessed January 21, 2011.

Weisman, Jonathan. 2009. "Signing Statements Reappear in Obama White House." *Wall Street Journal*, March 12.

Wolffe, Richard. 2010. *Revival: The Struggle for Survival Inside the Obama White House*. New York: Crown Publishers.

1

SOUND WORK IN A TOUGH ENVIRONMENT

Obama's Governing Achievements

John Kenneth White, Catholic University of America

As the Obama presidency enters its last quarter and Americans turn to the business of choosing a new president, it is altogether fitting to cast a parting glance at the Obama years. It has been, as historians are wont to say, a consequential presidency. Of course, that isn't saying much. After all, famous presidential failures have also been consequential—for example, the disastrous James Buchanan, who facilitated a civil war; Herbert Hoover, who presided over the Great Depression; or, more recently, Lyndon Johnson, whose Great Society is forever tainted by the Vietnam War; or Richard Nixon, who became the first president to turn in his resignation. Of course, there are the laudatory (and consequential) presidencies that are forever depicted on Mount Rushmore: George Washington, who was first in everything; Thomas Jefferson, whose Louisiana Purchase doubled the size of the United States; Abraham Lincoln, who won the Civil War; and Theodore Roosevelt, whose presidency has a contemporary resonance given his use of the bully pulpit to tackle corporate greed.

Barack Obama's presidency is unlikely to be depicted on Mount Rushmore (it would be hard to find room), nor will it be cataloged in a list of failures. But it is consequential. Obama rescued an economy on the brink of financial disaster; instituted health-care reform that eluded every prior president since Theodore Roosevelt; facilitated major social and cultural changes in the United States (especially in the area of gay rights);

extricated the United States from two disastrous wars in Iraq and Afghanistan; and killed Osama bin Laden, the terrorist who precipitated the events of 9/11. If that weren't enough, there have been other accomplishments as well. In the last quarter of his second term, Obama extended diplomatic recognition to the Castro government in Cuba, with embassies open for business in each country; conducted negotiations with Iran that resulted in an international agreement to monitor that nation's nuclear capability; negotiated a Trans-Pacific Partnership trade deal; and announced strict federal regulations designed to limit carbon emissions. Each is consequential, and all are likely either to be completed during the remaining days of Obama's second term or await the next president for final disposition. In many ways, the Obama presidency is best captured in lessons contained in three vignettes that occurred at the start of his remarkable rise to power.

THREE VIGNETTES FORETELL THE FUTURE

Election Night, 2008: Euphoria Tempered

The euphoria and sense of history being made was palatable on election night 2008. The early call (11 p.m. eastern time) that Barack Hussein Obama would become the forty-fourth president of the United States generated an outpouring of emotion. One part was relief—knowing that, finally, the George W. Bush years were about to end and the country would embark on a different path—an inevitable result given the enlarged partisan differences between Bush and Obama, and the change of parties and personnel that would follow the new president into the Oval Office. But an even greater wave of emotion came as broadcasters acknowledged the historical significance of the first African American elected to the presidency. This new reality elicited a river of tears—from Oprah Winfrey to Jesse Jackson, to unnamed African Americans pictured on television screens whose forebears (and they themselves) had been subjected to oppressive racial discrimination. Standing before 125,000 ecstatic supporters gathered at Chicago's Grant Park, Obama spoke to the moment: "If there is anyone out there who still doubts that America is a place where all things are possible, who still wonders if the dream of our founders is alive in our time, who still questions the power of our democracy, tonight is your answer" (Obama 2008b).

But just prior to bounding onto the stage, the newly elected president issued his first executive order, telling advisor David Axelrod to cut the fireworks display planned to coincide with the conclusion of his address: "I just want you to know I killed the fireworks. I don't think it's appropriate" (Wolffe 2009, 19). Later, Axelrod reflected that a festive display of pyrotechnics was incongruous to the grim work that lay ahead. During the campaign there had been gyrations in the US economy that all but assured Obama's election: a fluctuating stock market that lost much of its value; reeling financial markets; rising unemployment; impossible-to-obtain credit; and a bursting housing bubble. In October John McCain suspended his campaign and called for an emergency White House meeting—a peculiar session since McCain had so little to say once it happened. Congress was under pressure from the Bush administration to pass a Troubled Assets Relief Program (TARP), and Treasury Secretary Hank Paulson was on bended knee before House Speaker Nancy Pelosi begging her to act. In many ways Obama's fireworks cancellation heralded the beginning of a presidency awash in the blunders of his predecessor that would take years to fix. As Obama told cheering Chicagoans on the night of his victory: "The road ahead will be long. Our climb will be steep. We may not get there in one year or even in one term. But, America, I have never been more hopeful than I am tonight that we will get there" (Obama 2008b).

An Economic Meeting, December 16, 2008

Six weeks after that celebratory election night, Barack Obama found himself in a windowless conference room in Chicago receiving an economic briefing. With each passing minute, the news was ever-more grim. The president-elect was advised that the financial crisis had taken on the contours of a second Great Depression. Lawrence Summers, who would serve as director of the National Economic Council in the Obama White House, warned that any recovery, which usually took a V formation after a recession (meaning a steep drop followed by a quick recovery)—was unlikely (Axelrod 2015, 333). This was going to be one long, hard slog—something Obama later compared to digging one's way out of a deep ditch. For David Axelrod, this was a "holy shit" moment—something that the public had yet to grasp (Axelrod 2015, 332). As Obama lamented on the unfortunate hand he had drawn, Axelrod presciently replied that he would face "one hell of a tough midterm election" (Axelrod 2015, 335). Voters are impatient. Two centuries earlier Alexis de Tocqueville warned that Americans were especially impatient in times of economic prosperity (Tocqueville 1969, 536). Now with a second Great Depression looming, impatience for a quick fix would surely be magnified.

By the time George W. Bush surrendered the presidency on January 20, 2009, nearly six hundred thousand jobs were lost in that single month alone, the worst showing since December 1974 (Isidore 2009). As if this wasn't bad enough, in the last quarter of 2008, the gross domestic product (GDP) contracted at an 8 percent annual rate, a Depression-level free-fall (Grunwald 2014). It would be a long time before anything approaching a recovery would happen. Stanching the bloodletting of jobs and applying economic first aid became the new president's top priority. While Americans did not blame Obama for the economic catastrophe, they expected a quick recovery. But that would not happen.

Inauguration Night, January 20, 2009: Republicans Dine Out

The swearing-in of Barack Obama was an extension of the celebrations that began on election night 2008. Two million people converged on the Capitol grounds to witness Obama take the presidential oath on steps where slaves once baked the bricks, sawed the timber, and laid the stone for the foundations (*New York Times*, Obama 2009, 229). So many people in so little space led to hundreds of ticket holders finding themselves stuck in an underground tunnel, unable to get to the main event. In an inaugural speech with few built-in applause lines, Obama paid homage to his history-making election: "This is the meaning of our liberty and our creed, why men and women and children of every race and every faith can join in celebration across this magnificent mall. And why a man whose father less than sixty years ago might not have been served at a local restaurant can now stand before you to take a most sacred oath" (Obama 2009a).

But Obama was far from euphoric, soberly outlining the crises that lay before him and a chastened public: "Homes have been lost, jobs shed, businesses shuttered. Our health care is too costly, our schools fail too many, and each day brings further evidence that the ways we use energy strengthen our adversaries and threaten our planet. . . . Today I say to you that the challenges we face are real, they are serious, and they are many. They will not be met easily or in a short span of time. But know this America: They will be met" (Obama 2009a). This was one of the few moments when those gathered, even those stuck in the tunnel listening to the speech on old-fashioned transistor radios, gave the new president sustained applause.

But while Democrats were celebrating, Republicans were plotting. A group of influential lawmakers—including former House Speaker Newt Gingrich; Congressmen Paul Ryan, Eric Cantor, and Kevin McCarthy; Senators Jim DeMint, Jon Kyl, Tom Coburn, John Ensign, and Bob Corker; and GOP pollster Frank Luntz—gathered at a swank Capitol Hill restaurant to commiserate. All admitted their party was in trouble: They had lost the presidency decisively; Democrats were in charge of both houses of Congress; Republicans were saddled with an unpopular outgoing president; and the party's image was at an all-time low. As they munched on their meals, all agreed that attacking Barack Obama *personally* was not the answer—he was simply too popular at that moment. But, to a person, everyone decided that the best (and only) course of action was to express opposition to Obama's *policies* at every turn—even if that meant opposing measures they once supported. Paul Ryan, who would eventually become the party's 2012 vice presidential nominee and House Speaker, voiced the consensus: "The only way we'll succeed is if we're united. If we tear ourselves apart, we're finished" (Draper 2012, xviii). Future House majority leader Kevin McCarthy chimed in: "If you act like you're the minority, you're going to stay in the minority. We've gotta challenge them on every single bill and challenge them on every single campaign" (Draper 2012, xviii). Newt Gingrich concluded the evening with these words: "You will remember this day" (Draper 2012, xix).

Thus, when Obama proposed a $787 billion stimulus package to jump-start a stricken economy, every congressional Republican cast a "no" vote, even though one-third of the package contained tax cuts that Republicans presumably would have supported if proposed by a president from their own party. The GOP opposition hardened later in the year when Congress turned its attention to Obamacare, as *zero* Republicans in either chamber voted for final passage. This implacable (and unprecedented) opposition would become a hallmark of Obama's presidency and lead him to pursue other, nonlegislative means to fulfill his ambitions.

RESCUING THE ECONOMY AND ENACTING HEALTH CARE

A Second Great Depression

The job of rescuing the economy from a second Great Depression proved to be an enormous task—one that is not quite finished. Upon taking the oath of office, things went from bad to worse. The unemployment rate, which stood at 7.6 percent on Inauguration Day 2009, quickly climbed to more than 10 percent by the end of that year. And it remained near that double-digit mark for all of 2010—coinciding with the midterm elections and the worst unemployment numbers since the 1982 Reagan recession. The months ahead saw job losses in the range of seven hundred thousand per month, while the first six months of Obama's first term saw the worst GDP growth in sixty years (White House 2014). Stanching the outsourcing of jobs was priority number one, and the $787 billion stimulus package helped. While some believed the stimulus needed to be higher, Obama's incoming chief of staff, Rahm Emanuel, who had a good sense of what Congress would and would not approve, warned that any bill with a *T* (for trillion) would not win congressional support (Axelrod 2015, 334). During the summer of 2009, road signs alongside highway construction crews read: "Putting America to Work: The American Recovery and Reinvestment Act." By September 2010, 70 percent of the funds allocated under the law had been expended, including the largest investment in roads since the creation of the Interstate Highway System during the Eisenhower years (White House 2014).

Still, the economic headaches multiplied. George W. Bush left it to Obama to decide the fate of two of America's largest automobile companies, General Motors and Chrysler. Both faced bankruptcy, which would have compounded the extant economic difficulties several fold. Mitt Romney, whose father, George, had been the chief executive of American Motors, wrote a *New York Times* op-ed piece in late 2008 titled "Let Detroit Go Bankrupt." In it, he argued that the federal government should not rescue any car company: "If General Motors, Ford and Chrysler get the bailout that their chief executives asked for yesterday, you can kiss the American automotive industry goodbye" (Romney 2008). Instead, a "managed bankruptcy" (Romney's words) would be preferable, even if that meant thousands of automobile suppliers—from car dealerships to tire companies, battery and other auto-parts makers—would face foreclosure. Unwilling to let Detroit go belly-up, Obama stepped in with guaranteed loans. In addition, Congress passed a measure that upped the value of old automobiles—"clunkers"—in hopes that would spur demand for new automobiles.

In the summer of 2009, Obama announced a plan that would help citizens facing foreclosure who found themselves "underwater" with their home values (meaning that they paid more for their homes than they were worth). Many criticized the plan as doing too little, too late. The depression that hit the housing market in 2009 still lingers in certain parts of the United States, and it called into question the old adage that buying a home was a safe, secure investment.

The Tea Party and Occupy Wall Street

Even as these measures were enacted, revolts within both parties began to take hold. Republicans were first. As Obama announced his intentions to aid those about to default on their home mortgages, Rick Santelli, a CNBC correspondent, took to the floor of the Chicago Mercantile Exchange to denounce the plan:

> The government is promoting bad behavior! Because we certainly don't want to put stimulus pork and give people a whopping eight or ten dollars in their check and think they ought to save it. . . . This is America! How many of you people want to pay for your neighbor's mortgage that has an extra bathroom and can't pay their bills? Raise your hand [*boos*]. . . . We're thinking of having a Chicago Tea Party in July. All you capitalists who want to show up at Lake Michigan, I'm going to start organizing [*applause*]. . . . If you read our Founding Fathers, people like Benjamin Franklin and [Thomas] Jefferson, what we're doing in this country now is making them roll over in their graves (Santelli 2009, YouTube).

Santelli's "rant" went viral on the Internet, and it spawned the emergence of the Tea Party, whose acronym stands for "Taxed Enough Already." Spurred on by Fox News, the movement became more than a powerful critique of Obama. It was a *cri de coeur* against the Republican Party establishment that went along with George W. Bush's big government initiatives—including No Child Left Behind and a Medicare prescription drug benefit for the elderly. The Tea Party challenged the Republican Party to change and met with some early successes—winning primaries and ousting establishment candidates, including House Minority Leader Eric Cantor, Delaware Congressman Mike Castle, Utah Senator Bob Bennett, and Indiana Senator Richard Lugar. Initially, the Tea Party proved to be an effective stand-in for a still-disliked GOP. In the 2010 midterms, the Tea Party had a net favorable rating even as voters continued to view the Republican Party unfavorably (Edison Media Research and Mitofsky International 2010).[1] Over time, the government shutdowns and near-defaults of the US debt shifted public attitudes against the Tea Party, and the GOP establishment began to fight back. Today, only 18 percent say they have a positive view of the Tea Party while 43 percent are negative (NBC News/*Wall Street Journal* 2014). The intra-party fight between Tea Partiers and the Republican establishment is not yet finished and is being waged by proxy in the 2016 presidential primaries, with Donald Trump, Ben Carson, Ted Cruz, Jeb Bush, and Marco Rubio taking leading roles. But the prominence of the Tea Party—and the fear it inspired—kept Republican lawmakers in lockstep against Obama, thereby fulfilling the promise made by the party's congressional leaders on inauguration night that they would oppose Obama at every turn.

On the Democratic side, the Occupy Wall Street movement claimed to represent the "99 percent" who were stuck in low-paying jobs with stagnant wages; who were not rescued (or even thought of receiving help) from the government; and who were disillusioned with the extravagant role of money in politics—enhanced to insanity by the disastrous Supreme Court decision in the *Citizens United* case. Staging sit-ins in several major US cities and chanting "We are the 99 percent!" those who camped out with the Occupy Wall Streeters ignited a progressive resurgence within the Democratic Party led by senators Elizabeth Warren and Bernie Sanders, the latter a progressive who caucused with Senate Democrats but remained a socialist until he mounted a serious challenge to Hillary Clinton's quest for the 2016 Democratic presidential nomination. The Occupy Wall Street movement all but eliminated the so-called New Democrats, whose moderation and balanced budgeting came to characterize the Bill Clinton presidency. No longer would a Democratic president have to "triangulate" between Democratic and Republican parties forced to share congressional power. The Bill Clinton years ended with the success of this movement, and Hillary Clinton does not promise to reprise them.

The resurgence of the progressive wing created a stronger, more united Democratic Party—free of the Dixiecrats who once populated its congressional ranks. Now this united party under Obama's leadership could move toward regulatory reform. And the Democratic-controlled Congress did so, enacting the Dodd-Frank banking law in 2010. Named after Connecticut Senator Christopher Dodd and Massachusetts Congressman Barney Frank, Dodd-Frank imposed stricter regulations on the banks, including: (1) capital requirements to keep a certain amount of cash on hand as a cushion against further economic losses; (2) requiring banks that packaged loans made by other entities to retain some of the risk, thus keeping "skin in the game"; (3) limiting derivatives that became known as "financial weapons of mass destruction"; and (4) mandating banks to disband if any were deemed "too big to fail." The latter would be determined by the Financial Stability Oversight Council (chaired by the treasury secretary), which could ask the Federal Reserve to require such banks to increase their financial reserves. If a bank failed, the legislation creates the Orderly Liquidation Authority whereby the institution is placed into receivership and its officers and board of directors are dismissed. If the institution's debts remained outstanding, taxpayer funds *would not* be used to bail it out. Instead, the secretary of the treasury is mandated to recover those funds by assessing a tax on other financial institutions with $50 billion (or more) in assets. Finally, Dodd-Frank established the Consumer Financial Protection Bureau, which consolidated functions performed by other government agencies into one independent entity whose sole purpose is to protect consumers in all financial transactions—including ending shoddy mortgage-lending practices and offering credit card protection from lenders all too eager to increase consumer indebtedness (Frank 2015, 303–6).

Despite these efforts, unemployment remained stubbornly high. As the Obama presidency pressed forward, the discontent and restlessness that Alexis de Tocqueville once alluded to rose to the surface. Seeking reelection, Obama was an incumbent with the highest unemployment rate of any post–World War II president (even exceeding that of Ronald Reagan in 1984). While unemployment had fallen from its high of 10 percent in 2009, it remained at a stubborn 7.9 percent on Election Day 2012. Millions remained discouraged from seeking work, and those with jobs were unhappy with wages stuck in neutral. Republicans argued that giving Obama a second term would result in an unemployment rate well above 7 percent, gasoline prices approaching $5 per gallon, lagging consumer confidence, more government regulations that would curtail economic growth, and a burgeoning federal deficit that mortgaged our children's futures (Legum 2015). None of that happened.

Instead, voters sensed that Obama cared more about them and that responsibility for the nation's economic woes remained with George W. Bush. According to the 2012 exit polls, while Mitt Romney was slightly preferred over Obama when it came to handling the economy (51 percent to 47 percent), Obama held a whopping 81 percent to 18 percent advantage when voters were asked which candidate "cares about people like me" (Edison Research 2012). Meanwhile, Americans held George W. Bush in minimum regard: 53 percent said he was more to blame for the current economic problems; only 38 percent held Obama responsible (Edison Research 2012). During the campaign it was Vice President Joe Biden who neatly encapsulated Obama's argument for reelection: "Osama bin Laden is dead and General Motors is alive" (Hawkins 2012). This was a powerful slogan, and it helped Obama defy James Carville's famous aphorism coined during the 1992 Bill Clinton campaign, "It's the economy, stupid!" In 2012 Obama became the first Democratic president to twice win more than 50 percent of the vote since Franklin D. Roosevelt.

Today, the economic turnaround is nearly complete. Marking the fifth anniversary of the passage of the American Recovery and Reinvestment Act in 2014, the White House noted that for forty-seven consecutive months the economy added new private-sector jobs, and more than 8.5 million new jobs have been added since passage of the law (with 3.5 million directly attributable to it) (White House 2014). The unemployment rate has dipped to 5 percent—half what it was in 2010, and more than two points lower than when Obama assumed office. Republicans claim these improved figures happened *despite Obama*, and that enactment of his economic program actually hindered economic growth. But Obama and the Democrats counter that without the stimulus, measures saving the auto industry, TARP, Dodd-Frank, and other reforms, the economy would have plunged into a second Great Depression. The results speak for themselves. Under Obama the economy has created nearly five times more jobs than it did under George W. Bush. Remembering those early days in office, Obama reflected on the economic woes and the measures he undertook to stop them: "It was hard, but we ended up avoiding a terrible depression. That's an important legacy for me" (Walsh 2015).

"A Big Fucking Deal"

In the midst of the economic downturn, Obama was advised by Rahm Emanuel to go slow on health care. Americans, Emanuel argued, were preoccupied with the economic calamity before them and would understand if Obama took a piecemeal approach to health-care reform. But Obama overruled his chief of staff and decided to go all-in (Axelrod 2015, 371). One reason was personal: Obama witnessed his dying mother reviewing insurance company forms from her hospital bed, and vowed that no one, even those with life-threatening illnesses, should be denied coverage. By 2009 the problem was immense: 16 percent of all Americans (nearly fifty million people) lacked insurance, and 46 percent told the Gallup organization that "rising healthcare costs, including costs such as insurance premiums and out-of-pocket expenses," were a "major problem" (US Census 2010 and Gallup/*USA Today* 2009).[2] The time for action was long past. In a private letter written to Obama shortly before his death, Massachusetts Senator Edward M. Kennedy called health care "the great unfinished business of our society," and described it as "a moral issue, that at stake are not just the details of policy, but fundamental principles of social justice and the character of our country" (Kennedy 2009).

The more Obama pursued his dream of being the first president since Theodore Roosevelt wished it so to enact something approaching universal health-care coverage, the more the Tea Party wing (and others) within the Republican Party denounced his plan. Town hall meetings held during the summer of 2009 erupted into shouting matches between energized Tea Partiers and beleaguered lawmakers. Fearing reprisals from their base, Republican congressional leaders decided that they had to be unalterably opposed to *any* Obama-sponsored health-care measure. Senate Majority Leader Mitch McConnell remembered: "It was absolutely critical that everybody be together because if the proponents of the bill were able to say it was bipartisan, it tended to convey to the public that this is O.K., they must have figured it out" (Ornstein 2015). To that end,

McConnell threatened Republican senators Chuck Grassley and Mike Enzi that if they cooperated with Obama, their futures would be at risk. Both backed away from a bipartisan compromise (Ornstein 2015).

The combination of outrage from an angry Republican base and threats made to key legislators gave the GOP a boost in portraying Obamacare as another government intrusion that would take away liberties (including the right to choose one's own doctor, and dying patients subjected to "death panels") from society's "makers" while freely giving monies to the "takers"—that is, the poor and those on the margins of life (what Mitt Romney memorably called the "47 percent"). Obama's plan won congressional approval with *zero* Republican votes in either the House or Senate—a remarkable feat given that sixty votes had become a requirement to pass any Senate legislation. Not even Lyndon B. Johnson, whose mastery of the Senate is celebrated by biographer Robert Caro, had to deal with a Senate operating under this rule (Caro 2002).

When Obama sat down to sign the health-care law in 2010 (a delay that happened when Ted Kennedy died and Republican Scott Brown was elected to replace him), microphones caught Vice President Biden whispering in the president's ear, "This is a big fucking deal!" (Krugman 2014). Indeed it was. Among its key provisions: (1) Americans would be required to purchase health-care coverage or face increasing tax penalties, (2) young Americans could stay on their parent's health-care plans until age twenty-six (a popular provision given the paucity of jobs for young people), (3) health-care companies could no longer deny coverage based on any "preexisting condition," and (4) they could allocate no more than 15 percent of their incomes to administrative costs (a move designed to curb excessive executive salaries and bonuses).

But signing the law proved to be an albatross around Obama's political fortunes. Thinking he had done all he could, Obama ceded the bully pulpit to the Republicans, who continued to drive home the message that Obamacare was a huge government boondoggle. This message resonated in the 2010 midterms, and immediately upon taking control of the House in 2011, Republican members proceeded to pass bills to undo, repeal, or tweak Obamacare—a move they would undertake more than *fifty-four times* between 2011 and 2014 (O'Keefe 2014).

While Republicans continued to drive home their desire to "repeal and replace" Obamacare, the "replace" portion of their platform was lacking. Superficial GOP plans were constructed, none with any chance of gaining much legislative support. The more vocal Republicans became about repealing Obamacare, the more the Democratic base came to embrace it. And not only embrace it, but fear that a Republican-controlled Congress *and* a Republican president would make repeal their first priority. These fears are not unfounded. After all, a Republican-dominated Supreme Court took a swipe at Obamacare in 2012, with four GOP-appointed justices declaring the statute unconstitutional. (Only Chief Justice John Roberts demurred.) Another 2015 challenge was turned back by the Supreme Court, making it increasingly likely that Obamacare is here to stay. And a Democratic win in the 2016 presidential election would all but ensure the program's longevity.

All this happened as millions received health insurance for the first time. Estimates are that 10.2 million Americans are enrolled in Obamacare, with many receiving government subsidies to purchase health insurance (Kohn 2015). Despite the failure of the initial rollout, with the government-sponsored website failing to register eager applicants, the program eventually righted itself. Today, only one in twenty Americans thinks health care is the top problem facing the country, a fifth of the number during the Obamacare debate (Milbank 2015, A-2). Ironically, it is in places like Republican-red Kentucky where voters have seen the law's benefits. While voters there recoil at the word "Obamacare," they like their state-named program dubbed "Kynect," which actually *is* Obamacare. However, in 2015 Kentuckians elected a Tea Party–inspired governor who promised to do away with the program.

As the realization mounts that Obamacare is now woven into the fabric of society's safety net, Barack Obama has embraced the term Obamacare and sees it as an important legacy. Paul Pierson, a University of California–Berkeley political scientist, concludes: "When you add the ACA [Affordable Care Act] reforms in the stimulus package, Dodd-Frank, and his various climate initiatives, I don't think there's any doubt: On domestic issues Obama is the most consequential and successful Democratic president since LBJ. It isn't close" (Matthews 2015).

EXTRICATING THE UNITED STATES FROM IRAQ AND AFGHANISTAN

When Barack Obama assumed the presidency in 2009, the Iraq War had become a touchstone for the failures of the George W. Bush presidency. Initially popular, by Election Day 2008 the war was viewed as a mistake by 58 percent of those polled by the Gallup organization (Gallup/*USA Today* 2008). Democrats who once supported the war were quick to back away—the most prominent being Hillary Clinton, Obama's chief rival for the 2008 Democratic nomination. Many concluded that they had been sold a bill of goods, including the false intelligence claiming that Saddam Hussein was on the precipice of constructing a nuclear weapon. In October 2002 Bush stirred emotions, still raw in the wake of 9/11, by conjuring this powerful scenario: "Facing clear evidence of peril, we cannot wait for the final proof—the smoking gun—that could come in the form of a mushroom cloud" (Bush 2002). Frank Rich, then a *New York Times* columnist, wrote a best-seller about Bush's efforts to sell the public on the Iraq war titled *The Greatest Story Ever Sold* (Rich 2006). Twelve years after the start of the war, even many Republicans concluded it was a colossal error—including George W. Bush's brother Jeb, who, after being asked "Knowing what we know now," would he have ventured into Iraq, replied: "I would not have engaged; I would not have gone into Iraq" (Murray and Reston 2015).

Opposing the Iraq War in 2003, a young Illinois state senator pointedly noted he was not against all wars, just "dumb wars" (Obama 2006, 294). Barack Obama's classification of conflicts into smart and dumb categories is important because as a presidential candidate he never portrayed himself as a pacifist, a point Obama underscored in accepting the 2009 Nobel Peace Prize (Obama 2009b). During the 2008 campaign, Obama vowed: "We will kill bin Laden, we will crush al-Qaeda. This has to be our biggest national security priority" (Obama 2008a). Opposing Bush on Iraq and placing a renewed effort to decapitate al-Qaeda did not mean Obama objected to an expansive use of presidential power. Far from it. The use of drones is one example. As of January 2015, there were *nine times* as many drone strikes under Obama as there were during George W. Bush's two terms (Serle 2015). Drones not only hunted and killed leaders of al-Qaeda in Afghanistan, Yemen, Pakistan, and elsewhere, they also killed Americans overseas who, allegedly, had joined these terrorist organizations.

These actions outraged critics who saw Obama acting as judge and jury in a vast expansion of power far beyond the limits set by the US Constitution. Rand Paul, a leader in the libertarian wing of the Republican Party, was one. During the 2013 Senate confirmation hearings on the nomination of John Brennan to head the CIA, Paul staged a thirteen-hour talkathon as a protest, citing Brennan's contention that there was no limitation to US use of drone strikes anywhere in the world. Responding to congressional queries, CIA Director John Brennan stated, "There is nothing in international law that . . . prohibits us from using lethal force against our enemies outside of an active battlefield, at least when the country involved consents or is unable or unwilling to take action against the threat" (Moorhead 2013). Such reasoning continued to guide the Obama administration as it used drones as a principal weapon to kill those who would harm the homeland and inserted special forces to rescue captured Americans or kill suspected terrorists.

Another critic who challenged Obama's actions was Edward Snowden, a contractor assigned to the National Security Agency. While employed at the NSA, Snowden discovered that the United States was collecting phone records on every US citizen. To him, this represented a massive invasion of privacy that threatened to undermine the freedoms guaranteed in the Constitution. After disclosing mountains of information to the press, Snowden sought asylum in Russia, where Vladimir Putin welcomed him with open arms. Obama denounced Snowden as a "hacker," and sought to assure the public that his actions did not threaten their privacy but enhanced their security (Benac 2013). Administration officials claimed that to find a needle in a haystack (i.e., a terrorist), they had to have a haystack. And that meant acquiring phone records (not transcripts of phone conversations). Eventually, Congress ordered the phone companies to maintain these records, not the NSA. Shepard Fairey, the artist who created the iconic 2008 Obama "Hope" poster, acknowledged that Obama is "not even close" to having lived up to his promise: "I mean, drones and domestic spying are the last things I would have thought [he'd support]" (Lerner 2015).

Like other presidents, Obama undertook overseas actions without seeking congressional approval. A letter dated March 21, 2011, informing Congress of US air strikes against the Libyan regime of Muammar Gaddafi, contained this striking sentence: "For these purposes, I have directed these actions, which are in the national security and foreign policy interests of the United States, pursuant to my constitutional authority to conduct US foreign relations and as Commander in Chief and Chief Executive" (Obama 2011). Years later Obama again relied on a perceived inherent executive authority to strike against ISIL, a new terrorist threat in Syria and Iraq (more on this later), again without explicit legislative authority.

These actions—particularly those against ISIL—upset institutionalists in both parties, including Senators Timothy Kaine (D) and Jeff Flake (R), who struggled to pass a congressional resolution giving Obama authority to strike against ISIL. Obama ally Timothy Kaine was irate at his colleagues for failing to do their jobs, saying Congress "would rather hide from its constitutional duty to declare war than have a meaningful debate about whether and how the United States should militarily confront the Islamic state" (Kaine 2015, A-17). Kaine was also irritated at the president, calling Obama's reliance on the 2001 congressional resolution to wage war against al-Qaeda "ridiculous" and "weird" (Weiner 2015, B-3). Nonetheless, Kaine and Flake failed to overcome the legislative roadblocks—partly because no agreement could be found on proper wording of a resolution, and partly because the public appetite to reinsert US troops into the region was nonexistent. In December 2015 Obama finally declared his support for a congressional authorization to act against ISIL, telling the nation in a televised speech: "If Congress believes, as I do, that we are at war with ISIL, it should go ahead and vote to authorize the continued use of military force against these terrorists. I think it's time for Congress to vote to demonstrate that the American people are united, and committed, to this fight" (Obama 2015b).

As these actions make clear, Barack Obama's chief objection to George W. Bush was not his broad use of presidential power but his *judgment*. Obama offered himself to voters as someone who would not make snap decisions and, unlike Bush, be more deliberate in his thinking, especially when committing US forces abroad. That was appealing, since in 2008 voters were looking for someone completely different from Bush. This is a common phenomena: After eight years of Ronald Reagan, voters wanted a hands-on president and got one in George H. W. Bush. After George H. W. Bush, voters wanted an empathetic president who would understand their economic problems, and they found him in Bill Clinton.

And after Bill Clinton, voters wanted someone with high moral values, and George W. Bush fit the bill. In Obama's case, his deliberative judgment often served him well—keeping him cool in the midst of crises ("no drama Obama," as the saying went). One can almost literally see this quality at work in the famous photo of Obama and his team poised in their chairs in the White House Situation Room as the Navy SEALs were executing their raid within the walls of Osama bin Laden's Pakistani compound.

But Obama's judgment and overly deliberative style would fail him in Syria. As happened elsewhere in the Middle East, the Arab Spring spread to Damascus and Bashar al-Assad became a target. Having long ruled Syria (as his father did before him), the population rose up to overthrow his regime. But Assad would not go quietly. Pleas arose for the United States to help "moderates" dispose of Assad (who also happened to be a longtime Russian ally). Hillary Clinton favored US intervention, including providing arms to the rebels, calling Syria a "wicked problem" (Hillary Clinton 2014, 447–70). Clinton argued that US action was needed to prevent Assad from using chemical weapons against his own people, and to assure a peaceful transition of power (presumably to a government more favorably disposed to the United States). Obama dithered: first ruling out any US troop presence or assistance to moderates, whose moderation he doubted. When Assad used chemical weapons against his own people, Obama favored US air strikes, then pulled back, then decided there should be a congressional vote on the issue, and then decided there should not be such a vote when it became clear there would be no congressional consensus. This outraged the major US ally in the region, Israel, and Republicans charged, rightly, that Obama's indecision made the United States look weak. Eventually, Syria consented to international inspections and dismantled its stock of chemical weapons. But Obama's indecisiveness—as well as his reluctance to use significant numbers of US troops to deal with ISIL in Iraq and Syria—is a major critique of Obama's foreign policy record, even as Republicans themselves remain divided between neoconservatives (represented by former vice president Dick Cheney and most of the 2016 presidential candidates, including Jeb Bush and Marco Rubio), and isolationists (represented by Kentucky Senator and presidential candidate Rand Paul). While Republicans attack Obama's foreign policy as misguided (a charitable descriptor), the party remains divided when it comes to what the powers of the president should be and what future judgments should be rendered. Meanwhile, memories of the Vietnam War linger, and presidents have learned that without strong public backing, no war is sustainable for any lengthy period of time.

THREE FINAL FOREIGN POLICY INITIATIVES

Shortly after his party was routed in the 2014 midterm elections, President Obama noted that he is a gut player and that fourth quarters (both in his beloved basketball and in the presidency) are important: "Interesting things happen in the fourth quarter," he told a reporter with a grin (Miller 2014). Obama undoubtedly had in mind three important (and consequential) foreign policy initiatives already underway during the final twenty-six months of his presidency.

Cuba: "Cutting the Shackles"

The first initiative was to complete a piece of unfinished business that eluded previous presidents: granting formal diplomatic status to Cuba. One of Dwight D. Eisenhower's final acts as president was to sever diplomatic ties with Fidel Castro's Communist Cuba. A quarter century later Jimmy Carter entered the Oval Office with the desire to improve US relations around the world, including granting formal US diplomatic recognition of China in 1978. Carter wanted to do the same with Cuba, and he took the first step in 1977 with the establishment of the US Interests Section in Havana (Carter 2015, 186). But Cuban adventures in the African countries of Angola and Mozambique—along with the 1980 Mariel Boat Lift, which sent 120,000 Cuban refugees into the southern United States, including prisoners and other "undesirables" with criminal records or mental problems—ended plans to normalize relations (Clinton 2004, 274). Bill Clinton blamed the influx of refugees into his native Arkansas (and the rioting that followed) for his 1980 gubernatorial defeat (Clinton 2004, 274–78).

The intervention of Pope Francis proved instrumental in establishing a dialogue between Barack Obama and Fidel Castro's successor, his brother Raul. Those conversations produced the release of Alan Gross, a subcontractor for the US Agency for International Development and accused

US spy, who had been imprisoned by Cuban authorities for five years. His release—along with another US spy who had been jailed for two decades in return for three Cuban spies—were necessary preconditions. In addition, the US State Department removed Cuba from its list of nations as a State Sponsor of Terrorism. Using his constitutional authority, Obama unilaterally announced the restoration of US-Cuban diplomatic relations, stating, "America chooses to cut loose the shackles of the past so as to reach for a better future—for the Cuban people, for the American people, for our entire hemisphere, and for the world" (Obama 2014).

In July 2015 Cuban and US embassies were reopened in Havana and Washington, D.C., Secretary of State John Kerry traveled to Cuba to preside over the opening of the US embassy there (in the former US Interests Section). While Obama would like to end the trade embargo (something even some Republicans from agricultural states support), the 1996 Helms-Burton law prohibits him from doing so. Nonetheless, the day is coming when Congress is likely to end this failed policy. As Obama noted in his stunning announcement, the embargo "has failed to advance our interests," adding: "I do not believe we can keep doing the same thing for over five decades and expect a different result" (Obama 2014). However, several congressional Republicans and nearly all of the 2016 GOP presidential candidates criticized Obama for giving too much to the Castros. Marco Rubio led the charge: "Barack Obama is the worst negotiator we've had as president since at least Jimmy Carter—maybe in the history of the nation. . . . [W]hat the president is saying, by recognizing Cuba's government, is that in the twenty-first century being a Communist, brutal dictatorship is an acceptable form of government" (Kilgore 2014 and Welch 2014). Despite the harsh rhetoric, it is likely that Obama's recognition of Cuba will prevail for the foreseeable future, whether or not the next president is a Democrat or a Republican.

The Trans-Pacific Partnership

Another important Obama foreign policy initiative was to "pivot" US foreign policy interests toward the Pacific, where the rising powers of the twenty-first century—China and India, especially—will exert tremendous influence. This has resulted in the Trans-Pacific Partnership (TPP)—one of the most consequential trade deals since the North American Free Trade Agreement (NAFTA) was ratified in the early days of the Clinton administration. This deal establishes free trade zones between the United States and eleven other nations bordering (or located in) the Pacific Ocean. Together, these eleven Pacific Rim nations have an annual gross domestic product of nearly $28 trillion that represents roughly 40 percent of the global gross domestic product and one-third of all world trade (Granville 2015).

While not yet finalized, Obama won fast-track trade authority from the Republican-controlled Congress in 2015—one of the very few times Obama's interests and those of the GOP coincided. This authority gives Obama the power to present any eventual deal to Congress for an up or down vote without amendments. Many Democrats and their allies remain skeptical or outright opposed to TPP, including all of the 2016 Democratic presidential contenders. And Senate Majority Leader Mitch McConnell has vowed that the Senate will not take up the agreement prior to the 2016 presidential election (Kane and Nakamura 2015, A-1).

Thinking about this and other remaining decisions in Obama's fourth quarter, Bill Clinton presciently noted, "In a time when a lot of stuff's happening, a lot of foreign policy decisions are likely to be unpopular" (quoted in Gibbs and Duffy 2015, 39). This is especially true with TPP and the Democratic base. This schism is cheered by Republicans who see an opportunity to split the Democratic Party from Obama in advance of the 2016 elections. Whether this fourth-quarter press by Obama will succeed is dubious, and it is likely that the next president will have to conclude the deal. Still, the TPP represents a historic turning point in US foreign policy.

A Nuclear Deal with Iran

The final fourth-quarter Obama foreign policy initiative was the conclusion of a deal with Iran that limits that country's nuclear capacity in exchange for a gradual lifting of economic sanctions. Iran had been a pariah since the taking of hostages at the US embassy in November 1979—a saga that helped end the Jimmy Carter presidency and lasted until the day Ronald Reagan took office. US relations with Iran have remained almost nonexistent since. But during the 2008 campaign, Obama declared that, if elected, he would enter into a dialogue with Iran without any preconditions—a position that drew a strong rebuke from Hillary Clinton. Initially, the Obama administration sought (and won) additional congressional sanctions against Iran and persuaded both its European allies and its adversaries (notably China and Russia) to join. The sanctions crippled Iran's economy, which, in turn, brought the rogue nation to the negotiating table. In July 2015 an agreement was reached whereby Iran would submit to nuclear inspections conducted by the United Nations' International Atomic Energy Agency, and would dispose of its fissionable material. In exchange, economic sanctions would be gradually lifted as Iran complied with the agreement's provisions.

Obama argued that this agreement was the most consequential of his presidency, and he was preoccupied with making sure it would not be upset by recalcitrant Republicans who might find support among squishy Democrats. This was a hard sell, made harder when Israeli Prime Minister Benjamin Netanyahu labeled it a "capitulation" and "a mistake of historic proportions" (Beaumont 2015). Obama countered that Iran was mere months away from obtaining a nuclear weapon, which might necessitate using a military option to undo the deed. Rather than face this stark choice, Obama maintained the agreement postponed Iranian acquisition of nuclear weapons for at least ten to fifteen years, if not longer. Russia and China were important participants in this effort, and Obama argued that scuttling the Iran deal would split the United States from its partners—thereby making it impossible to reimpose sanctions. Critics contended that any easing of economic sanctions would give Iran a pile of money that would fund terrorist acts by Hezbollah against the Israelis and elsewhere. Obama countered that the stark economic realities facing Iran make it more likely that monies would be used to right that nation's listing economy.

In the end, Obama won the argument. The Senate fell short of the sixty votes needed to pass legislation voiding the deal, and the president did not have to issue a veto. This has not stopped Republicans from voicing their vitriolic opposition to Obama's actions. Former Arkansas Governor Mike Huckabee, a 2016 GOP presidential contender, maintained that Obama's actions would "take the Israelis and march them to the door of the oven"—a reference to the crematoria at the Nazi concentration camps during the Holocaust. Obama recoiled at the accusation, noting that the over-the-top GOP rhetoric was "ridiculous" and "sad," unbecoming of someone wanting the keys to 1600 Pennsylvania Avenue (Pace 2015). He later accused the Republican congressional caucus of making "common cause" with the Iranian hardliners who love to shout "Death to America!"

(Obama 2015a). The rhetorical sparring is likely to continue well into the 2016 campaign, with leading GOP presidential contender Donald Trump calling Obama "very stupid and incompetent" (Manjarres 2015).

REGRETS

Despite the many accomplishments of the Obama presidency, there are regrets. The "cancer" (Obama's word) represented by ISIL that will be left on the next president's desk is a sore point (Obama 2015b). Obama's inability to achieve a worldwide ban on nuclear weapons is a dream not realized. Guantanamo Bay remains open, despite a dwindling prison population there and Obama's repeated pledges to close it. Not pursuing comprehensive immigration reform—and hoping a delay would give Republican Congress members enough wiggle room to compromise—is another regret. A lack of money to support long-overdue infrastructure projects (including repairing dangerously unsafe roads and bridges) is one more. Also disappointing is the failure to achieve a comprehensive spending agreement with House Speaker John Boehner in 2011 (largely because the hapless Boehner could not control his party's raucous Tea Party faction). The need remains to curb entitlement programs, including Social Security and Medicare, and it will be up to the next president to do so. And in Obama's telling, his inability to overcome the power of the National Rifle Association following mass shootings in Tucson, Sandy Hook, Charleston, and Roseburg is high on his list of regrets. Obama described the killing of small children at Sandy Hook the "worst day of my presidency," and just prior to the Charleston massacre, he told the British Broadcasting Corporation that the one area "where I feel I've been most frustrated and most stymied" is that the United States "is the one advanced nation on earth in which we do not have sufficient commonsense gun safety laws, even in the face of mass killings" (Simmons 2015; Jackson 2015).

But perhaps the greatest regret of all was Obama's inability to transcend the partisan divide. This was his chief calling card when he first appeared on the national stage at the 2004 Democratic Convention. Speaking before an enraptured audience, Obama invoked the US motto "E pluribus unum" ("Out of many, one") and sought to reinvigorate it in the wake of the partisan chasm that had widened during George W.

Bush's presidency: "There's not a liberal America and a conservative America; there's the United States of America. . . . The pundits like to slice and dice our country into red states and blue states: red states for Republicans, blue states for Democrats. But I've got news for them too. We worship an awesome God in the blue states, and we don't like federal agents poking around our libraries in the red states. We coach Little League in the blue states and, yes, we've got some gay friends in the red states. There are patriots who opposed the war in Iraq, and there are patriots who supported the war in Iraq. We are one people, all of us pledging allegiance to the stars and stripes, all of us defending the United States of America" (Obama 2004).

But Obama's unifying rhetoric has fallen far short of achieving a broad sense of national unity. Instead, he became the second consecutive president unable to bridge the divide. In 2000 George W. Bush promised to be "a uniter, not a divider." But that disputed election, the war in Iraq, and Bush's failures in the wake of Hurricane Katrina further segregated Democrats and Republicans into their respective camps. Like Bush, Obama not only failed to heal the breach, he widened it. In 2013 the Gallup organization released data showing that the average gap in partisan approval of the Obama presidency was seventy points—nine points *higher* than the party gap of sixty-one points during George W. Bush's eight years (Jones 2013). As party loyalties become increasingly tied to racial and gender identification, geography, and cultural lifestyles, partisan perceptions have hardened. This has made it nearly impossible for any chief executive to govern in a divided government, and it has made the stakes surrounding the outcome of future presidential contests (including 2016) incredibly high.

Still, Obama's accomplishments outweigh the regrets. Think of it: If voters knew in 2008 that the economy (then on the precipice of a second Great Depression) would recover; that the dream of universal health care would edge much closer to reality; that the large-scale US-led wars in Iraq and Afghanistan would end; that Osama bin Laden would die; that Bill Clinton's Don't Ask, Don't Tell military policy would be repealed without incident; and that gay marriage would become legal, they would be astonished. On election night in 2008, speaking before thousands gathered in Chicago, Obama triumphantly declared, "It's been a long time coming, but tonight, because of what we did on this date, in this election, at this defining moment, change has come to America" (Obama 2008b).

On that night, not even Obama himself could fully contemplate the meaning of this sentence. Now everyone can.

As the end of his presidency draws nigh, Obama noted that when it comes to history's notations about him, scholars are likely to say:

> I have strengths and I have weaknesses, like every President, like every person. I do think one of my strengths is temperament. I am comfortable with complexity, and I think I'm pretty good at keeping my moral compass while recognizing that I am a product of original sin. And every morning and every night I'm taking measure of my actions against the options and possibilities available to me, understanding that there are going to be mistakes. . . . I am part of that tragedy occasionally, but that, if I am doing my very best and basing my decisions on the core values and ideals that I was brought up with and that I think are pretty consistent with those of most Americans, that, at the end of the day, things will be better rather than worse (Remnick 2015).

Citing an old proverb known to woodsmen, Carl Sandburg famously wrote of his hero, Abraham Lincoln, "A tree is best measured when it's down" (Sandburg 1969, 880). The Lincoln tree has long passed into posterity, with accolades from historians and fellow presidents alike. Obama has confessed that Lincoln remains his favorite president: "I think America was very lucky that Abraham Lincoln was President when he was President. If he hadn't been, the course of history would be very different. But I also think that, despite being the greatest President, in my mind, in our history, it took another hundred and fifty years before African-Americans had anything approaching formal equality, much less real equality. I think that doesn't diminish Lincoln's achievements, but it acknowledges that, at the end of the day, we're part of a long-running story. We just try to get our paragraph right" (Remnick 2015).

Now that the Obama tree is coming down, historians will take its measure. As Obama readily admits, the full consequences of his presidency will not be apparent for years, even decades. Thousands of paragraphs will be written about the Obama years, and many trees sacrificed for old-fashioned printed books covering this epoch of US history. But in this author's view, one thing is certain: The Obama tree is a very tall one indeed.

NOTES

1. Exit polls found that 41 percent approved of the Tea Party, with 92 percent of Republicans saying they "strongly supported" it. See Edison Media Research and Mitofsky International, exit poll, November 2, 2010.

2. In 2009, 16.1 percent of the population was uninsured, totaling 48,985,000 people.

WORKS CITED

Axelrod, David. 2015. *Believer: My Forty Years in Politics*. New York: Penguin Press.
Beaumont, Peter. 2015. "Netanyahu Denounces Iran Nuclear Deal but Faces Criticism from within Israel." *The Guardian*, July 14.
Benac, Nancy. 2013. "Obama Recasts Edward Snowden as 'Hacker' in Effort to Downplay Him." Huffington Post, June 28.
Bush, George W. 2002. Remarks by the president on Iraq. Cincinnati, OH, October 7.
Caro, Robert. 2002. *Master of the Senate: The Years of Lyndon Johnson*. New York: Alfred A. Knopf.
Carter, Jimmy. 2015. *A Full Life: Reflections at Ninety*. New York: Simon & Schuster.
Clinton, Bill. 2004. *My Life*. New York: Alfred A. Knopf.
Clinton, Hillary. 2014. *Hard Choices*. New York: Simon & Schuster.
Draper, Robert. 2012. *Do Not Ask What Good We Do: Inside the U.S. House of Representatives*. New York: Free Press.
Edison Media Research and Mitofsky International. 2010. Exit poll, November 2.
Edison Research. 2012. Exit poll, November 6.
Frank, Barney. 2015. *Frank: A Life in Politics from the Great Society to Same-Sex Marriage*. New York: Farrar, Strauss and Giroux.
Gallup/*USA Today*. 2008. Poll, October 31–November 2.
Gallup/ *USA Today*. 2009. Poll, September 11–13.
Gibbs, Nancy, and Michael Duffy. 2015. "Game of Thrones." *Time*, August 3.
Granville, Kevin. 2015. "The Trans-Pacific Partnership Trade Deal Explained." *New York Times*, May 11.
Grunwald, Michael. 2014. "Five Years After Stimulus, Obama Says It Worked." *Time*, February 16.
Hawkins, Rodney. 2012. "Biden: We Are Better Off, 'bin Laden Is Dead and General Motors Is Alive.'" CBS News, September 3.
Isidore, Chris. 2009. "Job Loss: Worst in 34 Years." CNN Money. February 6. http://money.cnn.com/2009/02/06/news/economy/jobs_january/.
Jackson, David. 2015. "Obama's Biggest Frustration: Gun Control." *USA Today*, July 24.
Jones, Jeffrey M. 2013. "Obama's Fourth Year in Office Ties as Most Polarized Ever." Gallup poll, press release, January 24.
Kaine, Tim. 2015. "Congress Sits on the Sidelines." *Washington Post*, August 9.
Kane, Paul, and David Nakamura. 2015. "McConnell Warns That Trade Deal Can't Pass Congress Before 2016 Elections." *Washington Post*, December 11.
Kennedy, Edward M. 2009. Final letter to President Obama. May 12.
Kilgore, Ed. 2014. "Action and Reaction on Cuba." *Washington Monthly*, December 17.
Kohn, Jonathan. 2015. "Obamacare Enrollment Is 10 Million, but Supreme Court Ruling Could Shrink It Dramatically." Huffington Post, June 2. www.huffingtonpost.com/2015/06/02/obamacare-enrollment_n_7493776.html.
Krugman, Paul. 2014. "In Defense of Obama." *Rolling Stone*, October 8.

Legum, Judd. 2015. "Four Things That Were Supposed to Happen by 2015 Because Obama Was Reelected." *Think Progress*, January 1.
Lerner, Adam B. 2015. "'Hope' Poster Artist Shepard Fairey Says Obama Let Him Down." *Politico*, May 28.
Matthews, Dylan. 2015. "Barack Obama Is Officially One of the Most Consequential Presidents in American History." *Vox*, June 26.
Manjarres, Javier. 2015. "Donald Trump Calls Obama 'Very Stupid and Incompetent.'" Shark-tank.com. September 10. See http://shark-tank.com/2015/09/10/donald-trump-calls-obama-very-stupid-and-incompetent-video/. Accessed May 31, 2016.
Milbank, Dana. 2015. "The Kindergarten Congress." *Washington Post*, June 11.
Miller, Zeke J. 2014. "Obama Looks to the '4th Quarter' of His Presidency." *Time*, December 10.
Moorhead, Molly. 2013. "Rand Paul Says CIA Director John Brennan Claimed No Geographic Limit on Drone Strikes." *PolitiFact*, March 12.
Murray, Sara, and Maeve Reston. 2015. "Jeb Bush Again Changes Iraq Answer." CNN Politics, May 15, 2015. www.cnn.com/2015/05/13/politics/jeb-bush-iraq-2016/.
NBC News/*Wall Street Journal*. 2014. Poll, December 10–14.
New York Times. 2009. *Obama: The Historic Journey*. New York: *New York Times* and Callaway Arts and Entertainment.
Obama, Barack. 2004. Keynote address to the Democratic National Convention. Boston, July 27.
Obama, Barack. 2006. *The Audacity of Hope: Thoughts on Reclaiming the American Dream*. New York: Crown Publishers.
Obama, Barack. 2008a. "Transcript of the Presidential Debate." October 7. See www.youtube.com/watch?v=kKHsjRzUTLQ. Accessed August 5, 2015.
Obama, Barack. 2008b. Victory speech. Chicago, November 4.
Obama, Barack. 2009a. Inaugural address. Washington, DC, January 20.
Obama, Barack. 2009b. "Remarks by the President at the Acceptance of the Nobel Peace Prize." Oslo, Norway, December 10.
Obama, Barack. 2011. "Letter from the President Regarding the Commencement of Operations in Libya." Office of the Press Secretary, March 21.
Obama, Barack. 2014. "Statement by the President on Cuba." Washington, DC, December 17.
Obama, Barack. 2015a. "Remarks by the President on the Iran Nuclear Deal." American University, Washington, D.C., August 5.
Obama, Barack. 2015b. "Address to the Nation by the President." Washington, DC, December 6.
O'Keefe, Ed. 2014. "The House Has Voted 54 Times in Four Years on Obamacare." *Washington Post*, March 21.
Ornstein, Norm. 2015. "The Real Story of Obamacare's Birth." *The Atlantic*, July 6.
Pace, Julie. 2015. "Obama Calls GOP Criticism of Iran Deal 'Ridiculous,' 'Sad.'" *Washington Post*, July 27.
Remnick, David. 2015. "Ten Days in June." *The New Yorker*, June 26.
Rich, Frank. 2006. *The Greatest Story Ever Sold: The Decline and Fall of Truth in Bush's America*. New York: Penguin Press.
Romney, Mitt. 2008. "Let Detroit Go Bankrupt." *New York Times*, November 18.
Sandburg, Carl. 1969 reprint. *Abraham Lincoln: The Prairie Years and the War Years, Volume 3*. New York: Harcourt Brace and Jovanovich.
Santelli, Rick. 2009. YouTube video. See www.youtube.com/watch?v=bEZB4taSEoA. Accessed November 23, 2015.
Serle, Jack. 2015. "Monthly Updates on the Covert War." *The Bureau of Investigative Journalism*, February 2.
Simmons, Bill. 2015. "President Obama and Bill Simmons: The GQ Interview." *GQ Magazine*, November 17.
Tocqueville, Alexis de. 1969 edition, ed., J. P. Mayer. *Democracy in America*. Garden City, NY: Doubleday.

US Census. 2010. "Table 8: People without Health Insurance Coverage by Selected Characteristics: 2009 and 2010." See www.census.gov/hhes/www/hlthins/data/incpovhlth/2010/table8.pdf. Accessed November 23, 2015.

Walsh, Kenneth T. 2015. "Building a Legacy," *U.S. News and World Report*, June 12.

Weiner, Rachel. 2015. "Kaine at War with an Undeclared War." *Washington Post*, August 7.

Welch, Matt. 2014. "Rand Paul Is More Right about Cuba than Marco Rubio." *Reason*, December 19.

White House. 2014. "The Recovery Act." See https://www.whitehouse.gov/economy/jobs/recovery-act. Accessed November 23, 2015.

Wolffe, Richard. 2009. *Renegade: The Making of a President*. New York: Crown Publishers.

2

OBAMA AND WASHINGTON

Fallen Hopes and Frustrated Change

John J. Pitney Jr., Claremont McKenna College

"For with what judgment you judge, you shall be judged: and with what measure you measure, it shall be measured to you against." This New Testament passage (Matthew 7:2) suggests that we should hold people to their own standards—a good starting point for appraising Barack Obama's presidency. During his 2008 campaign and his tenure in office, he created great expectations about what he would do and how he would conduct himself. On the night he clinched the Democratic nomination, he said that future generations would say "that this was the moment when we began to provide care for the sick and good jobs to the jobless; this was the moment when the rise of the oceans began to slow and our planet began to heal; this was the moment when we ended a war and secured our nation and restored our image as the last, best hope on Earth" (Obama 2008c).

Read my lips: Presidents sometimes break pledges. So is it fair to judge President Obama by his? The answer is yes, especially when one considers the circumstances of his 2008 election. He was promising not just competence and good policy but hope, change, and an entirely new way of doing the people's work. He said, "We are tired of business as usual in Washington. We are hungry for change and we are ready to believe again" (Obama 2008a). Just before his victory, he proclaimed that "we are five days away from fundamentally transforming the United States of America" (Obama 2008e). Years later journalist Barbara Walters (2013) recalled: "He made so many promises. We thought that he was going to be—I shouldn't say this at Christmastime—but the next messiah." Acting like a typical promise-breaking, hope-crushing, business-as-usual politician would thus be a breach of faith.

Unfortunately, that breach of faith started at the moment he announced his presidential candidacy. Right after his election to the Senate in 2004, he told a reporter: "So look, I can unequivocally say I will not be running for national office in four years, and my entire focus is making sure that I'm the best possible senator on behalf of the people of Illinois" (Fornek 2004). If we were to hold him strictly to his word, his presidency itself would have to count as a broken promise. He was hardly the first politician in this predicament: Bill Clinton made a similar pledge in 1990 and reneged two years later. Still, candidate Obama stressed that he was different from other politicians, and during the primary campaign, he emphasized that he was specifically not like the Clintons.

On issue after issue, the gap between promise and performance has been depressing. At Salon, Elias Isquith writes: "But even if the trajectory of the president's career is familiar, his first presidential campaign was so uniquely romantic, so willing to describe voting for Obama with the moralistic language of national self-redemption, that the consequences of his failure are not" (Isquith 2014).

ECONOMIC DISAPPOINTMENT

A few weeks after the 2008 election, NBC anchor Tom Brokaw asked the president-elect how fast his stimulus plan would create jobs. "Well, I think we can get a lot of work done fast," he said. "When I met with the governors, all of them have projects that are shovel ready, that are going to require us to get the money out the door, but they've already lined up the projects and they can make them work" (NBC News 2008). In the months ahead, he repeatedly spoke of "shovel-ready" projects. But implementation of the stimulus moved much more haltingly than he had promised. In a 2010 interview he tacitly acknowledged that his promise had been a mirage: "But the problem is, is that spending it out takes a long time, because there's really nothing—there's no such thing as shovel-ready projects" (Baker 2010).

The economy grew at a slow pace that mocked the administration's optimistic forecasts. In August 2009 the White House predicted annual real GDP growth of 4.3 percent in 2011, 2012, and 2013, followed by 4 percent in 2014 (US Office of Management and Budget 2009). The actual figures were 1.6 percent, 2.3 percent, 2.2 percent, and 2.4 percent.

In January 2009 the Obama transition team issued an analysis that described how the economy would fare through the next four years with and without his proposed fiscal stimulus policy (Romer and Bernstein 2009). It confidently predicted that the stimulus plan would keep unemployment under 8 percent. Without it, the forecast said, the rate could hit 9 percent. In fact, even with the passage of the stimulus, it hit 10 percent in October 2009. In the middle of the second Obama term, the Congressional Budget Office reckoned that any positive effect of the stimulus had largely melted away: Gross domestic product and full-time equivalent jobs were up less than 0.2 percent compared with what would have occurred otherwise. And in years to come, the effect of spending $831 billon on the scheme would be more troubling: "[The] long-run impact on the economy will stem primarily from the resulting increase in government debt. To the extent that people hold their wealth in government securities rather than in a form that can be used to finance private investment, increased debt tends to reduce the stock of productive private capital" (Congressional Budget Office 2015).

Around the time of that assessment, the unemployment rate had finally reached near-normal levels, prompting administration officials to claim success. This "success" came with asterisks. In October 2015 the labor force participation rate was 62.4 percent, which constituted more than a three-point drop since Obama took office and the lowest rate since 1977. Whatever the cause for the decline, it tended to mask the severity of unemployment. If the participation rate had remained where it stood at the start of the Obama administration—65.7 percent—the official unemployment rate would have been *9.8 percent*. As Federal Reserve Chair Janet Yellen put it, diplomatically, "the decline in the unemployment rate over this period somewhat overstates the improvement in overall labor market conditions" (Yellen 2014).

One reason for the shaky employment situation is that, under the Obama administration, the number of business deaths topped the number of business births among employer firms for the first time since 1977, when the Census started keeping such records (Hathaway and Litan 2014). One especially poignant example is Allentown Metal Works. In December 2009 President Obama visited the plant, holding it out as a symbol of hope for his jobs plan. A little more than a year later, it closed.

Even people with jobs had little reason to cheer. Real hourly wages fell 1 percent in 2011 and 1 percent in 2012. Changes in wage levels then edged into positive territory, but just barely: 0.5 percent in 2013 and 0.4 percent in 2014 (Gould 2015). Well into the second Obama term, American households were still worse off than they were before. Real median household income in 2014 was down 3 percent from its 2008 level and off 6.5 percent from the pre-recession year of 2007 (DeNavas-Walt and Proctor 2015). And the 2014 poverty rate of 14.8 percent topped the figures for either 2007 (12.5 percent) or 2008 (13.2 percent).

One group of Americans did fare well under Obama: the rich. A Pew Research Center analysis of 2013 statistics found the median wealth of the nation's high-income families was about seven times greater than that of middle-income families, the largest such gap in the thirty years that the Federal Reserve had gathered such data. Moreover, high-income families had a median net worth almost seventy times that of lower-income families, also the widest such gap in thirty years (Fry and Kochhar 2014).

In a 2015 Pew survey, majorities said that government policies had done a great deal or a fair amount to help large banks and financial institutions (71 percent), large corporations (67 percent), and wealthy people (66 percent). In contrast, 72 percent said the government's policies since the recession had done little or nothing to help middle-class people, and 65 percent said they had provided little or no help for the poor (Pew Research Center 2015).

"What was the point?" a 23-year-old Jacksonville grocery clerk told Robert Samuels of the *Washington Post*. "We made history, but I don't see change. . . . We got the president his job. But did he help us get any good jobs? I still need a raise" (Samuels 2015).

HEALTH CARE: "YOU CAN KEEP IT"

Early in the 2008 campaign, candidate Obama assured voters that he would not impose an individual mandate for health insurance: "I mean, if a mandate was the solution, we can try that to solve homelessness by mandating everybody to buy a house" (CNN 2008a). An Obama campaign spot attacked Hillary Clinton on this point: "Hillary Clinton's attacking, but what's she not telling you about her health-care plan? It forces everyone to buy insurance, even if you can't afford it, and you pay a penalty if you don't" (Holan 2008).

Early in his presidency, he reversed himself and endorsed the mandate. There was a problem with his new position: Enforcing the mandate would require taxes, and he had pledged that "no family making less than $250,000 a year will see any form of tax increase" (Holan 2010). So he simply denied that his law would raise taxes. In an interview with the president, ABC's George Stephanopoulos found his denial to be implausible, saying "the government is forcing people to spend money, fining you if you don't. How is that not a tax?"

Obama: What . . . what . . . if I . . . if I say that right now your premiums are going to be going up by 5 or 8 or 10 percent next year and you say, well, that's not a tax increase; but, on the other hand, if I say that I don't want to have to pay for you not carrying coverage even after I give you tax credits that make it affordable, then . . .

Stephanopoulos: I . . . I don't think I'm making it up. Merriam Webster's Dictionary: tax—"a charge, usually of money, imposed by authority on persons or property for public purposes."

Obama: George, the fact that you looked up Merriam's Dictionary, the definition of tax increase, indicates to me that you're stretching a little bit right now.

In defending the law before the Supreme Court, Solicitor General Donald Verrilli contradicted the president: "The practical operation of the minimum coverage provision is as a tax law. It is fully integrated into the tax system, will raise substantial revenue, and triggers only tax consequences for non-compliance" (Verrilli 2012). In videos that later came to light, economist Jonathan Gruber, an architect of the Affordable Care Act, was even more forthright about the individual mandate and other tax provisions of the bill (Nather 2014):

- March 16, 2011, on the "Cadillac tax" on expensive health-insurance plans: "The only way we could take it on was first by mislabeling it, calling it a tax on insurance plans rather than a tax on people when we all know it's really a tax on people who hold those insurance plans."

- January 18, 2012, on subsidies: "If you're a state and you don't set up an exchange, that means your citizens don't get their tax credits. But your citizens still pay the taxes that support this bill."
- October 30, 2012, on how a tax on insurance coverage affects consumers: "We just tax the insurance companies, they pass it on in higher prices that offsets the tax break we get. . . . It's a very clever, you know, basic exploitation of the lack of economic understanding of the American voter."
- October 17, 2013, on drafting legislative language: "This bill was written in a tortured way to make sure CBO did not score the mandate as taxes. If CBO scored the mandate as taxes, the bill dies."

In a 2008 debate, Senator Obama said: "So my job is to tell the truth, to be straight with the American people about . . . what I'm going to do with respect to providing health care for every American" (Sweet 2008). As we can see with his lack of candor about taxation, he failed at this job. Any serious health-care proposal involves tradeoffs of cost, access, and quality. You can improve one or two of these things at a time, but the improvement always comes at the expense of the third (Carroll 2012). One can surely argue that the tradeoffs of a particular policy are worthwhile, but it is disingenuous to suggest that those tradeoffs do not exist.

Time and again, President Obama did just that. In a national radio address, he made a promise to people who already had health insurance: "The only changes that you'll see are lower costs and better health care" (Obama 2009b). In many campaign speeches, he put a number on the pledge, vowing to "bring down premiums by $2,500 for the typical family" (Sack 2008). Things did not work out that way. Instead of falling, average family premiums went up $4,865 between 2008 and 2015 (Kaiser Family Foundation 2015). In 2015 a consulting firm found that premiums for some of the most popular insurance plans in the Affordable Care Act exchanges were heading for double-digit rate hikes in 2016 (Demko 2015).

President Obama's best-known broken promise was: "If you like your health-care plan, you'll be able to keep your health-care plan." He made variations of this pledge at least thirty-seven times (Jacobson 2013). As the Affordable Care Act went into effect, however, millions got cancellation notices. In the ensuing uproar, the president tried to redraft his promise after the fact: "Now, if you have or had one of these plans before the Affordable Care Act came into law and you really like that plan, what we said was, you could keep it *if it hasn't changed since the law was passed*" (Obama 2013b, emphasis added). None of his public statements up to that point had included that caveat. He had stressed that there were no caveats at all (Jacobson 2013):

- "If you like your health-care plan, you'll be able to keep your health-care plan, period. No one will take it away, no matter what."
- "If you like your current insurance, you keep that insurance. Period, end of story."
- "And if you like your insurance plan, you will keep it. No one will be able to take that away from you. It hasn't happened yet. It won't happen in the future."

How egregious were the president's misstatements? Former Representative Barney Frank (D-MA) told the Huffington Post in 2014: "[He] should never have said as much as he did, that if you like your current health care plan, you can keep it. That wasn't true. And you shouldn't lie to people. And they just lied to people" (Carter 2014).

FOREIGN POLICY

"The world wants to see the United States lead. They've been disappointed and disillusioned over the last seven, eight years," Senator Obama told CNN's Wolf Blitzer in mid-2008. "I think there is still a sense everywhere I go that if the United States regains its sense of who it is and our values and our ideals, that we will continue to set the tone for a more peaceful and prosperous world" (CNN 2008b). People across the world were so enthusiastic about his potential that he won the Nobel Peace Prize during his first year in office. "This is as far as I know the first Nobel Peace Prize awarded on spec, basically awarded for promise rather than accomplishment," American historian Allan Lichtman told Canadian television at the time (CTV 2009).

If members of the Nobel committee were hoping that Obama's accession would make the world more peaceful and free, they were in for a letdown. Between 2008 and 2014, fatalities in armed conflicts around the world more than tripled, from 56,000 to 180,000 (Inkster 2015). Freedom House found that tough tactics by authoritarian regimes and a rise in terrorist attacks fostered a decline in global freedom in 2014, the ninth straight year in which it found such a decline (Puddington 2015). Although it would be wrong to blame the president for these trends, it would also be hard to say that his performance on the global stage lived up to his billing.

For starters, consider superpower relations. Suggesting that President George W. Bush had bungled relations with Russia, President Obama vowed to "reset" them. In an awkward 2009 photo opportunity, Secretary of State Hillary Clinton gave Russian Foreign Minister Sergey Lavrov a mockup of a red button that was supposed to say "reset" in Russian. Lavrov gently pointed out that it actually said "overcharged." In an even more awkward moment in 2012, an open microphone captured Obama assuring Russian President Dmitry Medvedev: "This is my last election. . . . After my election I have more flexibility." Medvedev answered: "I understand. I will transmit this information to Vladimir" (Nakamura and Wilgoren 2012). At a fundraising event a few weeks later, he literally laughed off concerns about Russia: "But when you've got the leading contender, the presumptive nominee, on the other side suddenly saying our number-one enemy isn't al-Qaeda, it's Russia [*laughter*]. I don't make that up. [*Laughter*] I'm suddenly thinking, what—maybe I didn't check the calendar this morning. [*Laughter*] I didn't know we were back in 1975. [*Laughter*]" (Obama 2012).

By 2015 Vladimir Putin had seized Crimea and threatened the rest of Ukraine. President Obama's nominee to head the Joint Chiefs of Staff implicitly confirmed that his commander in chief had been wrong. "My assessment today, Senator, is that Russia presents the greatest threat to our national security," Marine General Joseph Dunford told Senator Joe Manchin (D-WV) at his confirmation hearing. "So if you want to talk about a nation that could pose an existential threat to the United States, I'd have to point to Russia" (Wong 2015).

As for another former Soviet republic, candidate Obama made an explicit promise. "As a senator, I strongly support passage of the Armenian Genocide Resolution (H.Res.106 and S.Res.106), and as President I will recognize the Armenian Genocide" (Armenians for Obama 2008). "What is amazing about Barack," said Obama adviser Samantha Power in a campaign video to the Armenian community, "is . . . his willingness as president to commemorate [the genocide] and certainly to call a spade a spade and to speak truth about it. . . . He's a person who can actually be trusted, which distinguishes him from some in the Washington culture" (Smith 2009). Obama broke his word. Over the next seven years, he never used the term "genocide" to describe the atrocity (Tapper 2015). "No U.S. president has ever made genocide prevention a priority, and no U.S. president has ever suffered politically for his indifference to its occurrence," wrote one leading scholar some years before. "It is thus no coincidence that genocide rages on." The scholar was Samantha Power, who became the president's ambassador to the United Nations (Power 2013, xxi).

In the Syrian civil war that started in 2011, President Bashar al-Assad's government killed at least one hundred thousand civilians. The administration's response was not a model of resolve. "Syria may well represent the single least-successful element of Mr. Obama's foreign policy," writes Brookings scholar and former Clinton adviser William Galston. "His declaration that 'Assad must go' was not backed by serious policy. His famous red line regarding the Assad regime's use of chemical weapons was breached without U.S. retaliation" (Galston 2015).

Complicating the situation was the rise of ISIS, whose operations spanned Syria and Iraq. Dozens of times between 2011 and 2014, President Obama took credit for ending the war in Iraq, sometimes using the first-person singular, as in "I ended the war in Iraq." He did indeed pull all American troops from the country, but withdrawal and peacemaking turned out to be two different things. In 2015 CIA Director John Brennan said of ISIS: "I don't think we are underestimating at all the capabilities of ISIS. Its growth over the last several years in particular—but as you know, that it had its roots in al-Qaida in Iraq. It was, you know, pretty much decimated when U.S. forces were there in Iraq. It had maybe 700-or-so adherents left. And then it grew quite a bit in the last several years, when it split then from al-Qaida in Syria, and set up its own organization" (Beckwith 2015).

The president touted a plan to back moderate Syrian rebels who would oppose both Assad and ISIS: "We're working with Congress to expand our efforts to train and equip the Syrian opposition" (Obama 2014a). A few days later he expressed pleasure that Congress had voted for "a key element of our strategy: our plan to train and equip the opposition in Syria so they can help push back these terrorists" (Obama 2014b). The following year Peter Baker reported in the *New York Times*: "By any measure, President Obama's effort to train a Syrian opposition army to fight the Islamic State on the ground has been an abysmal failure. The military acknowledged this week that just four or five American-trained fighters are actually fighting" (Baker 2015). But in spite of the president's own words, the White House contended that the outcome was actually a vindication. Baker again: "At briefings this week after the disclosure of the paltry results, Josh Earnest, the White House press secretary, repeatedly noted that Mr. Obama always had been a skeptic of training Syrian rebels."

During an interview with David Remnick early in 2014, the president dismissed the problem of "various rebel factions in Syria" (i.e., ISIS) with a flippant reference to basketball: "The analogy we use around here sometimes, and I think is accurate, is if a jayvee team puts on Lakers uniforms that doesn't make them Kobe Bryant" (Remnick 2014). Less than a year later, ISIS had grabbed huge swatches of land, exercising brutal control over millions. On the morning of November 13, 2015, ABC News aired an interview in which President Obama said: "I don't think they're gaining strength. From the start our goal has been first to contain, and we have contained them" (Saenz 2015). Just a few hours later, ISIS carried out a highly coordinated series of attacks in Paris, slaughtering more than a hundred.

Yet another problem in the Mideast was Iran's nuclear program. In a 2012 debate the president laid out a clear standard for an Iranian nuclear agreement: "And we hope that their leadership takes the right decision, but the deal we'll accept is they end their nuclear program. It's very straightforward" (Commission on Presidential Debates 2012). It is hard to argue that the agreement kept this promise. It did not close any of Iran's nuclear facilities, and limits on the expansion of the Iranian nuclear program expire within ten to fifteen years.

Administration officials tried to sell the deal by promising that inspectors would have "anytime, anywhere" access to the nuclear facilities. Ben Rhodes, deputy national security advisor, said that "we will have anytime, anywhere access [to] the nuclear facilities," referring to "the whole supply chain" (*Times of Israel* 2015). The deal fell short, allowing for a twenty-four-day delay in inspections. At that point the administration retroactively tried to redefine what it had promised. Said Rhodes: "We never sought in this negotiation the capacity for so-called anytime, anywhere where you can basically go anywhere in the country, look at whatever you wanted to do, even if it had nothing to do with the nuclear program" (CNN 2015). A senior administration official closed the circle by saying: "We don't think that 'anytime, anywhere' inspections are feasible. It's just not something that happens anywhere in the world" (Wilner 2015).

What of the Obama legacy in foreign policy? "We are at a point where I think the jury is still out," former Defense Secretary Leon Panetta said in the fall of 2014. "For the first four years, and the time I spent there, I thought he was a strong leader on security issues. . . . But these last two years I think he kind of lost his way" (Page 2014).

EXECUTIVE POWER

As a presidential candidate, Senator Obama frequently accused President Bush of exceeding his constitutional authority. In a 2008 campaign speech, he laid out what he thought Bush believed: "Well, I can basically change what Congress passed by attaching a letter saying 'I don't agree with this part' or 'I don't agree with that part.' I'm going to choose to interpret it this way or that way." He promised to be different: "I taught the Constitution for ten years, I believe in the Constitution, and I will obey the Constitution of the United States. We're not going to use signing statements as a way of doing an end run around Congress" (Obama 2008b). Between 2009 and 2014 he issued thirty-three signing statements. That number was smaller than the equivalent time period for Bush, in part because a badly divided Congress sent him fewer bills to sign. Notwithstanding his pledge, Obama did indeed use signing statements to nullify congressional instructions. When the 2014 National Defense Authorization Act put restrictions on the release of Guantanamo detainees, the president's signing statement declared that he could disregard those restrictions. He relied on this statement when he ordered the release of five detainees in exchange for Taliban-held soldier Bowe Bergdahl without telling Congress in advance, as the law requires (Carroll 2014).

Executive orders are another form of unilateral power. President Obama claimed that he had issued a below-average number of executive orders during his first six years, which was technically true but misleading. During the same period, he issued a record-high number of *presidential memoranda*, which have the same practical effect, albeit with a different administrative heading (Korte 2014, Lowande 2014). Presidents can also ask agency heads to issue their own memoranda, which are even harder to tally. President Obama did so with his highly controversial 2014 executive action on immigration, which took the form of a memorandum from the Department of Homeland Security.

Whether through executive order or memorandum, the bigger question was whether the president could unilaterally halt deportations. Reporter Glenn Kessler (2014) documented several occasions on which the president had clearly said no, explaining that he did not have the legal authority:

- "With respect to the notion that I can just suspend deportations through executive order, that's just not the case, because there are laws on the books that Congress has passed.
- "The problem is that you know I'm the president of the United States. I'm not the emperor of the United States. My job is to execute laws that are passed, and Congress right now has not changed what I consider to be a broken immigration system. And what that means is that we have certain obligations to enforce the laws that are in place, even if we think that in many cases the results may be tragic."
- "What we can do is then carve out the DREAM Act folks. . . . But if we start broadening that, then essentially, I would be ignoring the law in a way that I think would be very difficult to defend legally."

In November 2014 the president announced an executive action to shield millions of undocumented immigrants from deportation. "Well, actually, my position hasn't changed," he said, leading Kessler to award him "an upside-down Pinocchio." A federal court soon blocked the executive action, and a three-judge panel of the Fifth Circuit Court of Appeal upheld the lower court's injunction. The ultimate outcome remains in question.

On his first full day in office, President Obama said: "My Administration is committed to creating an unprecedented level of openness in Government" (Obama 2009a). Instead, the administration used its power to obscure its exercise of power. Michael A. Sollenberger and Mark J.

Rozell wrote: "The president has concealed information while avoiding formally invoking executive privilege, resulting again in White House assertions that he has issued fewer executive privilege claims than his predecessors all the while engaging in at least as much secrecy" (Sollenberger and Rozell 2014). In 2015 the *New York Times* reported on at least twenty internal investigations that the administration had hindered or blocked by denying access to information. "The bottom line is that we're no longer independent," Michael E. Horowitz, the Justice Department inspector general, told the *Times* (Lichtblau 2015).

According to an analysis of federal data by the Associated Press, the administration set a record in 2014 for censoring government files or denying access to them under the Freedom of Information Act (Bridis 2015). The Society of Professional Journalists reports: "Contact is often blocked completely. When public affairs officers speak, even about routine public matters, they often do so confidentially in spite of having the title 'spokesperson.' Reporters seeking interviews are expected to seek permission, often providing questions in advance. Delays can stretch for days, longer than most deadlines allow" (Society of Professional Journalists 2014). And for years the administration threatened *New York Times* reporter James Risen with imprisonment in order to get him to reveal a confidential source. The government dropped the demand early in 2015. "I plan to spend the rest of my life fighting to undo damage done to press freedom in the United States by Barack Obama and [Attorney General] Eric Holder," said Risen. "My son is a reporter. I don't want him to have to live in a country where there is less press freedom than when I started as a journalist" (Sullivan 2015).

QUESTIONS OF COMPETENCE

"For all of the talk about 'hope' and 'change'—and both were powerful slogans for Obama in 2008—the core of Obama's appeal to many independents and even some Republicans was the idea that he would restore competence back to the White House after President George W. Bush's eight years," writes Chris Cillizza of the *Washington Post*. "Obama openly embraced the idea that he was the anti-Bush on nothing much more than his commitment to putting the best people in the right places within his administration" (Cillizza 2014). Shortly after his 2008 election, 76 percent of the public agreed that he could manage the government effectively, but by the summer of 2014, that figure had dropped to 42 percent (CNN 2014).

One major reason for this loss of confidence was the botched rollout of the administration's online health-insurance marketplace. Throughout 2013 HHS Secretary Kathleen Sebelius repeatedly assured the public that everything was "on track," but as soon as people tried to use the site, it crashed. It took weeks to fix the biggest problems, and in the meantime, reporters found that the administration had disregarded warnings from those working on the site (Pear, LaFraniere, and Austen 2013). In spite of improvements, the Government Accountability Office warned as late as 2015 of "risk that future development will experience additional problems" (US Government Accountability Office 2015).

At the Department of Veterans Affairs, incompetence had deeper consequences. In 2009 the president told the Veterans of Foreign Wars: "I've pledged to build nothing less than a 21st-century VA. And I picked a lifelong soldier and wounded warrior from Vietnam to lead this fight, General Ric Shinseki. . . . And we're keeping our promise to fulfill another top priority at the VA, cutting the red tape and inefficiencies that cause backlogs and delays in the claims process" (Obama 2009c). Although such proclamations sounded good, the administration lacked follow-through. Even worse, it tied performance bonuses of VA hospital administrators to the new mandate, creating perverse incentives for agency officials to cook the books to make wait times look shorter (Bevan 2014).

In 2014, news accounts revealed that dozens of veterans had died while waiting for care at a Phoenix VA hospital. It turned out that backlogs were widespread and that bureaucrats had allegedly falsified records. Amid the brewing scandal, Shinseki resigned. In March of 2015 the president made a well-publicized visit to the Phoenix hospital. Despite the president's claims of progress, reporters from the *New York Times* got a different perspective from one of the whistle-blowers: "Very little has changed" (Shear and Philipps 2015). The problems went far beyond Phoenix, as a 2015 investigation found that about 867,000 pending records had not reached a final determination. VA's record-keeping was so bad that it was impossible to tell if the cases were still active or even if the veterans in question were still alive (U.S. Department of Veterans Affairs 2015). Normally, a department's inspector general (IG) would track down such maladministration, but for two years, VA had lacked a permanent IG. After the previous inspector general retired in late 2013, the president did not nominate a replacement until late 2015. In the meantime, the acting IG came under fire for failing to cooperate with lawmakers. After the scandal broke and a whistle-blower group spoke of a "horrifying pattern of whitewashing and deceit," the acting IG finally quit (Slack 2015).

There was an even longer gap at the State Department. For five years, including Hillary Clinton's entire tenure as secretary, State never had a permanent IG. In fact, of all the agencies with presidentially appointed IGs, only State had neither a confirmed nor nominated IG throughout that time (Tau and Nicholas 2015). During his five years as placeholder, the acting IG apparently did nothing to stop the secretary from using a private email account and "home brew" computer server for official correspondence, a practice that potentially created grave security risks. "For no one to raise concerns, it's almost impossible to believe," said Danielle Brian, the executive director for the Project on Government Oversight (John 2015).

"As President," Senator Obama said during his first presidential campaign, "I'll make cyber security the top priority that it should be in the 21st century" (Shactman 2008). The State Department mess is not the only reason to question the depth of this commitment. Because of lax security at the Office of Personnel Management, Chinese hackers were able to tap personal data on more than twenty-one million federal workers, mostly applicants for security clearances. The director of the office was a political appointee with no background in human resources or record-keeping.

There were other dubious appointments. In 2014 alone the nominee for ambassador to Norway did not appear to know at his confirmation hearing that the country is a constitutional monarchy. He also characterized one of the nation's ruling parties as a fringe group. A soap-opera producer slated for Hungary gave an incoherent answer when Senator John McCain asked her to explain America's strategic interests in the country. A prominent Obama bundler nominated to be ambassador to Argentina admitted that he had never been there (Philip 2014).

SPECIAL INTERESTS

Campaign fundraising was the common denominator of these ambassadorial picks. As a presidential candidate, however, Senator Obama had vowed to clean up politics, reducing the power of big money and special interests. "If I am the Democratic nominee," he said in the fall of 2007, "I will aggressively pursue an agreement with the Republican nominee to preserve a publicly financed general election" (Adair and Holan 2008). Instead, he became the first major-party nominee to decline public financing, along with the accompanying spending limits, since the system began in 1976. In the end, he vastly outspent McCain, who stayed within the system. When PolitiFact asked the Obama campaign to explain the contradiction, a spokesperson pointed to a news article noting that one of the campaign's lawyers had met with the McCain legal team. "But that account was sketchy and didn't sound to us like the 'aggressive pursuit' that Obama had promised," PolitiFact concluded. "The fact is that Obama said he would pursue public financing, but decided it wasn't in the campaign's tactical interest. That might have been a tactical decision, or even a wise one, but we see it as a Full Flop" (Adair and Holan 2008).

Four years later, after *Citizens United*, press secretary Jay Carney promised that the president would stay away from super PACs: "[The] President, Vice President, First Lady, Dr. Biden will not appear at any of these events associated with these organizations" (Carney 2012). Less than a month before the election, however, he attended a fundraising event for the Super PAC Priorities USA. The White House contended that it was a thank-you gathering for donors, but the distinction was murky at best (Terkel and Stein 2013). In the 2014 midterm campaign, he attended super PAC events openly (Zezima 2014).

Before becoming president Obama promised to keep lobbyists at bay. "I don't take a dime of their money," he said in 2007, "and when I am president, they won't find a job in my White House" (Obama 2007). The first part of that statement was true but trivial: lobbyists give relatively little campaign money anyway. Their *clients* are the big donors, and Obama said nothing about refusing money from lobbyist clients. The second part turned out to be less than true. In his first month in office, Obama signed an executive order stating that registered lobbyists would not be welcome on the payroll. The administration retreated, however, issuing several waivers. But the more important effect was that many lobbyists learned that they could lawfully deregister, largely doing the same things but without the L-word. Said Robert Gibbs, then Obama's press secretary: "If you're not registered to lobby, you can't be a lobbyist" (Gibbs 2009). The message was that the executive order would apply only to those who had to register as lobbyists, not to the broader Washington influence industry (Fang 2014).

"When I am president," said candidate Obama in 2008, "I will start by closing the revolving door in the White House that has allowed people to use their Administration job as a stepping stone to further their lobbying careers" (Obama 2008d). By 2015 the revolving door was spinning as fast as ever. Gibbs joined the McDonald's Corporation as global chief communications officer. His successor as press secretary, Jay Carney, signed on to a similar job at Amazon. Marilyn Tavenner, who helped oversee the rollout of the Affordable Care Act, became the top lobbyist for the health-insurance industry just six months after leaving the federal payroll. David Plouffe, the 2008 campaign manager, took a post at Uber to supervise policy and strategy. Other former administration officials landed in various Silicon Valley positions, doing lobbying or public relations on taxes, privacy, and related issues (Kang and Eilperin 2015). "Whether they are going to roles where they will be directly lobbying government or go into positions where they are directing lobbying, you have these extremely well-connected people who know the people in government to call to sort out problems for the company," said Bill Allison of the Sunlight Foundation. "Seven years into the Obama administration, this is the time when people are leaving and cashing in by joining companies. Obama was very clear—he didn't want people to switch between lobbying and the government, but that's what is happening" (Neate 2015).

During the 2008 campaign, he promised that he would curb special-interest influence by bringing policy making into the open. To great fanfare, he opened White House visitor logs to the public, but when staffers wanted to touch base with lobbyists without disclosure, they met at a nearby coffee shop or government conference center (Frates 2011). He promised that he could put health-care negotiations "on C-SPAN so that the American people can see what the choices are" (Federal News Service 2008). A health-care "summit" at Blair House was purely a media event that took place while the real bargaining was happening behind closed doors. White House adviser David Axelrod shrugged: "That's the way it has been. That's the way it will always be" (Amick 2009). In a talk to an economics conference, Jonathan Gruber was even more candid: "Lack of transparency is a huge political advantage, and basically, you know, call it the stupidity of the American voter or whatever, but basically that was really, really critical to getting the thing to pass" (Viebeck 2014).

A DIVIDER, NOT A UNITER

In 2004, when he was still a member of the Illinois Legislature, Barack Obama gained national fame with an electrifying Democratic keynote speech proclaiming that there is neither a liberal nor a conservative America but the *United* States of America. Ten years later a *Washington Post*–ABC poll asked Americans if President Obama had done more to unite or divide the country. By 55 percent to 38 percent, they said that he was more of a divider than a uniter (Blake 2014).

From the early days of his administration, the president's actions provided a jarring contrast with his rhetoric of unity. He spoke of reaching out to the GOP, then gave the reins of the stimulus legislation to House Speaker Nancy Pelosi, who shut Republicans out. Said Ray LaHood, the moderate Republican who served as Obama's Transportation Secretary: "The judgment to hand over decision making and legislative strategizing to Pelosi so early in the term on so critical a bill crippled efforts at bipartisanship on major policy initiatives for the next two years" (LaHood 2015, 231). LaHood saw a larger pattern: "I do not believe the White House ever committed fully to a genuine bipartisan approach to policy making, despite the president's words to the contrary" (LaHood 2015, 232).

Members of the president's party also noticed that he did not excel at outreach. Representative Dennis Cardoza (D-CA) wrote in 2011: "Early in his administration, President/Professor Obama repeatedly referred to 'teaching moments.' He would admonish staff, members of Congress and the public, in speeches and in private, about what they could learn from him. . . . President Obama projected an arrogant 'I'm right, you're wrong' demeanor that alienated many potential allies" (Cardoza 2011). When the president tried and failed to win Democratic support for trade legislation, Representative Peter De Fazio (D-OR) said: "The President tried to both guilt people and impugn their integrity. I was insulted." Another Democrat told CNN that the president "was fine until he turned it at the end and became indignant and alienated some folks" (Bradner and Walsh 2015).

If the president wanted to curb attack politics, he never sent that message to his political team. By the metric of broadcast ads, the Obama campaign in 2012 was the most negative candidate campaign in recent years, edging out the 2004 Bush campaign in the share of negative ads. Even though Obama was the incumbent, nearly three-quarters of his television spots were negative (Wesleyan Media Project 2012). In his 2015 State of the Union Address, he said: "A better politics is one where we debate without demonizing each other; where we talk issues and values, and principles and facts, rather than 'gotcha' moments, or trivial gaffes, or fake controversies that have nothing to do with people's daily lives" (Obama 2015a). Less than seventy-two hours later, CNN reported on what his party organization was up to: "While some members of the Democratic research team spend a good part of their day watching speeches and searching for public comments made by each potential GOP candidate, others comb through state and federal records, news stories, business dealings, campaign donations and social media accounts in search of damning or embarrassing information" (Preston 2015).

On September 20, 2009, the president said on *Meet the Press* that "we can disagree without being disagreeable, without, you know, questioning each other's motives. . . . And it starts with me, and I've tried to make sure that I've sent a clear signal and I've tried to maintain an approach that says, 'Look, we can have some serious disagreements, but at the end of the day I'm assuming that you want the best for America just like I do'" (NBC News 2009). He did not live up to his words. On August 20, 2011, he attacked his opponents for not backing his economic agenda: "The only thing holding them back is politics. The only thing preventing us from passing these bills is the refusal by some in Congress to put country ahead of party" (Obama 2011a). A few months later, he accused "some folks in Congress" of an "attitude that sees everything through the lens of the next election, that puts party ahead of country" (Obama 2011b). In speaking of health-care legislation in 2013, he was even more direct: "Now, I think the really interesting question is, why it is that my friends in the other party have made the idea of preventing these people from getting health care their holy grail, their number-one priority? The one unifying principle in the Republican Party at the moment is making sure that thirty million people don't have health care." (Obama 2013a).

In a 2015 address at American University (Obama 2015c), he linked Republican politicians to Iranian militants: "It's those hardliners chanting 'Death to America' who have been most opposed to the deal. They're making common cause with the Republican caucus [*Laughter*]." Columnist Ruth Marcus, who supported the Iran agreement, wrote: the president "has close to zero tolerance for those who reach contrary conclusions" (Marcus 2015).

When he began his quest for the presidency, he had cast himself as uniquely capable of uniting the country. "What right now I think the American people need is somebody who can bring the country together to overcome the gridlock that has become so pervasive in Washington" (NBC News 2007). Referring to Hillary Clinton during the primary campaign, Obama told Dan Balz of the *Washington Post*: "I think it is fair to say that I believe I can bring the country together more effectively than she can." He added: "I don't think there is anybody in this race who's able to bring new people into the process and break out of some of the ideological gridlock that we have as effectively as I can" (Balz 2007).

In 2015, however, he had a different memory of what he had promised. At a Beverly Hills fundraising event, he said that "when I ran in 2008, I in fact did not say I would fix it. I said we could fix it. I didn't say, 'Yes, I can.' I said, 'Yes, we can'" (Obama 2015b). And thus we see the same pattern that we saw with health care, immigration, and other issues: He made a promise, failed to keep it, and then claimed that he never really made the promise to begin with.

This chapter began with a passage from the New Testament, and we conclude with a passage from the Old Testament (Daniel 5:27): "You are weighed in the balances and are found wanting."

WORKS CITED

Adair, Bill, and Angie Drobnic Holan. 2008."He Said He'd Pursue It, but Opted Out." PolikitiFact, August 4. www.politifact.com/truth-o-meter/statements/2008/aug/04/barack-obama/he-said-hed-pursue-it-but-opted-out/.

Amick, John. 2009. "Axelrod Defends Merits of Senate Health Bill." *Washington Post*, December 20. http://voices.washingtonpost.com/44/2009/12/axelrod-defends-merits-of-sena.html.

Armenians for Obama. 2008. "Obama v. McCain." nd. http://armeniansforobama.com/obama_vs_mccain.php.

Baker, Peter. 2010. "Interview Excerpts: President Obama." *New York Times Magazine*, October 12, 2010. www.nytimes.com/2010/10/17/magazine/17obama-transcript.html.

Baker, Peter. 2015. "Finger-Pointing, but Few Answers, After a Syria Solution Fails." *New York Times*, September 17. www.nytimes.com/2015/09/18/world/finger-pointing-but-few-answers-after-a-syria-solution-fails.html.

Balz, Dan. 2007. "Obama Says He Can Unite U.S. 'More Effectively' Than Clinton." *Washington Post*, August 15. www.washingtonpost.com/wp-dyn/content/article/2007/08/14/AR2007081401939.html.

Beckwith, Ryan Teague. 2015. "Read the CIA Director's Thoughts on the Paris Attacks." *Time*, November 16. http://time.com/4114870/paris-attacks-cia-john-brennan/.

Bevan, Tom. 2014. "Obama's Broken VA Promise." RealClearPolitics, June 10. www.realclearpolitics.com/articles/2014/06/10/obamas_broken_va_promise_122927.html.

Blake, Aaron. 2014. "Obama, the Divider." *Washington Post*, September 12. www.washingtonpost.com/news/the-fix/wp/2014/09/12/obama-the-divider/.

Bradner, Eric, and Deirdre Walsh. 2015. "Democrats Reject Obama on Trade." CNN, June 13. www.cnn.com/2015/06/12/politics/white-house-tpp-trade-deal-congress.

Bridis, Ted. 2015. "Obama Administration Sets New Record for Withholding FOIA Requests." Associated Press, March 18. www.pbs.org/newshour/rundown/obama-administration-sets-new-record-withholding-foia-requests.

Cardoza, Dennis. 2011. "Dem Lawmaker Blasts 'Professor Obama' as Arrogant, Alienating." *The Hill*, December 13. http://thehill.com/blogs/congress-blog/cardozas-corner/198861-the-professorial-president.

Carney, Jay. 2012. Press briefing by Press Secretary Jay Carney, February 7. https://www.whitehouse.gov/the-press-office/2012/02/07/press-briefing-press-secretary-jay-carney-272012.

Carroll, Aaron. 2012. "JAMA Forum—The 'Iron Triangle' of Health Care: Access, Cost, and Quality." *JAMA*, October 3. http://newsatjama.jama.com/2012/10/03/jama-forum-the-iron-triangle-of-health-care-access-cost-and-quality/.

Carroll, Lauren. 2014. "After Ignoring Provision about Notifying Congress of Guantanamo Detainee Transfers, This Moves to Promise Broken." PolitiFact, June 4. www.politifact.com/truth-o-meter/promises/obameter/promise/516/no-signing-statements-nullify-instruction-congress.

Carter, Zach. 2014. "Barney Frank 'Appalled' by Obama Administration: 'They Just Lied to People.'" Huffington Post, August 1. www.huffingtonpost.com/2014/08/01/barney-frank-obama-lie_n_5642132.html.

Cillizza, Chris. 2014. "President Obama's Competence Problem Is Worse Than It Looks." *Washington Post*, July 28, https://www.washingtonpost.com/news/the-fix/wp/2014/07/28/president-obamas-competence-problem-is-worse-than-it-looks.

CNN. 2008a. "American Morning: Interview with Barack Obama." February 5. www.cnn.com/TRANSCRIPTS/0802/05/ltm.02.html.

CNN. 2008b. "Obama: World Wants to See U.S. Lead." May 8. www.cnn.com/2008/POLITICS/05/08/obama/index.html?iref=newssearch. CNN. 2014. CNN/ORC Poll. July 29. http://i2.cdn.turner.com/cnn/2014/images/07/27/cnn.orc.poll.pdf.

CNN. 2015. "Transcript: Erin Burnett Outfront." July 14. www.cnn.com/TRANSCRIPTS/1507/14/ebo.01.html.

Commission on Presidential Debates. 2012. Debate Transcript, October 22. www.debates.org/index.php?page=october-22-2012-the-third-obama-romney-presidential-debate.

Congressional Budget Office. 2015. "Estimated Impact of the American Recovery and Reinvestment Act on Employment and Economic Output in 2014." https://www.cbo.gov/sites/default/files/114th-congress-2015-2016/reports/49958-ARRA.pdf.

CTV. 2009. "Obama 'Deeply Humbled, Surprised' By Peace Prize." October 9. www.ctvnews.ca/obama-deeply-humbled-surprised-by-peace-prize-1.442121.

Demko, Paul. 2015. "Prices for Popular Obamacare Health Plans Rising Sharply." *Politico*, October 20. www.politico.com/story/2015/10/obamacare-cost-increase-215409.

DeNavas-Walt, Carmen, and Bernadette D. Proctor. 2015. "Income and Poverty in the United States: 2014." Washington: US Census Bureau. https://www.census.gov/content/dam/Census/library/publications/2015/demo/p60-252.pdf.

Fang, Lee. 2014. "Where Have All the Lobbyists Gone?" *The Nation*, March 10-17. www.thenation.com/article/shadow-lobbying-complex.

Federal News Service. 2008. Transcript: Democratic Debate in Los Angeles. *New York Times*, January 31. www.nytimes.com/2008/01/31/us/politics/31text-debate.html.

Fornek, Scott. 2004. "Obama for President? That's 'Silly.'" *Chicago Sun-Times*, November 4. www.highbeam.com/doc/1P2-1553463.html.

Frates, Chris. 2011. "W.H. Meets Lobbyists off Campus." *Politico*, February 24. www.politico.com/story/2011/02/wh-meets-lobbyists-off-campus-050081.

Fry, Richard, and Rakesh Kochhar. 2014. "America's Wealth Gap between Middle-Income and Upper-Income Families Is Widest On Record." Pew Research Center, December 17. www.pewresearch.org/fact-tank/2014/12/17/wealth-gap-upper-middle-income/.

Galston, William. 2015. "Obama's Wishful-Thinking Syria Policy." *Wall Street Journal*, October 6. www.wsj.com/articles/obamas-wishful-thinking-syria-policy-1444169695.

Gibbs, Robert. 2009. Press Briefing by Press Secretary Robert Gibbs and Secretary of Interior Ken Salazar. January 28. www.presidency.ucsb.edu/ws/?pid=85699.

Gould, Elise. 2015. "Average Real Hourly Wage Growth in 2014 Was No Better Than 2013." Economic Policy Institute, January 16. www.epi.org/blog/average-real-hourly-wage-growth-in-2014-was-no-better-than-2013.

Hathaway, Ian, and Robert E. Litan. 2014. "Declining Business Dynamism in the United States: A Look at States and Metros." Brookings Institution, May. www.brookings.edu/~/media/research/files/papers/2014/05/declining%20business%20dynamism%20litan/declining_business_dynamism_hathaway_litan.pdf.

Holan, Angie Drobnic. 2008. "Her Mandate Doesn't Mention Garnishment." PolitiFact, April 21. www.politifact.com/truth-o-meter/statements/2008/apr/21/barack-obama/her-mandate-doesnt-mention-garnishment.

Holan, Angie Drobnic. 2010. "No Family Making Less Than $250,000 Will See 'Any Form of Tax Increase.'" PolitiFact, April 8. www.politifact.com/truth-o-meter/promises/obameter/promise/515/no-family-making-less-250000-will-see-any-form-tax.

Inkster, Nigel. 2015. "Armed Conflict Survey 2015 Press Statement." International Institute for Strategic Studies, May 19. https://www.iiss.org/en/about%20us/press%20room/press%20releases/press%20releases/archive/2015-4fe9/may-6219/armed-conflict-survey-2015-press-statement-a0be.

Isquith, Elias. 2014. "Barack Obama's Worst Defeat: How the President Defined Dovishness Down." Salon, September 20. www.salon.com/2014/09/20/barack_obamas_worst_defeat_how_the_president_defined_dovishness_down.

Jacobson, Louis. 2013. "Barack Obama Says That What He'd Said Was You Could Keep Your Plan 'if It Hasn't Changed Since the Law Passed.'" PolitiFact, November 6. www.politifact.com/truth-o-meter/statements/2013/nov/06/barack-obama/barack-obama-says-what-hed-said-was-you-could-keep/.

John, Arit. 2015. "One More Question on Hillary Clinton E-Mails: Where Was the Watchdog?" Bloomberg News, March 24. www.bloomberg.com/politics/articles/2015-03-24/one-more-question-on-hillary-e-mails-where-was-the-watchdog-.

Kaiser Family Foundation. 2015. "2015 Employer Health Benefits Survey." September 22. http://kff.org/report-section/ehbs-2015-section-one-cost-of-health-insurance.

Kang, Cecilia, and Juliet Eilperin. 2015. "Why Silicon Valley Is the New Revolving Door for Obama Staffers." *Washington Post*, February 28. https://www.washingtonpost.com/business/economy/as-obama-nears-close-of-his-tenure-commitment-to-silicon-valley-is-clear/2015/02/27/3bee8088-bc8e-11e4-bdfa-b8e8f594e6ee_story.html.

Kessler, Glenn. 2014. "Obama's Royal Flip-Flop on Using Executive Action on Illegal Immigration." *Washington Post*, November 18. https://www.washingtonpost.com/news/fact-checker/wp/2014/11/18/obamas-flip-flop-on-using-executive-action-on-illegal-immigration/.

Korte, Gregory. 2014. "Obama Issues 'Executive Orders by Another Name.'" *USA Today*, December 17. www.usatoday.com/story/news/politics/2014/12/16/obama-presidential-memoranda-executive-orders/20191805/.

LaHood, Ray. 2015. *Seeking Bipartisanship: My Life in Politics*. Amherst, New York: Cambria Press, 2015.

Lichtblau, Eric. 2015. "Tighter Lid on Records Threatens to Weaken Government Watchdogs." *New York Times*, November 27. www.nytimes.com/2015/11/28/us/politics/tighter-lid-on-records-threatens-to-defang-government-watchdogs.html.

Lowande, Kenneth S. 2014. "After the Orders: Presidential Memoranda and Unilateral Action." *Presidential Studies Quarterly* 44 (December): 724–41. http://onlinelibrary.wiley.com/doi/10.1111/psq.12157/abstract.

Marcus, Ruth. 2015. "Barack Obama Embittered and unfair Over Iran. *Washington Post* August 11. www.washingtonpost.com/opinions/barack-obama-embittered-and-unfair/2015/08/11/8b8b4538-4049-11e5-8d45-d815146f81fa_story.html.

Nakamura, David, and Jodie Wilgoren. 2012. "Caught on Open Mike, Obama Tells Medvedev He Needs 'Space' On Missile Defense." *Washington Post,* March 26. https://www.washingtonpost.com/politics/obama-tells-medvedev-solution-on-missile-defense-is-unlikely-before-elections/2012/03/26/gIQASoblbS_story.html.

Nather, David 2014. "Will Jonathan Gruber Topple Obamacare?" *Politico*, December 7. www.politico.com/magazine/story/2014/12/will-jonathan-gruber-topple-obamacare-113369.

NBC News. 2007. "*Meet the Press* Transcript for November 11, 2007." www.nbcnews.com/video/meet-the-press-netcast/21737725.

NBC News. 2008. "*Meet the Press* Transcript for December 7, 2008." www.nbcnews.com/id/28097635/ns/meet_the_press/t/meet-press-transcript-dec#.VkPcLHarSUk.

NBC News. 2009. "*Meet the Press* Transcript for September 20, 2009." www.nbcnews.com/id/32935603/ns/meet_the_press/t/meet-press-transcript-sept/#.Vk0a13arSUl.

Neate, Rupert. 2015. "Washington Revolving Door Speeds Up as Obama Officials Head for Lobbying Jobs." *The Guardian*, March 7. www.theguardian.com/us-news/2015/mar/07/washington-revolving-door-lobbying-jobs-obama.

Obama, Barack. 2007. Remarks in Spartanburg, South Carolina: "A Change We Can Believe In." November 3. www.presidency.ucsb.edu/ws/index.php?pid=77018.

Obama, Barack. 2008a. Remarks in Columbia, South Carolina, January 26. www.cnn.com/2008/POLITICS/01/26/obama.transcript/index.html?eref=rss_latest.

Obama, Barack. 2008b. Remarks in Billings, Montana, May 19. https://youtu.be/nUh5SPWW8ak.

Obama, Barack. 2008c. Remarks in St. Paul, Minnesota, June 3. www.nytimes.com/2008/06/03/us/politics/03text-obama.html.

Obama, Barack. 2008d. Remarks in Green Bay, Wisconsin, September 22. http://speeches.demconwatchblog.com/2008/09/barack-obama-speech-from-green-bay-wi.html.

Obama, Barack. 2008e. Remarks in Columbia, Missouri, October 30. www.realclearpolitics.com/articles/2008/10/obama_rallies_columbia_missour.html.

Obama, Barack. 2009a. "Memorandum on Transparency and Open Government." January 21. www.presidency.ucsb.edu/ws/?pid=85677.

Obama, Barack. 2009b. The President's Weekly Address, June 13. www.presidency.ucsb.edu/ws/?pid=86270.

Obama, Barack. 2009c. Remarks at the Veterans of Foreign Wars Convention in Phoenix, Arizona, August 17. www.presidency.ucsb.edu/ws/?pid=86545.

Obama, Barack. 2011a. The President's Weekly Address, August 20. www.presidency.ucsb.edu/ws/?pid=92926.

Obama, Barack. 2011b. Remarks at a Democratic National Committee Fundraiser in Orlando, Florida, October 11. www.presidency.ucsb.edu/ws/?pid=96893.

Obama, Barack. 2012. Remarks at an Obama Victory Fund 2012 Fundraiser in McLean, Virginia, April 29. www.presidency.ucsb.edu/ws/?pid=100730.

Obama, Barack. 2013a. The President's News Conference, August 9. www.presidency.ucsb.edu/ws/?pid=104008.

Obama, Barack. 2013b. Remarks at the Organizing for Action Obamacare Summit, November 4. www.presidency.ucsb.edu/ws/?pid=104407.

Obama, Barack. 2014a. The President's Weekly Address, September 13. www.presidency.ucsb.edu/ws/?pid=107492.

Obama, Barack. 2014b. "Remarks on Congressional Passage of Legislation to Train and Equip Syrian Opposition Forces." September 18. www.presidency.ucsb.edu/ws/?pid=107533.

Obama, Barack. 2015a. Address before a Joint Session of the Congress on the State of the Union, January 20. www.presidency.ucsb.edu/ws/?pid=108031.

Obama, Barack. 2015b. Remarks at a Democratic National Committee Fundraiser in Beverly Hills, CA, June 18. www.presidency.ucsb.edu/ws/?pid=110363.

Obama, Barack. 2015c. Remarks at American University, August 5, www.presidency.ucsb.edu/ws/?pid=110537.

Page, Susan. 2014. "Panetta: '30-Year War' and a Leadership Test for Obama." *USA Today*, October 6. www.usatoday.com/story/news/politics/2014/10/06/leon-panetta-memoir-worthy-fights/16737615.

Pear, Robert, Sharon LaFraniere, and Ian Austen. 2013. "From the Start, Signs of Trouble at Health Portal." *New York Times*, October 12. www.nytimes.com/2013/10/13/us/politics/from-the-start-signs-of-trouble-at-health-portal.html.

Pew Research Center. 2015. "Most Say Government Policies Since Recession Have Done Little to Help Middle Class, Poor." March 4. www.people-press.org/2015/03/04/most-say-government-policies-since-recession-have-done-little-to-help-middle-class-poor.

Philip, Abby D. 2014. "5 Most Cringe-Worthy Blunders from Obama's Ambassador Nominees." February 7. http://abcnews.go.com/blogs/politics/2014/02/5-most-cringe-worthy-blunders-from-obamas-ambassador-nominees/.

Power, Samantha. 2013. *A Problem From Hell: America and the Age of Genocide*. New York: Basic Books.

Preston, Mark. 2015. "With Opposition Research, Democrats Look to Define GOP Candidates." CNN, January 23. www.cnn.com/2015/01/23/politics/democrats-use-opposition-research-on-gop/.

Puddington, Arch. 2015. "Discarding Democracy: A Return to the Iron Fist." Freedom House, January 28. https://freedomhouse.org/report/freedom-world-2015/discarding-democracy-return-iron-fist.

Remnick, David. 2014. "Going the Distance: On and Off the Road with Barack Obama." *The New Yorker*, January 27. www.newyorker.com/magazine/2014/01/27/going-the-distance-david-remnick.

Romer, Christina, and Jared Bernstein. 2009. "The Job Impact of the American Recovery and Reinvestment Plan." January 9. http://otrans.3cdn.net/45593e8ecbd339d074_l3m6bt1te.pdf.

Sack, Kevin. 2008. "Health Plan from Obama Spurs Debate." *New York Times*, July 23. www.nytimes.com/2008/07/23/us/23health.html.

Saenz, Arlette. 2015. "President Obama Vows to 'Completely Decapitate' ISIS Operations." ABC News, November 13. http://abcnews.go.com/Politics/president-obama-vows-completely-decapitate-isis-operations/story?id=35173579.

Samuels, Robert. 2015. "Disillusioned Black Voters Ask: Is Voting Even Worth It?" *Washington Post*, June 9. https://www.washingtonpost.com/local/disappointment-in-obama-leads-some-blacks-to-ask-is-voting-even-worth-it/2015/06/09/5922363c-052b-11e5-bc72-f3e16bf50bb6_story.html.

Shactman, Noah. 2008. "Obama Wages Cyberwar." *Wired*, July 16. www.wired.com/2008/07/obama-wages-cyb/.

Shear, Michael, and Dave Philipps. 2015. "Progress Is Slow at V.A. Hospitals in Wake of Crisis." *New York Times*, March 13. www.nytimes.com/2015/03/14/us/obama-va-hospital-phoenix.html.

Slack, Donovan. 2015. "Embattled VA Watchdog Stepping Down." *USA Today*, June 30. www.usatoday.com/story/news/politics/2015/06/30/va-inspector-general-to-resign-this-week-in-face-of-criticism'/29525497.

Smith, Ben. 2009. "'A Person Who Can Actually Be Trusted,'" *Politico*, April 24, www.politico.com/blogs/ben-smith/2009/04/a-person-who-can-actually-be-trusted-017808.

Society of Professional Journalists. 2014. "Letter Urges President Obama to Be More Transparent." July 8. www.spj.org/news.asp?ref=1253.

Sollenberger, Michael A., and Mark J. Rozell. 2014. "The Art of Disguised Unilateralism." *The Hill*, December 23. http://thehill.com/opinion/op-ed/227887-obama-the-art-of-disguised-unilateralism.

Sullivan, Margaret. 2015. "Why a Reporter's 'Epic Rant' on Twitter Gets No Argument Here." *New York Times*, February 19. http://publiceditor.blogs.nytimes.com/2015/02/19/why-a-reporters-epic-rant-on-twitter-gets-no-argument-here/.

Sweet, Lynn. 2008. "Sweet: At Las Vegas Debate, Obama Addresses Smears." *Chicago Sun-Times*, January 16. chicagobeta.suntimes.wordpress-prod-wp.aggrego.com/news/7/71/808263/sweet-at-las-vegas-debate-obama-addresses-smears.

Tapper, Jake. 2015. "For 7th Year in a Row, Obama Breaks Promise to Acknowledge Armenian Genocide." CNN, April 24. www.cnn.com/2015/04/24/politics/armenia-genocide-obama-broken-promise-jake-tapper.

Tau, Byron, and Peter Nicholas. 2015. "State Department Lacked Top Watchdog during Hillary Clinton Tenure." *Wall Street Journal*, March 24. www.wsj.com/articles/state-department-lacked-top-watchdog-during-hillary-clinton-tenure-1427239813.

Terkel, Amanda, and Sam Stein. 2013. "Obama Broke Super PAC Pledge during Campaign." Huffington Post, November 4. www.huffingtonpost.com/2013/11/04/obama-super-pac_n_4214466.html.

Times of Israel. 2015. "Top Obama Adviser Dismisses Idea That Better Iran Deal Is Possible." April 6. www.timesofisrael.com/top-obama-adviser-dismisses-idea-that-better-iran-deal-is-possible/.

US Department of Veterans Affairs, Office of the Inspector General. 2015. "Review of Alleged Mismanagement at the Health Eligibility Center." September 2. www.va.gov/oig/publications/report-summary.asp?id=3586.

US Government Accountability Office. 2015. "Healthcare.gov: CMS Has TakenSteps to Address Problems, but Needs to Further Implement Systems Development Best Practices." GAO-15-238, March. www.gao.gov/assets/670/668834.pdf.

US Office of Management and Budget. 2009. Mid-Session Review: Budget of the U.S. Government, Fiscal Year 2010. August 25. https://www.whitehouse.gov/sites/default/files/omb/assets/fy2010_msr/10msr.pdf.

Verrilli, Donald, et al. 2012. *Department of Health and Human Services v. State of Florida*, No. 11-398. Brief for Petitioners (Minimum Coverage Provision), January 4. www.americanbar.org/content/dam/aba/publications/supreme_court_preview/briefs/11-398_petitioner.authcheckdam.pdf.

Viebeck, Elise. 2014. "ObamaCare Architect: 'Stupidity' of Voters Helped Bill Pass." *The Hill*, November 10. http://thehill.com/policy/healthcare/223578-obamacare-architect-lack-of-transparency-helped-law-pass.

Walters, Barbara. 2013. "We Thought He Was Going to Be the Next Messiah." CNN interview with Piers Morgan, December 17. www.realclearpolitics.com/video/2013/12/17/barbara_walters_on_obama_we_thought_he_was_going_to_be_the_next_messiah.html.

Wesleyan Media Project. 2012. "2012 Shatters 2004 and 2008 Records for Total Ads Aired." October 24. http://mediaproject.wesleyan.edu/releases/2012-shatters-2004-and-2008-records-for-total-ads-aired.

Wilner, Michael. 2015. "Six World Powers Adopt Nuclear Deal with Iran." *Jerusalem Post*, July 14. www.jpost.com/Middle-East/Iran-nuclear-deal-reached-408871.

Wong, Kristina. 2015. "Joint Chiefs Nominee: Russia Is Our 'Greatest Threat.'" July 9. http://thehill.com/policy/defense/247362-general-russia-is-the-greatest-threat-to-us-national-security.

Yellen, Janet L. 2014. "Labor Market Dynamics and Monetary Policy." Federal Reserve Bank of Kansas City Economic Symposium, Jackson Hole, Wyoming, August 22. www.federalreserve.gov/newsevents/speech/yellen20140822a.htm.

Zezima, Katie. 2014. "Obama Is Attending Events for Super PACs He Once Railed Against. Here's What He Said." *Washington Post*, July 24. https://www.washingtonpost.com/news/post-politics/wp/2014/07/24/obama-is-attending-events-for-super-pacs-he-once-railed-against-heres-what-he-said/.

3

BARACK OBAMA'S ELECTORAL LEGACY

In a Polarized Era, Democrats Poised for Success in 2016 and Beyond

Alan I. Abramowitz, Emory University

Like almost everything involving his presidency, Barack Obama's electoral legacy has become a subject of intense controversy. Critics of Obama's electoral record point to the undeniable fact that Democrats today find themselves in a weaker position in the US Congress and in state governments than at any time since the onset of the Great Depression (Greenfield 2015; Kraushaar 2015). Republicans currently control both chambers of Congress, and their majority in the House is the largest since the late 1920s. And GOP gains have been just as dramatic in the states. Republicans currently hold thirty-one of the nation's fifty governorships and control sixty-nine of its ninety-nine state legislative chambers. Republicans have complete control of the state government—majorities in both chambers of the legislature and control of the governorship—in twenty-four states while Democrats have complete control in only seven states. All of those numbers are records for the post-Depression era (Stolberg, Shear, and Blinder 2015).

Despite its current weakness in Congress and in state governments, however, a strong case can be made that the Obama years have left the Democratic Party in much better condition than the Republican Party. Democrats are well positioned to not only hold the White House in 2016 but to make substantial gains in Congress and to regain at least some of the ground that the party has lost in the states since 2008. In this chapter I will focus on four important results of Barack Obama's presidency that bode well for Democratic prospects in 2016 and beyond: a significant advantage in party identification among the public, a high level of unity among both party elites and rank-and-file party supporters, a strong record of policy achievements, and a high level of approval from rank-and-file Democrats.

One of the most important advantages that Democrats have going into the 2016 election is a clear advantage in party identification in the overall electorate. Moreover, this advantage is greatest among voter groups whose importance will be growing over time: young people and racial minorities. Over the next several election cycles, as the inevitable process of generational replacement proceeds, the nonwhite share of the American electorate is going to continue to increase. By some time in the 2040s, the United States is expected to have a majority minority population, although it will take considerably longer before nonwhites make up a majority of voters (Frey 2014). Nevertheless, in 2016 nonwhites are expected to make up between 30 and 31 percent of the electorate, up from 28 percent in 2012, with Latinos accounting for the largest share of the increase.

Republican candidates have typically won less than a tenth of the African American vote and less than a third of the Latino and Asian American vote in recent years, so the steady growth in the nonwhite share of the electorate clearly poses a long-term challenge to the competitiveness of the Republican Party in national elections. And the message some of the leading Republican presidential candidates for 2016 are sending to minority voters could very well exacerbate the GOP's problems with nonwhite voters. At the same time, however, the growing dependence on the votes of young people and minorities has created problems for Democrats in midterm elections because these voters are disproportionately likely to drop out of the electorate when there is no presidential contest on the ballot (Brownstein 2014).

A second positive result of the Obama presidency for Democrats is that the Democratic Party at the mass level, as well as at the elite level, is much more unified than in the past and much more unified than the Republican Party. Rank-and-file Democrats are far more supportive of their party's leadership and policies than rank-and-file Republicans. In contrast to Republicans, the large majority of Democrats actually like their party and its top leaders. This difference between the two major parties has been very evident in the current presidential nomination campaign in which Democrats have quickly coalesced behind a strong front-runner in Hillary Clinton while Republicans have remained badly divided—split among a large field of candidates, many of whom are running against their own party's establishment in order to appeal to a rather disgruntled GOP base (Milligan 2015).

A third positive result of the Obama presidency for Democrats, and one that is likely to be especially important in 2016, is that President Obama is leaving his party a legacy of major domestic and foreign policy achievements, including a strong economic recovery from the worst economic crisis since the Great Depression, health-care reform that has extended access to care to millions of Americans, the ending of two major wars, and a nuclear agreement with Iran that should keep that country from developing nuclear weapons for many years. This situation contrasts dramatically with the legacy of foreign policy disasters and economic collapse that George W. Bush left to his party in 2008.

Barack Obama's record of major policy achievements is closely connected to the fourth positive result of the Obama presidency for Democrats: solid public approval ratings including strong support from rank-and-file Democratic voters. While John McCain had to run away from George W. Bush's record and keep Mr. Bush out of sight as much as possible during the 2008 campaign, the Democratic presidential nominee in 2016 will be able to proudly run on the Obama record and welcome the president to appear alongside her on the campaign trail. And the president will be an invaluable asset to the Democratic presidential nominee and to Democratic candidates at all levels when it comes to energizing and mobilizing one of the most important components of the Democratic electoral base, African American voters.

Along with these positive results of the Obama years, it is important for Democratic Party leaders and elected officials to recognize that their party faces some long-term challenges, and I will discuss these as well. Three challenges in particular loom large as Democrats seek to reverse losses in Congress and the states since 2008: increasing reliance on groups of voters—young people and racial minorities—who are difficult to motivate to turn out when there is not a presidential race on the ballot; the growing nationalization of subpresidential elections, which has helped Republicans to increasingly dominate state politics in parts of the country where the national Democratic Party is unpopular; and the inefficient geographic distribution of Democratic voters due to the heavy concentration of key Democratic voting groups, especially racial minorities, in large urban areas—a problem exacerbated by the effects of Republican gerrymandering in many states following the 2010 midterm elections (Wang 2014).

SETTING THE RECORD STRAIGHT: CHOOSING AN APPROPRIATE BASELINE FOR MEASURING ELECTORAL TRENDS

Much of the criticism of the president's electoral legacy emphasizes steep Democratic losses in the US House and Senate between 2008 and 2014. And indeed, Democrats have taken a big hit in both chambers since Mr. Obama's initial election. From 256 seats in the House and 59 seats in the Senate in the 111th Congress, Democrats were reduced to only 188 seats in the House and 46 seats in the Senate in the 114th Congress. The Democrats' losses of 68 seats in the House and 13 seats in the Senate in only six years certainly appear to be enormous by modern standards. But there is a fundamental problem with these numbers: Using Democratic strength in the 111th Congress is a very unrealistic and unfair baseline for evaluating Obama's electoral legacy. That's because those 256 House seats and 59 Senate seats represented the largest Democratic contingents in both chambers since the 103rd Congress, which took office following the 1992 election.

Those huge Democratic majorities in the 111th Congress reflected the impact of very strong short-term forces favoring Democratic candidates, including Barack Obama. In 2006 and 2008 Democrats made big gains in the House and Senate as voters took out their anger and frustration at President Bush and congressional Republicans over the Iraq War in 2006 and the worst economic crisis since the Great Depression in 2008. But those strong short-term forces favoring Democrats in 2006 and 2008 were bound to fade once Mr. Bush himself was out of office. Indeed, it is generally unfair to any president to use the number of seats his party wins in his initial election as a baseline for evaluating his party's performance during the rest of his presidency. A more realistic standard is the number of seats in the House and Senate that the new president's party held in the four previous elections. In the case of President Obama, those would be the 2000–2006 elections.

Table 3.1 compares changes in presidential party strength in the US House and Senate during every two-term presidential administration between Eisenhower and Obama. For each administration, the baseline period is the four elections prior to the president's election, and the end point is the second midterm election during each administration. Using this new and more realistic baseline, the results in Table 3.1 show that the falloff in Democratic strength under President Obama was hardly unusual. Indeed, the decline of twenty-five House seats and three Senate seats between the baseline period and the second midterm was only slightly larger than the declines experienced by the Republican Party under George W. Bush and considerably smaller than the declines experienced by the Democratic Party under Bill Clinton and the Republican Party under Dwight Eisenhower. And in comparing the performance of the Democratic Party during the Obama years to the performance of the Republican Party during the Bush years, it should be kept in mind that

Table 3.1. Changes in Presidential Party Strength on U.S. House and Senate

Presidents	*Chamber*	*Baseline*	*After Second Midterm*	*Change*
Obama	House	213	188	-25
	Senate	49	46	-3
G. W. Bush	House	214	198	-16
	Senate	51	49	-2
Clinton	House	260	211	-49
	Senate	53	45	-8
Reagan	House	150	177	+18
	Senate	40	45	+5
Nixon-Ford	House	170	144	-26
	Senate	34	37	+3
JFK-LBJ	House	240	248	+8
	Senate	52	64	+12
Ike	House	202	153	-49
	Senate	45	34	-11

Note: Baseline is average of four elections prior to a president's first election.
Source: Statistical Abstract of the United States.

Republicans suffered major losses in both chambers of Congress in 2008 under President Bush. It remains to be seen how congressional Democrats will fare in 2016, but it appears more likely that Democrats will gain seats in both chambers rather than lose seats in both for reasons discussed below.

What the results in Table 3.1 show very clearly is that there is often a presidential penalty in American politics. Especially when the president's party starts from a position of unusual strength in Congress, as was true for Barack Obama, some loss of strength is very likely during the course of the next eight years. That is partly a result of the normal tendency of the president's party to lose seats in Congress in midterm elections (Trygstad 2013). In President Obama's case there have been two midterms since his initial election, both of which resulted in substantial seat losses in Congress. However, Mr. Obama has thus far experienced only one presidential election since his own initial election. In 2012, as Mr. Obama was winning a second term in the White House, Democrats made up some but not nearly all of the ground that they had lost in the 2010 midterm election. And they almost certainly would have made up even more of that lost ground if it hadn't been for Republican gerrymandering of House districts in many states following their gains in state legislatures in 2010—Democrats gained only a handful of seats in the House even though Democratic House candidates received more than a million more votes than Republican House candidates in 2012.

It is very likely that in 2016, Democrats will regain at least some of the ground lost in the House and Senate in the 2014 midterm election, especially if the Democratic candidate at the top of the ticket is successful. Democratic pickup opportunities in 2016 are likely to be limited—there are only thirty-one members of the House of Representative who represent districts carried by the opposing party's presidential candidate in the 2012 presidential election. However, twenty-six of those thirty-one mismatched members are Republicans while only five are Democrats. Given the very strong relationship between presidential partisanship and House election outcomes and the fact that the 2016 presidential electorate will almost certainly be considerably younger, less white, and more Democratic than the 2014 midterm electorate, Democrats are very likely to regain at least some of the ground lost in the House in 2014.

On the Senate side Democrats also stand to make gains in 2016: Twenty-four of the thirty-four Senate seats up for election in 2016 are currently held by Republicans, and several of those seats are in Democratic-leaning or swing states including Florida, Illinois, New Hampshire, Pennsylvania, and Wisconsin. The political geography of the 2016 Senate elections along with the fact that Republican incumbents elected in a midterm year will now have to face a larger, more diverse, and younger presidential electorate almost guarantee that Democrats will gain seats in the Senate. By the end of his presidency, it is quite possible that Barack Obama's legacy when it comes to Democratic strength in the House and Senate will look considerably more positive than it does today.

THE PARTIES IN THE ELECTORATE: A PERSISTENT DEMOCRATIC ADVANTAGE

In the current era of polarization and strong partisanship, the single-most important factor influencing the outcomes of elections at all levels is the balance of party identification in the electorate. Given this fact, a crucial part of Barack Obama's electoral legacy is the continued Democratic advantage in party identification in the American electorate. One of the best sources of data on the distribution of party identification in the American electorate today comes from the combined results of numerous national surveys conducted by the highly respected Pew Research Center during 2014 (Pew Research Center 2015a). These data, which are displayed in Table 3.2, are based on over twenty-five thousand interviews with eligible voters. This makes it possible to obtain reliable information on the party preferences of a wide variety of subgroups. In this table, independents who indicated that they leaned toward a party are combined with regular party identifiers since these leaning independents typically behave very similarly to regular party identifiers.

The most important finding here is that even in 2014, a year in which Democratic candidates suffered major setbacks at the polls, Democratic identifiers and leaners outnumbered Republican identifiers and leaners by a fairly substantial margin. A nine-point Democratic margin in party identification among eligible voters obviously did not prevent Republicans from gaining ground in the House and Senate as well as in many state contests in a very low-turnout midterm election. As we will see, low turnout among key Democratic voting groups was a major problem for Democratic candidates in 2014. But a nine-point margin in party identifi-

Table 3.2. Party Identification in 2014

	Dem/Lean Dem %	Rep/Lean Rep %	Pure Ind %
Total	48	39	13
Region			
Northeast	53	34	13
Midwest	47	40	13
South	46	42	12
West	49	38	13
Race/Ethnicity			
White, Non-Hispanic	40	49	11
Black, Non-Hispanic	80	11	9
Hispanic	56	26	18
Asian, Non-Hispanic	65	23	12
Generation			
Millennial (age 18-33)	51	35	14
Generation X (34-49)	49	38	13
Baby Boomer (50-68)	47	41	11
Silent (69-86)	43	47	19
Gender			
Men	44	43	13
Women	52	36	12
Education			
Post-College	57	35	8
College Grad	49	42	9
Not College Grad	47	39	14
Gender of Whites			
Men	36	53	11
Women	44	45	11

Education of Whites			
College Grad	47	46	7
Not College Grad	37	50	13

Source: Pew Research Center.

cation among eligible voters would potentially be much more important in a high-turnout presidential election in which the partisan composition of the electorate would be expected to more closely reflect the partisan composition of the voting-age population.

The data displayed in Table 3.2 show that not only did Democrats enjoy a solid advantage in party identification in the nation, they enjoyed at least a modest lead in every region of the country, including the South. Even among non-Hispanic whites, the overall nine-point Republican advantage in party identification was based largely on support from men and from those without a college degree. Among white women and white college graduates, there was close to an even split between Democrats and Republicans.

But the most important findings in Table 3.2 in terms of their implications for 2016 and beyond involve the partisan preferences of nonwhites and younger Americans. These data show that in 2014, Democrats continued to enjoy an overwhelming advantage among African Americans and very large advantages among the two most rapidly growing racial and ethnic groups in the population—Latinos and Asian Americans. And the huge Democratic advantage among nonwhites helps to explain the fact that younger Americans were much more Democratic than older Americans. While Democrats enjoyed a sixteen-point lead in party identification among members of the millennial generation, the only age group favoring the GOP was the silent generation—those ages sixty-nine and older.

Demographic data show that the generations of Americans who will be entering the electorate over the next several election cycles are considerably more diverse than the millennial generation. Indeed, among the very youngest group of Americans, those born since 2010, non-Hispanic whites are outnumbered by nonwhites (Smialek and Giroux 2015). If whites and nonwhites entering the electorate over the next ten to twenty years continue to support the two major parties in the same proportions as whites and nonwhites today, the Republican Party faces a bleak future indeed (Greenberg 2015). And that's not even taking into account the fact that younger whites today are considerably less likely to identify with the GOP than older whites.

What makes the current Democratic advantage in party identification in the electorate so important in the current era is the fact that party loyalty in voting has reached record levels in recent elections and that Democratic identifiers are now just as loyal to their party as Republicans, if not more loyal (Abramowitz and Webster 2015). The data in Figure 3.1 show the trends in consistent party loyalty among Democratic and Republican voters, including independents leaning toward a party, since the 1980s. Consistent loyalty here refers to voting for your party's candidates for US president, House of Representatives, and US Senate in the same election. What these results show is that there have been dramatic increases in party loyalty among both Democratic and Republican identifi-

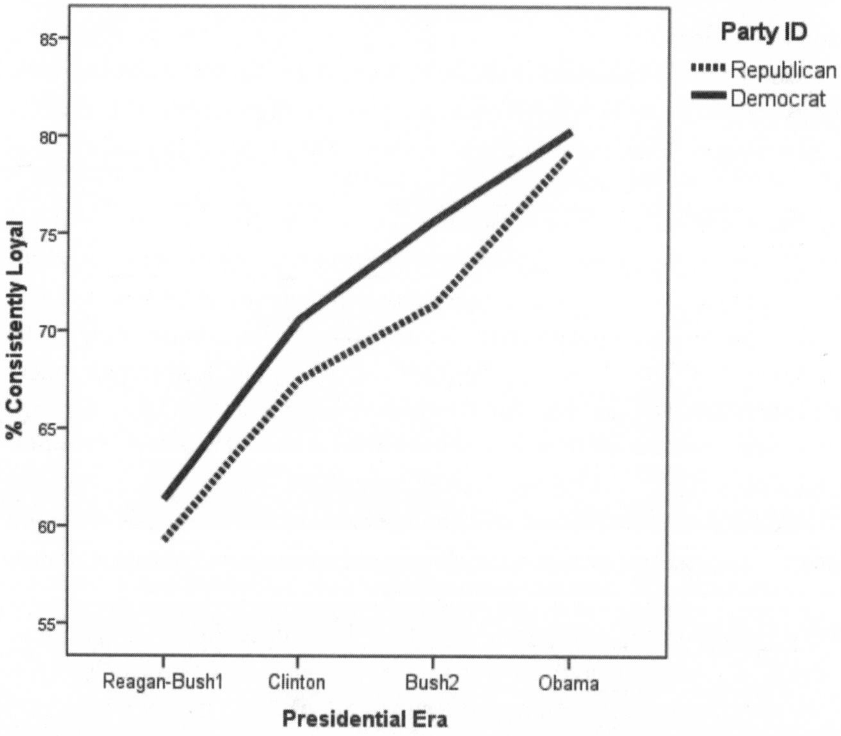

Figure 3.1. American National Election Studies Cumulative File.

ers since the 1980s with loyalty rates reaching record levels during the Obama years.

Party loyalty has increased in all types of elections, but the most dramatic increase has been in presidential loyalty among Democrats. During all of the presidential elections of the 1970s and 1980s, a fifth or more of Democratic identifiers voted for Republican presidential candidates. Democratic defection rates were especially high in the 1972, 1980, and 1984 presidential elections, with large proportions of moderate-to-conservative Democrats supporting Republicans Richard Nixon in 1972 and Ronald Reagan in 1980 and 1984. Since 1992, however, defection rates of Democrats and Republicans in presidential elections have been roughly equal. In both 2008 and 2012, over 90 percent of Democratic identifiers voted for the Democratic nominee, Barack Obama. Over 90 percent of Republican identifiers voted for the Republican nominees in those two elections, John McCain and Mitt Romney, but the Democratic edge in party identification was large enough in both years to produce victories for Obama. And in 2012 the six-point Democratic advantage in party identification was large enough to produce a four-point overall popular-vote margin for Obama despite the fact that Mitt Romney won the independent vote by a five-point margin according to the national exit poll.

A UNIFIED DEMOCRATIC PARTY

The Democratic Party is more unified today than it has been at almost any time in the past sixty years and is considerably more unified than the Republican Party. This difference is readily apparent in the way the parties' presidential nomination races have played out during 2015. Without an incumbent in the race, one would normally expect vigorous competition in both major parties for the 2016 presidential nomination. There has been competition in both parties, but the nature of that competition has been very different on the Republican side than on the Democratic side.

The Republican nomination race has been highly divisive with a large field of candidates. But the most striking development in the GOP race has not been the presence of a large number of candidates, many with little apparent support according to national polls, but the fact that two of the candidates—businessman and reality TV star Donald Trump and retired neurosurgeon Ben Carson—have been individuals with no political experience who have been running against the established leadership of the party. With no support from Republican elected officials or party leaders, Trump and Carson, along with another antiestablishment candidate, Texas Senator Ted Cruz, have been winning well over half of the vote among likely Republican primary voters nationally and in the key early states of Iowa, New Hampshire, and South Carolina. It is unclear whether these antiestablishment candidates will be able to translate this early support in the polls into actual votes in the caucuses and primaries. However, the fact that candidates running against the party establishment have been doing so well, while the candidate with the most support among Republican elected officials and major donors, former Florida Governor Jeb Bush, has been doing so poorly, clearly reflects a high level of discontent among rank-and-file Republicans with their party's leadership. That discontent also contributed to the resignation of the Republican Speaker of the House of Representatives, John Boehner—something that had not happened in over a century.

In contrast to the situation on the Republican side, the Democratic presidential nomination race quickly settled into a two-person contest between former first lady, senator, and secretary of state Hillary Clinton and Vermont Senator Bernie Sanders. From the outset, Clinton was the heavy favorite for the nomination among Democratic elected officials and party leaders—gobbling up almost all of the endorsements of members of the party establishment. And from the outset, Clinton was also the clear leader among rank-and-file Democratic voters as reflected by the results of national polls. Despite some differences between the policy views of Clinton, a mainstream liberal, and Sanders, a self-described democratic socialist, the contest between the two has not been very divisive. Most Democratic voters appear to like both candidates.

It is no accident that the Republican nomination contest has been far more divisive than the Democratic contest. The differences between the two contests reflect important underlying differences between the two parties in 2015. The Republican Party is divided between mainstream, pro-business economic conservatives and far-right, antiestablishment, Tea Party conservatives. The entire party is far more conservative than it was during the 1970s and 1980s (Mann and Ornstein 2012). But despite the overwhelming conservatism of the party's leadership and its electoral base, there are sharp divisions between these two factions in their approach to governing. Essentially, the mainstream conservatives want the government to work and are willing to compromise with Democrats if necessary to make that happen. Tea Party conservatives, in contrast, prefer confrontation to compromise. They are willing to shut down the government or force a default on the national debt rather than work with Democrats. The antiestablishment faction is also much more focused on pushing the conservative agenda on cultural issues such as abortion and gay rights than the mainstream faction—a focus that could pose serious electoral risks to the Republican Party in 2016 and beyond given the growing liberalism of the American public on social issues (Jones 2015).

There are policy differences among Democrats, of course. Those backing Bernie Sanders in the presidential race are generally more supportive of dramatically increased spending on entitlement programs and sharply increased taxes on the wealthiest Americans than those supporting Hillary Clinton. But there is broad agreement among supporters of both candidates on policies aimed at protecting the environment, addressing climate change, reforming campaign finance, expanding the welfare state, and increasing taxes on the rich in order to reverse a long-term trend in the United States toward growing economic inequality. And there is strong agreement among Democrats on support for liberal policies on immigration and on social issues such as abortion and gay rights. There is even fairly broad agreement on a focus on diplomacy and working with allies rather than unilateral reliance on American military power in dealing with potential threats from abroad. On a wide range of issues, Democratic voters, activists, and elites appear to be more united now than at any time in the post–World War II era and considerably more unified than Republican voters, who seem to be united on little more than their dislike of President Obama (Kopicki 2014).

In addition to being more united than Republicans on major issues and on their party's presidential candidates, Democrats also feel better about their party than Republicans. In fact, the Democratic Party today has a much more positive image among the public in general than the Republican Party. In a 2015 national survey, the Pew Research Center found that 48 percent of Americans had a favorable opinion of the Democratic Party while only 32 percent had a favorable opinion of the Republican Party. Part of the Democratic advantage was due to the fact that while 86 percent of rank-and-file Democrats had a favorable opinion of the Democratic Party, only 68 percent of rank-and-file Republicans had a favorable opinion of the Republican Party (Pew Research Center 2015b).

Given their intense dislike of the Democratic Party and its leaders, the fact that many Republicans are not very happy with their own party and its leaders probably will not prevent them from voting for Republican candidates. But this sense of frustration among rank-and-file Republicans is clearly fueling the candidacies of antiestablishment and extremist candidates—candidates who may cause the GOP problems in the general election in which Republicans will probably have to hope for low turnout among nonwhites and young voters in order to take back the White House. Even if support for candidates like Trump, Carson, and Cruz fades once the caucuses and primaries begin, their presence in the race has already caused several of the establishment candidates, like Jeb Bush and Marco Rubio, to take positions on issues such as immigration and abortion that fire up the GOP base but will cause problems in 2016 by helping Democrats to fire up their own base.

MAJOR POLICY ACHIEVEMENTS

Even when the incumbent is not on the ballot in a presidential election, the incumbent's record and standing among the public can have a powerful influence on the outcome. That was clearly the case in 2008 when George W. Bush's unpopularity made it almost impossible for John McCain to keep the White House in Republican hands. It will certainly be true in 2016 as well. Barack Obama will not be on the ballot, but the election will undoubtedly be in large part a referendum on his presidency.

There is no doubt that Barack Obama has been a consequential but also a controversial president. In the current era of partisan polarization, it is impossible that any president could be consequential without also being controversial (Abramowitz 2013). Opinions about the most significant domestic policy achievement of Mr. Obama's presidency, the Affordable Care Act, continue to divide Americans deeply along party lines. Democrats overwhelmingly support the law and, if anything, would like to see it expanded. On the other hand, the large majority of Republicans still would like to see it completely or partially repealed and perhaps replaced, although there is little agreement among Republican leaders about what to replace it with.

The ACA has been a highly successful policy by almost any standard—dramatically reducing the percentage of Americans without health insurance and producing measurable improvements in health-care outcomes while holding health-care costs to their lowest rates of increase in many years (Sommers, Gunja, Finegold, and Musco 2015). None of the dire predictions of the law's opponents that it would stifle economic growth and result in massive job losses have come true (Krugman 2014). Nevertheless, the ACA remains very unpopular with Republicans. But that did not stop Barack Obama from winning a second term in the White House by a fairly decisive margin in 2012, much to the surprise of his conservative critics. And it should not stop the Democratic nominee from extending the Democratic hold on the White House in 2016.

Without question, the most important part of Barack Obama's record has been his handling of the US economy, and Mr. Obama's economic record is one that a Democratic candidate will be able to point to with considerable pride in 2016. Taking office at the height of the nation's worst economic crisis since the Great Depression, President Obama and the Democratic majority in the 111th Congress put policies in place that ended the recession, reversed massive job losses, and produced seven years of sustained economic growth and job creation (Hartung 2014). Unemployment, which peaked at just over 10 percent in 2009, has been cut in half. And notwithstanding the constant inflation fear-mongering of conservative critics, actual inflation has remained well in check at under 2 percent.

Of course there are still major problems with the US economy, including declining participation in the labor force, very slow growth in real incomes, heavy concentration of income gains among the top 10 percent of earners, and growing inequality of income and wealth. The president's economic record might be considerably better if it had not been for the overwhelming opposition to his economic proposals from Republicans, especially after the GOP takeover of the House of Representatives in the 2010 midterm election. But many of the economic problems facing the country reflect very long-term trends, such as the retirement of millions of members of the post–World War II baby boom generation, increasing automation, and loss of manufacturing jobs to emerging economies with lower labor costs. And there is little indication that the president's conservative critics have better ideas about how to address these challenges. Indeed, every candidate seeking the 2016 Republican presidential nomination has simply doubled down on traditional conservative economic policies emphasizing deregulation and tax cuts for the wealthy—policies that were tried and failed miserably under the last Republican president (Madland 2015).

When it comes to foreign policy and national security, the Democratic nominee in 2016 will also be able to point to important achievements by the Obama administration (Kriesberg 2015). These include, most notably, winding down two major wars and bringing hundreds of thousands of American troops home while aggressively pursuing terrorists intent on harming the United States and its allies. Working closely with US allies, the Obama administration reached a major agreement with Iran to limit its nuclear program, greatly reducing the possibility that Iran would obtain nuclear weapons for the foreseeable future. The Obama administration also reopened diplomatic relations with Cuba, ending fifty years of failed efforts to isolate the Castro regime and bringing new hope for improved relations and expanded trade. Last but not least, President Obama has led the way in persuading the nations of the world to address what may well be the greatest danger facing all of humanity in the twenty-first century: the threat of climate change.

Many challenges remain, of course, especially the continued threat of terrorism emanating from the Middle East and ongoing disputes with Russia and China. Much more needs to be done to effectively address the issue of climate change. And as with almost everything that President Obama has accomplished in his time in office, his record on foreign policy and national security has come under sharp attack from Republicans. But this is a record that the Democratic nominee in 2016 will be able to run on rather than away from.

PUBLIC SUPPORT IN A POLARIZED ELECTORATE

Ultimately, the real test of President Obama's policies will involve his standing with the American public in 2016. This is the test that will have the most direct bearing on the electoral prospects of Democratic candidates at all levels in 2016 and especially on the prospects of the Democratic presidential nominee. An examination of weekly data from the Gallup tracking poll based on interviews with approximately thirty-five hundred voting-age Americans per week shows that Mr. Obama's average approval rating has been remarkably stable since the late summer of 2015, ranging between 46 and 49 percent. This is slightly higher than his average approval rating from late 2014 and early 2015.

What is most striking about President Obama's standing with the American public is the continued sharp divide between Democrats and Republicans. For the five weeks between October 12 and 18 and November 9 and 15, 2015, Mr. Obama's average approval rating was 84 percent among Democrats, 44 percent among independents, and 10 percent among Republicans. And Obama's 44 percent approval rating among independents is very misleading since analyses of other recent surveys show that there is also a sharp divide between Democratic-leaning independents and Republican-leaning independents, with the former overwhelmingly approving of the president's performance and the latter overwhelmingly disapproving.

The sharp partisan divide in public approval of President Obama is reflected in the findings of numerous recent polls regarding approval of President Obama among various subgroups in the population. Groups that lean heavily Democratic, such as liberals, secular whites, unmarried women, nonwhites, and those under the age of thirty, give Mr. Obama high marks; groups that lean heavily Republican, such as conservatives, white evangelicals, and older white males, rate him very poorly. All of these results are very consistent with the voting patterns of these groups in both 2008 and 2012. Groups that supported Mr. Obama strongly in those two elections support him strongly now; groups that opposed him strongly in those two elections oppose him strongly now. And these patterns of support and opposition are very unlikely to change by November 2016.

The key question, of course, is whether the president's popularity will be high enough next November to allow the Democratic nominee to do something that has been very hard to do in American politics: win a third consecutive term in the White House for her party. Since World War II there have been six presidential elections like 2016 with no incumbent in the race: in 1952, 1960, 1968, 1988, 2000, and 2008. The only one in which the candidate of the president's party was victorious was 1988. On the other hand, Al Gore did win the national popular vote in 2000 and almost certainly would have won the electoral vote if not for voter errors caused by a confusing ballot design in the state of Florida (Cauchon and Drinkard 2001). And both Richard Nixon in 1960 and Hubert Humphrey in 1968 came very close to winning a third consecutive term for their party.

The two open-seat elections in which the president's party lost badly, 1952 and 2008, involved incumbents with approval ratings well below 40 percent—Harry Truman in 1952 and George W. Bush in 2008. By the end of their presidencies, both Truman and Bush had lost considerable support even among their own party's voters. That almost certainly will not be the case for Barack Obama in 2016. However, given the deep partisan divide in American politics today, it is also very unlikely that President Obama's approval rating will be much higher than 50 percent in November 2016.

In all likelihood, the Democratic and Republican electoral coalitions in 2016 will look very similar to the Democratic electoral coalitions in 2012, and the vast majority of states will again support the same party as in the last four presidential elections. In those elections, forty out of fifty states voted for the same party four times. The outcome will therefore depend primarily on the partisan composition of the electorate. Based on the results of Pew Research Center surveys during 2014, Democrats should have the advantage in that regard if heavily Democratic voting groups such as younger Americans and nonwhites turn out at rates similar to those seen in 2008 and 2012 as opposed to those seen in 2010 and 2014. In an era of deep partisan polarization, partisan turnout is likely to be more important than the persuasion of swing voters in determining the outcomes of the 2016 presidential and congressional elections.

LONG-TERM CHALLENGES

While Democrats have a good chance of extending their hold on the White House and gaining seats in both the House of Representatives and Senate in 2016, the Democratic Party clearly does face some serious challenges in trying to regain ground lost in Congress and the states since 2008. With Barack Obama at the top of the ticket, Democratic candidates in both 2008 and 2012 benefited from strong turnout among racial minorities and younger voters inspired by Obama's personality and policies. In 2012, according to data from the National Exit Poll, nonwhites made up 45 percent of Democratic voters, and by 2020 if not 2016, the Democrats will become a majority minority party. That is a good position to be in given the growing nonwhite share of the American electorate. But it is also a big challenge for Democrats in midterm and other off-year elections because younger voters and nonwhites are more likely to drop out of the electorate than older voters and whites when there is not a presidential contest on the ballot (Brownstein 2014). In 2012 just over 130 million Americans, an estimated 58 percent of eligible voters, turned out to vote. Two years later, without a presidential contest on the ballot but with control of the Senate very much in play, only eighty-three million Americans, an estimated 37 percent of eligible voters, turned out. Forty-seven million Americans dropped out of the electorate between 2012 and 2014. It was the lowest turnout in a midterm election since 1942. And the decline in turnout between 2012 and 2014 was the largest since the 1940–1942 elections.

While turnout was substantially lower in 2014 than in 2012 among every voter group, the decline in turnout was considerably greater among some key Democratic voter groups. Table 3.3 compares the age, racial, and partisan composition of the 2012 and 2014 electorates based on national exit polls. The differences are striking. Voters under the age of

Table 3.3. Composition of Presidential and Midterm Electorates

	2012 %	2014 %
Age		
18-29	19	13
30-44	27	22
45-64	38	43
65+	16	22
Race		
White	72	75
Nonwhite	28	25
Party ID		
Democrat	38	35
Independent	29	28
Republican	32	36

Source: National Exit Polls.

forty-five made up a much smaller share of the electorate in 2014 than in 2012, while voters over the age of forty-five and especially over the age of sixty-five made up a much larger share of the electorate in 2014 than in 2012. Similarly, whites made up a larger share of the electorate and nonwhites made up a smaller share of the electorate in 2014 than in 2012. The result of these differential turnout trends was that the Democratic share of the electorate fell from 38 to 35 percent while the Republican share rose from 32 to 36 percent. A six-point Democratic advantage turned into a one-point Democratic deficit—enough to cost Democrats about a dozen seats in the House of Representatives and nine seats in the Senate. And this decline in Democratic turnout also resulted in big Republican gains in state elections since the large majority of governors and other statewide elected officials are now chosen in midterm years rather than presidential years.

The Democratic turnout problem in midterm elections was exacerbated by another long-term problem affecting Democrats in House elections: the heavy concentration of Democratic voters in densely populated urban areas. And this problem was compounded by the results of redistricting following the 2010 midterm election, which gave Republicans control of the redistricting process in a large number of states, including several with large numbers of House districts, such as Florida, Ohio, Pennsylvania, and Wisconsin. The consequences of this were clearly evident in the 2012 election results. Despite the fact that Barack Obama won the national popular vote by about 4 percentage points, Mitt Romney carried 227 House districts to only 208 for Obama. And despite winning about 1.2 million more votes than Republicans nationwide in the House elections, Democrats gained only a handful of seats in the House and fell far short of a majority.

The problems of low midterm turnout and inefficient voter distribution are unlikely to go away anytime soon. Fortunately for Democrats, the next election preceding a redistricting year will occur in 2020, a presidential election year. The 2020 Census will undoubtedly reveal continued growth in the nonwhite share of the population in almost every state, presenting potential opportunities for Democrats to make gains in subsequent elections, especially if Democrats have more say in the redistricting process than they did following the 2010 midterm election. Democratic strategists are well aware of the significance of this opportunity to undo some of the damage done after the 2010 midterm election and are planning to make a major effort to win back governorships and state legislative seats (Roller 2015). A strong Democratic presidential candidate at the head of the ticket will be essential for success in that endeavor.

One other trend in American electoral politics has had a detrimental impact on Democratic results in state and local elections in some parts of the country, especially the South. That is the increasing nationalization of subpresidential elections (Abramowitz and Webster 2015). With the increasing partisanship of the electorate, more and more voters are choosing state and local candidates based on their national party preferences. This development has sometimes helped Democratic candidates for state and local offices in strongly Democratic states like California, New York, and Massachusetts. But more often it has hurt Democratic candidates for state and local office in traditionally Democratic but conservative states in the South and Appalachia. As recently as the 1990s, Democrats continued to hold the large majority of seats in most state legislatures in southern states that regularly voted for Republican presidential candidates, but that is no longer the case. Republicans now control every state legislative chamber in the eleven states of the old Confederacy.

It should be emphasized that these long-term challenges facing Democrats have little or nothing to do with Barack Obama's presidency. They preceded his election in 2008 and they will undoubtedly continue after he leaves the White House. And despite these challenges, the long-term prospects for Democrats, even in the House of Representatives and in state elections, are promising. The same demographic trends that have helped Democrats win the popular vote in five of the last six presidential elections and that give Democrats a good chance to retain the White House in 2016 will also eventually shift more House seats, state legislatures, and governorships into the Democratic column. But demographic trends take time to produce significant shifts in electoral outcomes, so Democrats will likely continue to experience difficulty in House elections and in many state elections for the next several election cycles.

CONCLUSION: EVERYTHING DEPENDS ON 2016

In the end, Barack Obama's electoral legacy, along with his policy legacy, very much depend on what happens in November 2016. If Mr. Obama is succeeded by a Republican, and especially if Republicans also maintain control of the House and Senate, many of the president's domestic policy achievements will be in serious jeopardy. There is little doubt, for example, that a Republican president and Congress would move quickly to enact large tax cuts on upper-income Americans, drastically reduce spending on a wide range of domestic social programs, and sharply increase military spending. Needless to say, the president's signature domestic policy achievement, the Affordable Care Act, would be at great risk. Even if they were unable to totally repeal "Obamacare," a Republican president and Congress would undoubtedly make major changes in the Affordable Care Act that would greatly reduce its benefits by replacing direct subsidies for those unable to pay for coverage with tax credits and scaling back access to Medicaid for individuals and families with incomes above the poverty line. And while Democrats will certainly have at least forty-one votes in the Senate, it is very likely that Republicans would seize the opportunity presented by unified party control to end the filibuster once and for all.

Regardless of which party controls the House and Senate, a Republican president would be able to move US foreign policy in a much more hawkish direction, with much greater emphasis on unilateral use of American military force and much less reliance on coordination with US allies and diplomacy. One of President Obama's most important foreign policy achievements, the Iran Nuclear Deal, might well be jeopardy. And a Republican president would certainly rescind many of President Obama's executive orders and directives on immigration and the environment.

It goes without saying that the individuals who would be appointed by any Republican to key positions in the executive branch would be much more business friendly. Even more importantly, given the lifetime tenure of federal judges, individuals appointed to the federal courts, including the Supreme Court, would almost certainly be strong conservatives. Given the advanced age of several of the liberal justices on the Supreme Court, there is a real chance that a Republican president would be able to shift the ideological balance on the court sharply to the right with potentially long-lasting consequences.

A very conservative Republican in the White House combined with very conservative Republican majorities in the House and Senate would be a nightmare scenario for Democrats and their political allies, and President Obama would undoubtedly be blamed, fairly or unfairly, for allowing that to happen. On the other hand, a Democratic victory in the 2016 presidential election would be seen as a major political victory for Mr. Obama, especially if it is combined with a Democratic takeover of the Senate and substantial gains in the House and in state elections. A Democratic president would certainly seek to build on President Obama's policy achievements by expanding the benefits of the Affordable Care Act, moving forward with efforts to combat climate change, and working to achieve comprehensive immigration reform, including a path to citizenship for millions of undocumented immigrants, making it likely that key elements of President Obama's policy legacy would endure far beyond 2016.

I have argued that the president's record of achievement and especially his strong support from key Democratic voting groups should make it possible for Democrats to achieve a successful result in 2016. But nothing is certain. The presidential election is likely to be close, and the outcome will depend on several factors that won't be known for some time: economic conditions, the president's approval rating, the appeal of the Democratic candidate, and whether Republicans choose a mainstream or radical conservative as their nominee. Unpredictable events such as scandals and terrorist attacks could also affect the outcome.

More than anything else, though, the outcome of the 2016 election will depend on who actually votes. In an era of deep partisan polarization, the partisan composition of the electorate is the single strongest predictor of election outcomes. Democrats start out with an advantage in this regard—Democrats outnumber Republicans in the voting-age population. But Democratic candidates at every level, from the White House to the state and local levels, will need strong turnout from traditionally Democratic voting groups such as young people, African Americans, Latinos, Asian Americans, and unmarried women in order to translate that underlying advantage in the voting-age population into an advantage in the actual electorate.

President Obama's continued popularity with key Democratic constituencies should help considerably with the task of mobilizing the Democratic electorate in 2016. But he will need a lot of help from state and local party organizations, organized labor, and other progressive groups to maximize Democratic turnout in 2016. However, the sharp rightward tack of the Republican Party and the hostility of prominent Republican leaders to immigrants and racial minorities should make that task easier.

Given the stark differences between the domestic and foreign policies of the two major parties today, one thing almost all political observers can agree on is that a great deal will be at stake when Americans go to the polls in 2016. There will be no excuse for staying home.

WORKS CITED

Abramowitz, Alan I. 2013. *The Polarized Public: Why American Government Is So Dysfunctional*. New York: Pearson Longman.

Abramowitz, Alan I., and Steven W. Webster. 2015. "The Rise of Negative Partisanship and the Nationalization of U.S. Elections in the 21st Century." Paper presented at the Annual Meeting of the American Political Science Association, Washington, DC.

Brownstein, Ronald. 2014. "Shellacking: The Sequel." *National Journal*, November 7. www.nationaljournal.com/politics/2014/11/07/Shellacking-Sequel. Accessed November 20, 2015.

Cauchon, Dennis, and Jim Drinkard. 2001. "Florida Voter Errors Cost Gore the Election." *USA Today*, May 11. http://usatoday30.usatoday.com/news/politics/2001-05-10-recount-main.htm. Accessed November 20, 2015.

Frey, William H. 2014. *Diversity Explosion: How New Racial Demographics Are Remaking America*. Washington, DC: Brookings Institution Press.

Greenberg, Stanley B. 2015. *America Ascendant: A Revolutionary Nation's Path to Addressing Its Deepest Problems and Leading the 21st Century*. New York: St. Martin's Press.

Greenfield, Jeff. 2015. "Democratic Blues: Barack Obama Will Leave His Party in Its Worst Shape Since the Great Depression—Even If Hillary Clinton Wins." *Politico*, August 21. www.politico.com/magazine/story/2015/08/democratic-blues-121561. Accessed November 22, 2015.

Hartung, Adam. 2014. "Obama Outperforms Reagan on Jobs, Growth and Investing." *Forbes*, September 5. www.forbes.com/sites/adamhartung/2014/09/05/obama-outperforms-reagan-on-jobs-growth-and-investing/. Accessed November 20, 2015.

Jones, Jeffrey M. 2015. "On Social Ideology, the Left Catches Up to the Right." Gallup Poll, May 22. www.gallup.com/poll/183386/social-ideology-left-catches-right.aspx. Accessed November 20, 2015.

Kopicki, Allison. 2014. "Democrats Are Unified; GOP Is Unified Only in Opposing Obama." *New York Times*, May 14. www.nytimes.com/2014/05/15/upshot/democrats-are-unified-gop-is-unified-only-in-opposing-obama.html. Accessed November 20, 2015.

Kraushaar, Josh. 2015. Democrats' Vanishing Future. *National Journal*, May 21. www.nationaljournal.com/daily/2015/05/21/democrats-vanishing-future. Accessed November 22, 2015.

Kriesberg, Louis. 2015. "Constructive Conflict Applications in Obama's Foreign Policies." *Foreign Policy in Focus*, November 11. http://fpif.org/constructive-conflict-applications-in-obamas-foreign-policies/. Accessed November 22, 2015.

Krugman, Paul. 2014. "Obamacare Fails to Fail." *New York Times*, July 13. www.nytimes.com/2014/07/14/opinion/paul-krugman-obamacare-fails-to-fail.html. Accessed November 20, 2015.

Madland, David. 2015. "Unwavering Fealty to a Failed Theory: The Republican Presidential Candidates Still Cling to Trickle-Down Economics." *U.S. News and World Report*, August 6. www.usnews.com/opinion/economic-intelligence/2015/08/06/republican-2016-candidates-cling-to-failed-trickle-down-economics-theory. Accessed November 20, 2015.

Mann, Thomas E. and Norman J. Ornstein. 2012. *It's Even Worse Than It Looks: How the American Constitutional System Collided with the New Politics of Extremism*. New York: Basic Books.

Milligan, Susan. 2015. "Who Speaks for the GOP?" *U.S. News and World Report*, October 23. www.usnews.com/news/the-report/articles/2015/10/23/the-republican-party-has-no-leader. Accessed November 20, 2015.

Pew Research Center. 2015a. "A Deep Dive into Party Affiliation." Pew Research Center, April 7. www.people-press.org/files/2015/04/4-7-2015-Party-ID-release.pdf. Accessed November 20, 2015.

Pew Research Center. 2015b. "GOP's Favorability Rating Takes a Negative Turn." Pew Research Center, July 23. www.people-press.org/files/2015/07/07-23-15-Politics-release.pdf. Accessed November 20, 2015.

Roller, Emma. 2015. "Can Democrats Ever Win Back State Legislatures?" *National Journal*, February 24. www.nationaljournal.com/daily/2015/02/24/can-democrats-ever-win-back-state-legislatures. Accessed November 20, 2015.

Smialek, Jeanna, and Gregory Giroux. 2015. "The Majority of American Babies Are Now Minorities." *Bloomberg Business*, June 25. www.bloomberg.com/news/articles/2015-06-25/american-babies-are-no-longer-mostly-non-hispanic-white. Accessed November 20, 2015.

Sommers, Benjamin D., Munira Z. Gunja, Kenneth Finegold, and Thomas Musco. 2015. "Changes in Self-Reported Insurance Coverage, Access to Care, and Health Under the Affordable Care Act." *Journal of the American Medical Association*, 314 (4), 366–74. http://jama.jamanetwork.com/article.aspx?articleid=2411283. Accessed November 20, 2015.

Stolberg, Sheryl Gay, Michael D. Shear, and Alan Blinder. 2015. "In Obama Era, GOP Bolsters Grip in the States." *New York Times*, November 12. www.nytimes.com/2015/11/13/us/politics/obama-legacy-in-state-offices-a-shrinking-democratic-share.html?_r=1. Accessed November 20, 2015.

Trygstad, Kyle. 2013. "History Shows Midterm Elections a Hard Slog for President's Party." *Roll Call*, January 21. www.rollcall.com/news/history_shows_midterm_elections_a_hard_slog_for_presidents_party-220970-1.html. Accessed November 20, 2015.

Wang, Sam. 2014. "Has Gerrymandering Made It Impossible for Democrats to Win the House?" *The New Yorker*, October 31. www.newyorker.com/news/news-desk/gerrymandering-made-impossible-democrats-win-house. Accessed November 20, 2015.

4

WITH ENEMIES LIKE THIS, WHO NEEDS FRIENDS?

How Barack Obama Revived the Republican Party

William G. Mayer, Northeastern University

To appreciate just how bad Barack Obama has been as a party and electoral leader, it is helpful to recall the mood that prevailed just after Election Day, November 6, 2008. To say that the Democrats were jubilant then is a significant understatement. Not only had that party succeeded in electing the first black president—and perhaps the most openly left-wing president ever—Democratic candidates had triumphed up and down the ballot. Republicans lost twenty-one seats in the US House of Representatives and eight seats in the Senate. Coming on top of the substantial Republican losses in 2006, this meant that:

- Republican strength in the House of Representatives had been reduced to its lowest level since 1993.
- Republican strength in the Senate had been reduced to its lowest level since 1979.
- Obama himself had received the highest percentage of the total popular vote of any Democratic candidate since 1964.

More than just a victory, many commentators interpreted the 2008 election as the onset of a realignment: a sharp, decisive change in the parties' relative fortunes that would usher in an extended period of Democratic electoral dominance. John Judis and Ruy Teixeira had predicted an "emerging Democratic majority" in 2002, and six years later it actually seemed to be taking place. As Judis (2008) proclaimed in the post-election issue of the *New Republic*:

> [Obama's] election is the culmination of a Democratic realignment that began in the 1990s, was delayed by September 11, and resumed with the 2006 election. This realignment is predicated on a change in political demography and geography. Groups that had been disproportionately Republican have become disproportionately Democratic, and red states like Virginia have turned blue. Underlying these changes has been a shift in the nation's "fundamentals"—in the structure of society and industry, and in the way Americans think of their families, jobs, and government. The country is no longer "America the conservative."

Judis was not the only person to draw this conclusion from the 2008 tea leaves. Consider the verdict of Hendrik Hertzberg (2008, 39–40), editor of the *New Yorker*:

> This election was so extraordinary in so many ways that its meaning will take many years to play out and many more to be understood. But there is already the feel of the beginning of a new era. As in 1932 and 1980, a crisis in the economy opened the way for the rejection of a reigning approach to government and the forging of a new one. Emphatically, comprehensively, the public has turned against conservatism at home and neoconservatism abroad. The faith that unfettered markets and minimal taxes on the rich will solve every domestic problem, and that unilateral arrogance and American arms will solve every foreign one, is dead for a generation or more. And the electoral strategy of "cultural" resentment and fake populism has been dealt a grievous blow.

Or Harold Meyerson (2008), writing in the *Washington Post*:

> Even though Obama's victory was nowhere near as numerically lopsided as Franklin Roosevelt's in 1932, his margins among decisive and growing constituencies make clear that this was a genuinely realigning election. . . . Republicans stumble from Tuesday's contest, then, in worse shape than they've been in decades.

Seven years later it is, I believe, impossible to sustain the fiction that a stable, durable Democratic electoral majority has emerged. Perhaps, as

Alan Abramowitz argues in his chapter, demographic trends favor the Democrats to such an extent that they will develop a reliable majority in the future (though I am skeptical of this as well). But it most certainly hasn't happened yet. With the notable exception of 2012 (which I will examine in more detail below), the election news for Democrats since 2008 has been not just disappointing but dreadful. While the party of the president normally loses some ground in midterm elections—though this pointedly did not occur in 1934 during the last Democratic realignment—the scale of Democratic losses in 2010 and 2014 went well beyond "business as usual." In US House elections, for example, the Democrats lost sixty-three seats in 2010—the largest midterm seat loss since 1938—won back just eight of those seats in 2012, then lost thirteen more in 2014. Add the three elections together, and by the end of 2014 Republicans held:

- 247 seats in the House of Representatives, their largest total since 1928
- 54 seats in the Senate, not a historic number, but close to it
- 31 governorships, not far off their post–Herbert Hoover high point
- majorities in both houses of thirty state legislatures, as compared to the fourteen state legislatures they controlled in 2009.

Though media attention has, for obvious reasons, focused on the federal-level results, Republican gains at the state level may well be more significant as a harbinger of future election outcomes. On the one hand, as Gary Jacobson has shown (1980, 2013), congressional candidates who have already run for and won at least one other elective office do substantially better than those who are seeking their first electoral victory. The sizable number of Republican governors and state legislators thus provides the party with the political equivalent of a good "farm system": a pool of potentially strong candidates they can turn to if their existing set of US senators and House members retire or run for higher office or to challenge Democratic incumbents. Second, unless Republican dominance at the state level is reversed in the next three elections, Republicans will also have a larger-than-usual role in drawing the new congressional district lines in 2020, which, all other things equal, will give them an advantage in House elections for the next ten years.

For those who do not believe that a trend is real unless all the various numbers can be crunched together into a single metric, Sean Trende and David Byler (2015) of realclearpolitics.com have computed just such an index, which combines the results of presidential, US House, US Senate, gubernatorial, and state legislative elections. Their conclusion: As of mid-2015, the Republican Party was at its strongest position since 1928. Or as political analyst Jeff Greenfield (2015) summed up the Obama record: "No president in modern times has presided over so disastrous a stretch for his party, at almost every level of politics."

If this is a Democratic realignment, the Republicans should always be so fortunate.

THE ANOMALOUS CASE OF 2012

As noted above, the lone exception to the pattern of substantial Republican gains during the Obama presidency was the 2012 election. Even this was scarcely a resounding victory for a purported majority party. The Democrats picked up just eight seats in the House, about one-eighth of the number they had lost two years earlier, and two seats in the Senate. Barack Obama was reelected—but here, too, the victory was hardly of historic proportions. Obama won just 51.1 percent of the popular vote (52.0 percent of the two-party vote), almost 2 percentage points *less* than he had received in 2008.

Impressive or not, the 2012 election deserves a closer examination. Why *did* the Democrats fare so much better in 2012 than they did in 2010 and 2014? There are, I think, three major factors that worked to the Democrats' advantage that year.

First, as Professor Abramowitz (1988) himself was the first to point out, it is extraordinarily difficult to defeat an incumbent president when his party has only been in the White House for the previous four years. As Table 4.1 shows, since 1952 eight presidential candidates have been in this position and seven of them were elected. Over the same period, eight presidential candidates were nominated by a party that had held the presidency for at least eight years—and only one of them won the election. In 2012 this factor, which Abramowitz has estimated can add between 4 and 5 percentage points to a favored party's vote, aided the Democrats. In 2016, however, it will no longer work in their favor.

Second, one source of the electoral advantage that accrues to a party that has only been in the White House for four years is that they can credibly shift some of the blame for the country's problems to their opposite-party predecessors. Ronald Reagan in 1984, Bill Clinton in 1996, and George W. Bush in 2004 all argued, at least with respect to some issues, that while current conditions were far from ideal, their policies had only had four years to work and they deserved another term to "finish the job." But Obama was especially fortunate in this regard, because his predecessor's performance was seen in a particularly unfavorable light.

To an extent that many party members are still unwilling to acknowledge, the presidency of George W. Bush was a disaster for the Republican Party. Even with the stratospheric ratings that Bush received in the immediate aftermath of the September 11 terrorist attacks, July 2005 was the last time during his presidency, at least in the Gallup polls, when those who approved of his performance exceeded the number who disapproved. During his last two years in office, the *highest* approval rating Bush achieved in Gallup surveys was a dismal 38 percent. (His average rating during this period was 32 percent.) Bush's father, the forty-first president, also left office with low approval ratings, but George H. W. Bush was at least seen as quite successful in some policy areas, particularly foreign policy. In George W. Bush's case, by contrast, the aura of failure and incompetence touched almost every major issue. The federal budget was way out of balance; the economy slipped into recession in December 2007, then confronted a major financial crisis in the final months of 2008; his signature domestic initiative, the No Child Left Behind education act, was sharply criticized by both liberals and conservatives; and his mishandling of the war in Iraq largely negated the Republican Party's traditional advantage as the party perceived to be better at protecting American national security. To top it all off, the second presi-

Table 4.1. How Long a Party Has Been in the White House Affects How Likely They Are to Win the Upcoming Election, 1952-2012

	Incumbent Party Has Been in the White House for Just Four Years	Incumbent Party Has Been in the White House for Eight or More Years
Incumbent party wins	7	1
Incumbent party loses	1	7

dent Bush also received low marks for his personal honesty and integrity, largely due to the perception that he had lied about the existence of weapons of mass destruction in Iraq.

Against that background, it should come as no surprise that Barack Obama spent a good part of the 2012 campaign running against George W. Bush. And it worked. During his first term, for example, Barack Obama had run up the largest total deficit in any presidential term in American history. Yet who were the Republicans to attack him on this count? Bush had actually inherited a $236 billion *surplus* from his predecessor, quickly squandered it, then ran up the second-largest one-term deficit during his second term. Thus, when Americans were asked in January 2012 who was "mostly to blame for most of the current federal budget deficit," 43 percent put the onus on Bush while just 14 percent blamed Obama (19 percent blamed Congress). Similarly, a question in the 2012 National Election Pool exit poll asked voters who was "more to blame for current economic problems," Obama or Bush. The results were: Bush 53 percent, Obama 38 percent.

In 2016 Democrats will no doubt try once again to run against George W. Bush, but if history is any guide, they will find it a difficult sell. The "blame your predecessor" tactic really does have a time limit. By 2016 Bush will have been out of office for eight years, and as Abramowitz's results show, voters will increasingly blame the country's problems on the party that has actually held the presidency since 2009.

Even in 2012 Mitt Romney's presidential campaign might have reduced the damage of the Bush legacy somewhat had they directly addressed this issue and detailed the specific ways that Romney would be different from Bush, as many conservative commentators recommended at the time (see, in particular, Goldberg 2012). But the Romney campaign resolutely ignored all such warnings. The only time I am aware of that Romney spoke about his differences with Bush was in the second presidential debate, when that issue was the subject of a question from one of the "town hall" audience members. Romney's answer that night was good, though not great—but one two-minute answer, even one broadcast on national television, hardly suffices to overcome months of pounding from the other side.

This is just one illustration of the third reason Obama did so well in 2012: Romney ran a terrible campaign.[1] For all his other gifts, Romney himself has never been a very skillful politician (which is why he lost three of the four elections in which he was a candidate). To make matters worse, the campaign team he hired in 2012—Stuart Stevens, Beth Meyers, Neil Newhouse, Lahnee Chen, et al.—was perhaps the weakest ever assembled for a modern presidential general election, and they proceeded to run a remarkably flawed, mistake-ridden campaign. Apparently relying on Newhouse polls that assured them, contrary to everybody else's numbers, that they were comfortably ahead of Obama, the Romney high command seem to have premised their campaign on the belief that Obama was so unpopular that they merely had to sit back and let the public register their dissatisfaction. As a result, they ran an especially vacuous campaign, as if their principal challenge was not to make a strong case against a potentially vulnerable incumbent, but to avoid squandering a big lead. The 2012 Republican national convention was particularly issueless, without a single speech that offered a detailed critique of the Obama record or a clear sense of what Romney would do differently. Chris Christie spent more time talking about himself than about Romney or Obama. Anne Romney talked about love. Romney himself presented a long and directionless reflection on the American dream, made a few exceedingly mild criticisms of Obama's performance, then provided a rushed litany of unspecific promises, most of which the voters had heard over and over again in recent elections.

Throughout the fall campaign, a small army of conservative commentators and pundits wrote articles or columns in which they lamented how poorly the Romney campaign was being run. Yet the Romney high command never indicated that they took these criticisms seriously, much less that they intended to alter their strategy or leadership. In one especially puzzling incident that occurred during the final presidential debate, Romney was offered a golden opportunity to criticize Obama's handling of the attack on the American embassy in Libya, which had left four Americans dead. But Romney refused to swing at a hanging curve. Instead, after saying that "our hearts and minds go to" the victims, Romney rattled off a vague, four-point strategy to deal with the Middle East that was, in the unspecific terms Romney stated it, not very different from what Obama claimed to be doing.

In general, American political scientists are inclined to think that the importance of presidential general election campaigns is exaggerated, that presidential elections are determined more by such fundamentals as the state of the economy and the performance of the incumbent president than by the parading and posturing that occur in the months immediately preceding the final voting (for a particularly good development of this argument, see Campbell 2008). But 2012 is an exception to the general rule: an election where all of the factors that political scientists look to suggested a very close election, potentially winnable by either side. That the Republicans lost is, I believe, largely attributable to the incompetence of the Romney campaign.

A MESSIAH WITH CLAY FEET

Why did the Democratic Party fare so poorly during the period when Barack Obama was its principal decision-maker and spokesperson? The short but sufficient answer is that he just wasn't a very good president. Other chapters in this volume have detailed his major policy failures: the weakest economic "recovery" in modern American history; the poorly designed, poorly executed national health-care law he pushed through Congress; the extraordinary disarray that has ensued from his foreign policies, especially in the Middle East; the record-breaking federal deficits; the numerous domestic terrorist attacks that have occurred during his presidency; the wholesale disregard he has shown for the rule of law.

For the purposes of this chapter, however, the relevant question is not how Obama's performance would be assessed by a panel of experts, but how it has been evaluated by the American public. As of December 2015, when this article was written, Obama's ratings were not quite as negative as those registered by George W. Bush—perhaps because Obama had managed to retain the loyalty of a hard core of blacks, liberals, and Democrats, perhaps because Obama received substantially softer press coverage than his Republican predecessor. But it is clear that Obama has come nowhere near satisfying the high expectations that surrounded his 2008 presidential campaign and subsequent inauguration. If one had to sum up the public's assessment of the Obama presidency in one word, that word would be *disappointing*.

Consider two prime pieces of evidence:

1. Obama started his presidency with considerable public goodwill. The first Gallup poll conducted after Obama's inauguration found that 67 percent of its sample approved of how Obama had handled

his job thus far, significantly higher than the initial approval ratings of his four immediate predecessors. Just 17 percent disapproved. Unfortunately for the Democrats, it was all downhill from there. Like his immediate predecessor, Obama has spent most of his second term "underwater": that is, with a plurality of the public viewing his performance unfavorably. In the realclearpolitics.com running average of presidential approval polls, June 8, 2013, was the last time that the number who approved of Obama's performance exceeded the number who disapproved. Indeed, Obama's approval ratings haven't been consistently positive since July 2010.

2. Even more striking are the results of a series of Gallup poll questions that asked respondents how they thought each of the last eight presidents "will go down in history—as an outstanding president, above average, average, below average, or poor?" As shown in Table 4.2, when this question was first asked in mid-January 2009—about a week *before* Obama was inaugurated—lots of Americans clearly believed that Obama had the mark of greatness upon him. Sixty-two percent of the Gallup respondents thought that Obama would be either an outstanding president (24 percent) or an above average one (38 percent). When this question sequence was repeated in November 2013, however (it apparently has not been asked since then), a dramatic change had taken place in public assessments of Obama. After seeing Obama at work for five years, only 28 percent of the public thought he would go down in history as an outstanding or above average president, with just 6 percent giving him an outstanding rating. A comparative assessment of the eight presidents rated in Table 4.2 is perhaps even more telling. Before Obama took office, Americans expected him to be among the very best of the modern presidents. Of all the presidents since Richard Nixon, Obama was ranked second highest, just a notch below Ronald Reagan. By late 2013, by contrast, Obama was ranked sixth of eight, below Reagan, Bill Clinton, George H. W. Bush, Gerald Ford, and even Jimmy Carter.

Table 4.2. Public Assessments of How Recent Presidents Will Go Down in History

	Outstanding	*Above Average*	*Average*	*Below Average*	*Poor*	*Don't Know*	*Overall Assessment*
Jan. 9-11, 2009							
Ronald Reagan	25	39	26	4	5	2	3.76
Barack Obama	24	38	25	5	6	3	3.70
Bill Clinton	13	37	29	10	10	0	3.33
Gerald Ford	4	19	58	7	4	8	3.13
George W. Bush	5	23	49	10	11	2	3.01
Jimmy Carter	6	20	39	15	14	5	2.88
Richard Nixon	2	13	32	23	25	4	2.41
George W. Bush	4	13	23	23	36	0	2.25
Nov. 7-10, 2013							
Ronald Reagan	19	42	27	6	4	2	3.67
Bill Clinton	11	44	29	9	6	1	3.45
George H.W. Bush	3	24	48	12	10	2	2.98
Gerald Ford	2	14	56	15	5	8	2.92
Jimmy Carter	4	19	37	20	15	6	2.76
Barack Obama	6	22	31	18	22	1	2.72
George W. Bush	3	18	36	20	23	1	2.58

	Outstanding	*Above Average*	*Average*	*Below Average*	*Poor*	*Don't Know*	*Overall Assessment*
Richard Nixon	2	13	27	29	23	6	2.38

Note: Question wording was: "How do you think each of the following presidents will go down in history—as an outstanding president, above average, average, below average, or poor?" "Overall assessment" figures were computed by assigning a value of 5 for "outstanding" responses, 4 for "above average," 3 for "average," 2 for "below average," and 1 for "poor," and then calculating a mean value for each president. Source: The Gallup Poll.

WHY THE EMERGING DEMOCRATIC MAJORITY NEVER EMERGED

With Obama as their leader, it's no wonder the Democratic majority never emerged. And the key flaw in Judis and Teixeira's analysis—and the reason I am also skeptical about Professor Abramowitz's predictions—is that neither makes an allowance for the importance and the difficulties of governing.

To approach the issue from a somewhat more theoretical angle, the major disagreement between Judis, Teixeira, and Abramowitz and me concerns the question of why realignments occur.[2] In the vast realignments literature, two major answers have been given to this question. One theory holds that realignments are the product of *accumulated social change*. Every party system, it is argued, is established to deal with one particular constellation of policy issues and related social groups. As society changes, however, the existing system begins to seem increasingly irrelevant to the new conditions and challenges and the new voting groups. The result is that the old party system finally implodes and a new one emerges to take its place. A second theory links realignments to *major governing crises*, such as severe economic depressions or the Civil War. When the party in power seems incapable of dealing with this crisis, the argument goes, it is likely to suffer a harsh drubbing at the polls. If the party that replaces it is perceived to cope with the problem(s) more successfully, a realignment will then take place as large numbers of people, especially young people, align themselves with that party. These two theories, of course, are not mutually exclusive. A fair number of party scholars have accordingly fallen back on that old, reliable chestnut from their undergraduate days, the balanced answer: In order for a realignment to take place, *both* social change and a governing crisis are necessary.

No fence-sitter I, my reading of American electoral history indicates that governing crises play a far more important, more determinative role in giving rise to realignments than social changes do. To be sure, since social change is a ubiquitous feature of American history, every realignment has been preceded by some sort of important social change that can, after the fact, be linked to the realignment. But this hardly proves that social change *caused* the realignment or made it inevitable.

Consider a specific case: the realignment of 1932. Though the years between 1896 and 1932 witnessed a panoply of important social changes—immigration, urbanization, industrialization—there is no evidence that the fourth-party system was teetering on the brink of dissolution until the stock market crashed in October 1929 and the US economy plunged into a deep recession. In the 1928 elections Herbert Hoover won 58 percent of the popular vote and carried forty of forty-eight states. Republicans also won a one-hundred-seat majority in the US House and a 56-to-39 advantage in the Senate. It is true that Alfred E. Smith, as the first Catholic presidential nominee of a major party, ran unusually well among Catholic voters that year. But in the absence of the Great Depression, there is no reason to think that the Catholic surge toward the Democrats would have been lasting (unless the Democrats continued to nominate Catholic presidential candidates). Had the American economy continued to behave about the way it had between 1921 and 1928, there is every reason to believe that Hoover would have been comfortably reelected in 1932.

If my argument is correct in placing great emphasis on the performance of government in causing realignments, a second important conclusion follows: Whether any particular election is later seen as realigning depends to a great extent on what happens *after* the election. A governing crisis such as the Depression of 1929 typically produces a widespread revulsion against the party in power. And in a classic demonstration of retrospective voting, the public's immediate instinct is to vote the miscreants out and turn the reins of power over to the other party. But this one act doesn't make them instant Democrats (or, in 1896, instant Republicans). Voters transfer their allegiance from one party to the other—they become reliable party voters—only after the new power holders have shown that they can cope with the nation's problems more effectively. If they, too, fail, it is likely that the voters will turn back to the original party or perhaps to some new third party. From this perspective, the 1932 election merely gave Democrats the opportunity to gain new adherents. They achieved that goal, probably beyond their highest expectations, only because Franklin Roosevelt was perceived to have done a substantially better job than Hoover at ending the Depression and giving aid to the unemployed and destitute.[3] In a similar way, the 1860 election resulted in a Republican realignment only because Lincoln actually won the Civil War and kept the Union together. It is unlikely that the northern states would have continued to vote Republican if the South had won the war.

If all of this seems rather obvious and commonsensical, there is very little allowance for such matters in the framework of the *Emerging Democratic Majority*. Judis and Teixeira's predictions are driven almost entirely by social changes. The Democrats would become the new majority party, they argued, because of three important social trends: the surging number of nonwhite minorities; the "feminist revolution"; and the growing number of democratically inclined professionals produced by the postindustrial economy. They say very little about whether future Democrats would govern the country effectively. It could hardly have been otherwise, since Judis and Teixeira were writing their book in 2002 about changes they expected/hoped would occur in 2004 or 2008. They could have no reliable information about whom the Democrats would nominate in those elections, what kinds of platforms they would run on, or how effectively they would govern if elected.

While I think that the severity of the so-called Great Recession of 2007–2009 has been exaggerated—it was nowhere near as bad as the depressions that began in 1893 or 1929 or even the economic mess that Jimmy Carter handed off to Ronald Reagan in 1981—perhaps economic conditions plus public resentments over the war in Iraq gave the Democrats a reasonable opportunity to convert a significant number of independents and weakly committed Republicans to the Democratic fold. Since the United States was then widely thought to be a "50:50 nation," even a relatively small increase in the number of Democratic partisans, assuming it lasted, might have created a durable Democratic majority. But the Democrats needed Obama to be a good president: to restore American prosperity, to protect our national security, to convince the country that Democratic government did not inevitably mean large deficits, huge new government bureaucracies, and the unrestrained excesses of the cultural left.

By and large, Obama failed the test.

OBAMA'S FAILURES: A CLOSER LOOK

Public opinion surveys taken during the Obama presidency, especially during his second term, reveal a wide variety of public complaints, but behind most of them, I would argue, are three basic problems. First, a quite large number of Americans believe that Obama's policies are simply too liberal. As shown in Table 4.3, this was always a potential vulnerability for the 44th president, as it probably is for all Democratic presidents. In March 2009, according to a question posed by the Opinion Research Corporation, 36 percent of the respondents said that "Obama's views and proposed programs for the country" were "too liberal," but 58 percent then thought that his policies were "just about right." When the same question was asked in March 2011, however, and the public had actually had a chance to watch Obama govern, a plurality, 46 percent, now thought he was too liberal, while just 39 percent said his views and programs were about right. Note that only a small minority—about 10 percent, on average—claimed that Obama's policies weren't liberal enough.

This finding deserves special emphasis, for it highlights the problem noted earlier with Judis and Teixeira's prediction of an emerging Democratic majority. Judis and Teixeira, as I have already observed, didn't pay a lot of attention to questions of governance, but to the extent they did address this issue, they assumed that the next Democratic presidency would be a straight-line extrapolation of the Clinton presidency, or at least its last six years. The "new Democrats," they insisted, would be "centrists." They would favor "incremental, careful reforms that will substantially increase health-care coverage and perhaps eventually universalize it, but not a large new bureaucracy that [would] replace the entire

Table 4.3. Is Obama Too Liberal?

Sampling Dates	Too Liberal	Just About Right	Not Liberal Enough	Don't Know
March 12-15, 2009	36	58	5	1
July 31-Aug. 3, 2009	40	50	8	2
Oct. 30-Nov. 1, 2009	42	44	14	1
Jan. 8-10, 2010	46	42	10	2
Aug. 6-10, 2010	46	39	13	3
March 11-13, 2011	46	39	12	3

CNN/Opinion Research Corporation: "In general, would you say that President Obama's views and proposed programs for the country are too liberal, not liberal enough, or just about right for the country?"

private health-care market. . . . They [would] worry about budget deficits" (Judis and Teixeira 2002, 5–6).

While judgments about whether Obama is "*too* liberal" depend on a person's own position on the ideological spectrum, I find it difficult to believe that many fair-minded observers would claim Obama was a centrist. On issue after issue—welfare reform, criminal sentencing, free trade, business regulation, the value of entrepreneurship—Obama has governed from a position far to the left of the "new Democrats" that Judis and Teixeira celebrate. As several commentators have observed, Bill Clinton probably couldn't win a presidential nomination in the contemporary Democratic Party.

Perhaps no issue shows the difference between Clinton and Obama more vividly than their attitudes and policies with regard to the federal deficit. Though it was not a major issue in his 1992 campaign, in between his election and his inauguration, Clinton became convinced that reducing the deficit was the key to reviving the American economy. In pursuit of that goal, he soon jettisoned several of his more conspicuous campaign promises, including both a middle-class tax cut and a good deal of additional domestic spending. In the end, Clinton was able to boast that the federal budget actually ran a surplus during his last three years in office, as well as in George W. Bush's first year. According to Judis and Teixeira, this emphasis on fiscal restraint, which they say actually began with Walter Mondale in 1984, "marked the end of the Democrats as the party of indiscriminate big spenders and the beginning of the party's commitment to more incremental reform. It was the first intimation of the Democrats' progressive centrism" (Judis and Teixeira 2002, 48–49).

If so, the word never got through to Barack Obama—or, for that matter, to John Kerry, whose 2004 presidential campaign included almost a trillion dollars in new spending promises. Obama can credibly be accused of many things, but fiscal restraint isn't one of them. Putting aside fiscal year 2009, for which George W. Bush bears most of the responsibility, the first four Obama budgets (2010–2013) ran up a total deficit of $4.36 trillion, busting the previous record for a single presidential term by more than $2 trillion. Small wonder, then, that in six separate polls conducted in 2014, only 31 percent of the public approved of the way Obama was handling the federal deficit.

Second, Obama is seen as too weak in his dealings with foreign governments and terrorist groups. In a Fox News poll conducted in September 2014, only 34 percent of the respondents thought that Obama was a "strong and decisive leader" in foreign policy; 57 percent called him "weak and indecisive." A March 2015 survey that asked specifically about Obama's performance as a "negotiator with foreign leaders" produced almost identical results: 34 percent said he was a "strong negotiator" versus 59 percent who thought him a "weak negotiator."

Thus, while Obama does not get high marks for his handling of domestic policy issues, he gets even lower marks on foreign policy. In a November 2015 CBS poll, for example, 42 percent approved of his overall performance and 44 percent approved of the way he was "handling the economy." But 36 percent approved of his handling of the "threat of terrorism," and just 31 percent approved of the way he was "handling the situation with ISIS (Islamic) militants in Iraq and Syria."

Finally, many Americans have concluded that Obama just isn't very competent. This was, of course, also seen as one of George W. Bush's major shortcomings. After witnessing the bungled occupation in Iraq, the inept response to Hurricane Katrina, the widely criticized nomination of Harriet Miers to the Supreme Court, and numerous other glaring mistakes, the perception gradually developed that Bush just wasn't capable of mastering the many difficult tasks that confront a modern president. By the middle of Obama's second term, the public had also come to entertain serious doubts about his competence. As was the case with George W. Bush, this perception developed from a long list of embarrassing incidents: the administration's inability to create a functioning Obamacare website through which uninsured Americans could sign up for health insurance; the "red line" Obama laid down for the Syrian government's use of chemical weapons—and then declined to enforce; the admission that all those "shovel ready" jobs that were supposed to be funded by the 2009 stimulus bill weren't actually shovel ready; the widely repeated, subsequently broken promise that "if you like your doctor, you can keep your doctor."

In March 2006 NBC News and the *Wall Street Journal* asked respondents whether the "Bush administration" was very competent, somewhat competent, not too competent, or not competent at all in "managing the federal government." They then asked an identically worded question about the "Obama administration" in June 2014. As shown in Table 4.4, the general assessment of the two administrations is quite similar. Very few Americans thought either administration to be "very competent." But

Bush does have a slight advantage at the very bottom of the scale: 31 percent said Obama was "not competent at all," while just 24 percent rated Bush that poorly. A Fox News poll, also conducted in June 2014, confronted the issue head-on by asking respondents, "Do you think the Obama administration is more or less competent than the George W. Bush administration?" Forty-two percent said Obama was more competent, 48 percent said less competent. Lest one conclude that all presidents are seen as pretty much alike on this dimension ("They're all just politicians"), it is worth noting another question in that same Fox poll, which asked respondents to compare the competence of the Obama and Clinton administrations. The public verdict was clear: 68 percent thought the Clinton administration was more competent, while just 18 percent gave the nod to the Obama administration.

CONCLUSION: THE COMPETENCE GAP

So where does this leave the country in 2016?

In the 1970s and early 1980s, America was sometimes said to be suffering from a "confidence gap": a situation in which public trust in all of the country's major institutions—business, labor, and government—had declined (see, in particular, Lipset and Schneider 1983). For the last sixteen years, I would argue, the United States has suffered from a "competence gap": two successive presidents who were just not very qualified to hold the office to which each was twice elected.

If this diagnosis is accurate, the future belongs to that party that can actually demonstrate the capacity to govern the nation effectively. On this

Table 4.4. How the Public Rated the Competence of the Bush and Obama Administrations*

	"Bush Administration" (March 2006)	"Obama Administration" (June 2014)
Very competent	14	11
Somewhat competent	39	39
Not too competent	22	19
Not competent at all	24	31
Number	1,005	1,000

matter, both parties have much to be modest about, both in terms of recent past performance and in their outlook for the future. As this chapter is being finished, Donald Trump has just clinched the 2016 Republican presidential nomination. The GOP has thus chosen as its standard-bearer a man with no previous governmental experience, minimal knowledge of most of the issues the next president will have to confront—and a highly checkered business career. On paper, Hillary Clinton, who will be the Democratic nominee, has a far more impressive résumé: eight years in the US Senate, four years as secretary of state, plus her service as head of the task force that drafted the Clinton administration's health-care bill. Unfortunately, her record in each position is conspicuously devoid of actual achievements.

But whatever happens in 2016, it is clear that Obama's eight years in the White House have dug an enormous hole for the Democrats.

NOTES

1. The next three paragraphs make an argument that is laid out in more detail in Mayer 2012.

2. In posing this question, I am assuming that realignment is still a valid and useful tool for analyzing American partisan and electoral history. That assumption, once all but universally shared among political scientists, has recently been dealt a severe body blow in a book by David Mayhew (2002). Space does not permit an extended reply to Mayhew's nuanced and well-documented argument. Suffice it for now to say that I disagree with him. For my own take on the realignment issue, which I believe is still generally valid, see Mayer 1995.

3. In reaching this conclusion, I am not overlooking the clear evidence that American unemployment continued at an unacceptably high level throughout the 1930s and that it was the national mobilization for World War II, not the New Deal, that finally brought an end to the Great Depression. As I have already emphasized with respect to Obama's record, from an electoral standpoint, it is public perceptions that matter, not the reality of economic conditions as these might have been assessed by the National Bureau of Economic Research. Whatever the weaknesses of Roosevelt's anti-Depression program, his record as "manager of prosperity" was substantially better than that of Herbert Hoover and seems to have been assessed largely on that basis. And there is no denying that the American public viewed Roosevelt's performance very favorably. How else can one explain the Democratic Party's unprecedented gains in the 1934 midterm elections or Roosevelt's crushing reelection victory in 1936? Even during the

depths of the 1937–1938 recession, early Gallup polls indicate that Roosevelt had an approval rating of over 50 percent.

WORKS CITED

Abramowitz, Alan I. 1988. "An Improved Model for Predicting Presidential Election Outcomes." *PS: Political Science and Politics* 21 (Autumn): 843–47.

Campbell, James E. 2008. *The American Campaign: U.S. Presidential Campaigns and the National Vote*. 2nd ed. College Station: Texas A&M University Press.

Goldberg, Jonah. 2012. "De-Bushing Romney." *National Review Online*, August 3. www.nationalreview.com/article/313043/de-bushing-jonah-goldberg. Accessed December 12, 2012.

Greenfield, Jeff. 2015. "Democratic Blues." *Politico*, August 20. http://politico.com/magazine/story/2015/08/democratic-blues-121561. Accessed December 9, 2015.

Hertzberg, Hendrik. 2008. "Obama Wins." *New Yorker*, November 17.

Jacobson, Gary C. 1980. *Money in Congressional Elections*. New Haven: Yale University Press.

Jacobson, Gary C. 2013. *The Politics of Congressional Elections*. 8th ed. Boston: Pearson.

Judis, John B. 2008. "America the Liberal." *New Republic*, November 5.

Judis, John B., and Ruy Teixeira. 2002. *The Emerging Democratic Majority*. New York: Scribner.

Lipset, Seymour Martin, and William Schneider. 1983. *The Confidence Gap: Business, Labor, and Government in the Public Mind*. New York: Free Press.

Mayer, William G. 1995. "Changes in Elections and the Party System: 1992 in Historical Perspective." In *The New American Politics: Reflections on Political Change and the Clinton Administration*, ed. Bryan D. Jones. Boulder, CO: Westview, 19–50.

Mayer, William G. 2012. "How the Romney Campaign Blew It." *The Forum* 10 (December): 40–50.

Mayhew, David R. 2002. *Electoral Realignments: A Critique of an American Genre*. New Haven: Yale University Press.

Meyerson, Harold. 2008. "A Real Realignment." *Washington Post*, November 7, A19.

Trende, Sean, and David Byler. 2015. "The GOP Is the Strongest It's Been in Decades." www.realclearpolitics.com/articles/2015/05/19/the_gop_is_the_strongest_its_been_in_decades_126633.html. Accessed December 10, 2015.

5

OBAMA'S FOREIGN POLICY

Securing America's Position, Avoiding Costly Errors

Lawrence Korb and Peter Juul,
Center for American Progress

In his two terms in office, President Barack Obama has consistently pursued a foreign policy designed to lay the foundation for continued American global leadership for decades to come by putting America's security engagement in the Middle East on more sustainable footing and enhancing diplomatic, economic, and security engagement with the Asia-Pacific region. Though it has been criticized for its allegedly feckless response to crises like the emergence of the Islamic State or Russia's aggression in Ukraine, the Obama administration has maintained a consistent focus on this overarching goal. President Obama has centered his foreign policy on securing America's position as the world's preeminent power over the long term while attempting to avoid costly errors in the short term.

The contours of this foreign policy can be seen in the Obama administration's policies toward the Middle East and the Asia-Pacific. In the Middle East President Obama has sought to move away from costly ground wars like Iraq and Afghanistan. Instead, he has reconfigured America's security engagement with the region to rely more on airpower, special operations, and local partners. In contrast with this security-heavy engagement, the Obama administration has pursued a policy of renewed diplomatic, economic, and security engagement with the Asia-Pacific. All the while, the administration has pursued an aggressive campaign against terrorist groups around the world.

It's too early to determine whether or not President Obama's bet on the long game will pay off. The failure to adequately address immediate challenges like the Islamic State could serve to undermine the long-term goals of his foreign policy, and President Obama's confidence in the long-run triumph of liberal values can appear complacent at times. But if the Obama administration's foreign policy has shortcomings, its critics fail to diagnose them correctly. Misapprehending the purposes of President Obama's foreign policy, they accuse him of leading an "American retreat" (Stephens 2015) from the world.

Nothing could be further from the truth. Though events have not entirely cooperated with President Obama's long-term vision, he and his administration have sought to give their successors a United States in a better strategic position than they found it. By and large, they have succeeded: President Obama will leave his successor an America in a far better position to cope with the challenges of the future than the America he inherited.

RECONFIGURING SECURITY ENGAGEMENT IN THE MIDDLE EAST

In his campaign for the presidency, then-senator Barack Obama clearly did not view lengthy ground wars in the Middle East as serving America's strategic interests. Candidate Obama argued that the Bush administration possessed a "mindset that focuses on Iraq and ignores the rest of the world." Iraq represented "the path of unending war and unilateral action," a path that would "sap our strength and standing." At the same time, however, he cautioned against "the path of disengagement" that would "cede our leadership" (Obama 2008). In Obama's view, the United States would have to end its costly ground wars in order to maintain the power necessary to retain global leadership.

Indeed, when President Obama took office in 2009, the United States had over 180,000 troops on the ground in Iraq and Afghanistan (Belasco 2014, 85). More than 4,200 American service-men and service-women had died in both wars (iCasualties.org 2015a and 2015b), and the United States had spent a combined $892 billion to pay for them (Belasco 2014,

15). These commitments could not be sustained over the long term, and the global financial crash of late 2008 and the need to invest in domestic economic recovery added greater impetus to President Obama's intention to reconfigure America's security engagement in the Middle East.

Critics have claimed that President Obama's Middle East policy represents a retreat from the region (Mead and Gallagher 2015). But these critics confuse the end of expensive, large-scale American ground deployments in Iraq and Afghanistan with military disengagement from the region as a whole. They fail to recognize that the Obama administration has adopted a different model to secure America's interests in the Middle East, one that relies on airpower, special operations forces, and local partners rather than hundreds of thousands of American troops on the ground.

The nature of this shift in strategy would not become apparent until well into Obama's second term, but its contours could be glimpsed as the president outlined his Iraq policy shortly after taking office. In a February 2009 speech at Camp Lejeune, a Marine Corps base in North Carolina, Obama announced that the "combat mission" of America's troops in Iraq would come to an end by August 31, 2010 (Obama 2009a). Though often considered a political sop to the antiwar wing of the Democratic Party (Gordon and Trainor 2012, 574), in retrospect the Iraq policy announced at Camp Lejeune offers insight into President Obama's strategic thinking.

At Camp Lejeune Obama made clear that he intended to shift the role of American forces deployed to Iraq. When Obama made his Iraq policy announcement, the United States had nearly 150,000 troops on the ground in Iraq (Belasco 2014, 85). But by the end of August 2010, American force levels would drop below 50,000 and focus primarily on "training, equipping, and advising Iraqi Security Forces" to fight for themselves (Obama 2009b). American troops would no longer be on the frontlines in Iraq; they would instead support local partners taking their place. Indeed, in an address marking the end of combat operations on August 31, 2010, Obama announced that "the Iraqi people now have lead responsibility for the security of their country" (Obama 2010).

President Obama's strategic shift can be seen more clearly in the failed negotiations to extend the American military presence in Iraq beyond the date of December 31, 2011, that had been agreed upon at the end of the Bush administration. Military commanders in Iraq and the Pentagon recommended force levels of between 10,000 and 24,000 troops, assuming the security agreement between Iraq and the United States was extended (Gordon and Trainor 2012, 655–56). Obama, however, ruled out troop levels above 7,000, and eventually settled on a 3,500-strong American military presence to train and equip Iraqi forces (Gordon and Trainor 2012, 669–70). This plan ultimately came to naught due to the failure of the Iraqi government to provide legal immunity to the US troops that would have remained in Iraq, but it does reflect President Obama's desire to minimize the direct involvement of US ground forces in conflicts in the Middle East.

President Obama's late 2009 decision to send additional troops to Afghanistan appears to contradict this strategic shift. However, as Obama made clear in his December 2009 speech announcing his Afghanistan policy, the purpose of this surge of forces was not to conduct a long-term counterinsurgency campaign. Rather, additional American troops would "help create the conditions for the United States to transfer responsibility to the Afghans" (Obama 2009b). By July 2011, US troops would begin drawing down and transition to an advise-and-assist mission (Woodward 2010, 387–88). As in Iraq, the United States would support Afghan government forces but no longer put its troops on the frontlines.

In other words, President Obama ordered the surge to enable a transition to a more sustainable military mission in Afghanistan. But the surge itself proved costly in both lives and money: Some 1,425 American service-men and service-women died in Afghanistan in the six years that followed the surge (iCasualties.org 2015b), and the United States incurred some $523 billion in war costs over the same time period (Belasco 2014, 15). The US troop drawdown did indeed begin in 2011, and the international combat mission in Afghanistan came to a close at the end of 2014. The subsequent advise-and-assist mission continued into 2015, with some 12,900 troops—6,800 of them American—serving in the NATO-led Resolute Support Mission (Resolute Support Mission 2015).

Taken together, the total number of US troops deployed to both Iraq and Afghanistan declined from 180,000 in January 2009 to roughly 10,300 in December 2015 (Carter 2015). The combined financial cost of both wars dropped from $149 billion in fiscal year 2009 (Belasco 2014, 15) to almost $59 billion in fiscal year 2015 (Shane III and Gould 2015).

President Obama's new Middle East security strategy faced its sharpest test in 2014 when the terrorist army of the Islamic State overran Mosul—Iraq's second-largest city—and threatened genocide against the

Yazidi religious minority in northern Iraq. The first American air strikes against Islamic State positions in Iraq began in early August and expanded to Islamic State targets in Syria in September. By the end of the year, Obama had ordered some 3,100 US military personnel to Iraq to train and equip Iraqi security forces that had crumbled during the initial Islamic State advance (Stewart and Rampton 2014). At the core of the Obama administration's approach to the Islamic State has been the proposition that, as President Obama told the nation in September 2014, "American power can make a decisive difference, but we cannot do for Iraqis what they must do for themselves" (Obama 2014).

This indirect approach has seen successes and setbacks. When the Islamic State threatened to overrun the Syrian Kurdish town of Kobani in late 2014 and early 2015, American air strikes proved vital in helping the YPG, the Syrian Kurdish militia, halt the Islamic State's advance and expel it from Kobani (Everstine 2015). Indeed, air strikes by the US-led coalition have proven crucial in Iraqi advances in Tikrit and Sinjar and Syrian Kurdish offensives in northeastern Syria, and have put a dent in the Islamic State's chain of command (Naylor 2015).

But there have been setbacks. In mid-2015 the Islamic State captured Ramadi, the capital of Anbar Province, and the historic site of Palmyra in Syria. It also launched terrorist attacks around the world, killing hundreds in attacks in Beirut, the Sinai Peninsula, and Paris in October and November 2015. Moreover, the Obama administration's effort to train and equip a force of Syrian fighters to take on the Islamic State ended with little to show for the $500 million invested by the United States (Shear, Cooper, and Schmitt 2015).

Before the Paris attacks, however, the administration began an "intensification" of the military campaign against the Islamic State (Jaffe and Gibbons-Neff 2015). Additional American warplanes were sent to Incirlik air base in Turkey, and a small contingent of special operations forces were deployed inside Syria to assist Kurdish and other forces fighting the Islamic State. Air strikes began targeting the Islamic State's oil facilities, aiming to shut down the terrorist army's main source of revenue (Gordon and Schmitt 2015). As of late 2015, however, it remains unclear whether or not President Obama has the time and political space necessary to pursue this strategy of strangulation amid increasing public concern about the terrorist threat from the Islamic State.

What is clear at this point, though, is that President Obama aims to safeguard America's security interests in the Middle East at a lower—and therefore more acceptable—cost to the United States. As Obama put it in his December 2015 address to the nation on terrorism and the Islamic State, "We should not be drawn once more into a long and costly ground war in Iraq or Syria." Rather, the United States would pursue a strategy involving "air strikes, Special Forces, and working with local forces who are fighting to regain control of their own country" to "achieve a more sustainable victory" (Obama 2015).

And as of late 2015, the campaign against the Islamic State has in fact proven far less costly than the wars in Iraq and Afghanistan. Since the start of the campaign on August 8, 2014, the Pentagon estimates that the war against the Islamic State has cost the United States $5.2 billion (US Department of Defense 2015). In addition to the handful of special operations forces deployed in Syria, the United States has around 3,500 troops deployed to Iraq to rebuild the Iraqi security forces (Carter 2015)—ironically enough, around the same number President Obama intended to leave in Iraq after 2011.

Though the United States and its international partners have not been able to defeat the Islamic State as of December 2015, they have halted its advances in both Syria and Iraq and punctured its aura of invincibility in the process. Air strikes and ground offensives by Iraqi and Syrian Kurdish forces have rolled back some of the Islamic State's gains, and the terrorist army's resources have come under considerable strain as a result. But the strangulation strategy pursued by the Obama administration requires time to work, which gives the Islamic State the opportunity to carry out terrorist atrocities like the November 2015 attacks in Paris. Further attacks could serve to undermine President Obama's new approach to securing America's interests in the Middle East and prepare the United States to cope with the challenges of the future.

Nonetheless, the Obama administration's strategy of airpower, special operations, and local partners on the ground has prevented worst-case outcomes in the Middle East at relatively low cost in American lives and money. For all the threat the Islamic State poses to the world as a terrorist organization, its conventional military expansion in Iraq and Syria has been halted and, in some places, reversed. Afghan government forces have bent but not broken in the face of new Taliban offensives, and

American air and naval forces remain present in the Persian Gulf to deter Iranian adventurism.

What's more, the extraordinarily destabilizing prospect of an Iranian nuclear weapon has been put off indefinitely thanks to a combination of diplomatic pressure and economic coercion orchestrated by the Obama administration. After Tehran rejected offers of negotiation early in President Obama's first term, the United States, together with the European Union and United Nations, levied increasingly restrictive sanctions on Iran—and in particular its oil exports (Katzman 2015, 19–21). With its economy contracting under the pressure of sanctions, in 2013 Iran reached an interim agreement with the P5+1—the five permanent members of the UN Security Council and Germany—that provided modest sanctions relief in exchange for a freeze on certain nuclear activities and a work toward a final agreement. That final deal was reached in July 2015 and provided for intrusive inspections of and restrictions on Iran's nuclear activities for more than a decade in exchange for a lifting of nuclear-related sanctions (White House 2015).

While the Obama administration will not be leaving its successor a more stable Middle East, the United States is better positioned to protect its security interests in the region than it was when President Obama took office. The specter of an Iranian nuclear bomb has been delayed for the foreseeable future, and the threat of war between the United States and Iran over Tehran's nuclear program has been averted. More importantly, the United States no longer has hundreds of thousands of ground troops fighting costly counterinsurgency campaigns in Iraq and Afghanistan. President Obama has abandoned neither country; rather, he has pursued a more sustainable strategy of supporting local partners as they fight for the security and stability of their own societies.

REBALANCING TO THE ASIA-PACIFIC

President Obama's reconfiguration of America's security strategy in the Middle East hasn't happened in isolation. It's part of a broader foreign policy that aims to protect American security interests in that region while refocusing attention on a rising Asia-Pacific region and repairing the domestic foundations of international power. Resources not spent on counterinsurgency campaigns in the Middle East can be better applied shoring up America's long-term position in the Asia-Pacific or making necessary investments at home.

Yet critics like Fareed Zakaria argue that the Obama administration has been drawn deeper and deeper into the "Middle East morass" despite its stated desire to shift focus to the Asia-Pacific. "The Obama administration," Zakaria contends, "needs to start believing in its own grand strategy" (Zakaria 2015). In other words, the Obama administration is caught between critics that accuse it of abandoning the Middle East and critics like Zakaria who accuse it of investing too much in that same region.

It's true that the Obama administration has not been able to fully consummate its intention to shift America's foreign policy focus from the Middle East to the Asia-Pacific. But any honest evaluation of the so-called "pivot" to the Asia-Pacific ought to include the reconfiguration of America's security engagement in the Middle East. That strategic shift has freed up resources—if not necessarily top-level attention—that the next administration can use to complete America's rebalance to the Asia-Pacific. The more sustainable security engagement the Obama administration has pursued in the Middle East will allow the United States to, as then–secretary of state Hillary Clinton stated it, "put ourselves in the best position to sustain our leadership, secure our interests, and advance our values" (Clinton 2011).

While President Obama's strategic shift in the Middle East may be his most important contribution to a renewed American focus on the Asia-Pacific, it's hardly his administration's only one. By simply making what Obama called "a deliberate and strategic decision" for the United States to "a play larger and long-term role in shaping this region and its future" (Obama 2011b), the Obama administration has set the United States on a strategic course that will be difficult for future administrations to substantially alter. More concretely, however, the shift in focus to the Asia-Pacific has played out along three primary dimensions: military, economic, and diplomatic.

Militarily, the Pentagon has committed to stationing 60 percent of Navy and Air Force assets in the Asia-Pacific by 2020 (Davidson 2014). Already, a new Marine rotational force has been stationed in Darwin, Australia (Taylor 2014), and four of the Navy's new Littoral Combat Ships are scheduled to be deployed to Singapore by 2017 (LaGrone 2015). Enhanced Defense Cooperation Agreements have been signed with the Philippines (Bacon 2015) and Singapore (Minnick 2015). The United States has already flown P-8 maritime surveillance aircraft on missions over the South China Sea from bases in both countries (De Luce 2015).

This enhanced military commitment to the Asia-Pacific has been accompanied by the multiyear negotiation of the Trans-Pacific Partnership trade agreement. Obama administration officials have framed the twelve-nation agreement as "giving the United States a leading role writing the rules of the road for tomorrow's global economy" (Froman 2015). Though many of President Obama's own supporters remain critical of its economic merits (Bernstein 2015), the agreement's importance is as much strategic and diplomatic as it is economic. Whatever faults the TPP may have, the fact remains that the United States has been able to lead negotiations on a substantial multinational economic agreement that includes major economies on both sides of the Pacific. While the Obama administration's economic engagement with the Asia-Pacific has not been an entirely resounding success—its failure to stop America's allies and partners from joining China's Asian Infrastructure Investment Bank, for instance, ranks high on the list of administration foreign policy defeats (Zakaria 2015)—the successful negotiation of the TPP represents an important victory for America's global and regional leadership.

America's renewed military and economic engagement with the Asia-Pacific are, of course, deeply tied to its renewed diplomatic engagement in the region. Indeed, Chinese overreach in territorial disputes with its neighbors has given the United States a golden opportunity to build or solidify diplomatic and security relationships with countries like the Philippines and Vietnam (Mehta 2015). The United States has also sought to push back against expansive Chinese claims against Japanese islands by making clear that that territory falls under the purview of the US-Japan mutual defense treaty (Panda 2014). Less contentiously, the Obama administration has increased US participation in regional diplomatic events like the East Asia Summit, which President Obama attended as a full participant for the first time in 2011 (White House 2011).

To be sure, the pivot to the Asia-Pacific did not live up to its early hype. The Obama administration could have better prepared both pundits and the public for the difficulty inherent in such an undertaking. Making matters worse, events in the Middle East have demanded increasing attention from policymakers in Washington. Even friendly critics like Fareed

Zakaria could reasonably wonder, "Whatever happened to the pivot to Asia?" (Zakaria 2015).

However, it's important to recognize that America's strategic position in the Asia-Pacific will be markedly stronger by the time President Obama leaves office in January 2017. America is no longer spending hundreds of billions of dollars every year on inconclusive counterinsurgency campaigns in the Middle East, freeing resources to support a renewed focus on the Asia-Pacific. American military might be increasingly concentrated in the region, and economic ties between the United States and the Asia-Pacific will likely be stronger than ever. China's strategic blunders in the region have made the United States an increasingly attractive strategic partner for the countries of Southeast Asia.

In short, with its moves in the Middle East and the Asia-Pacific, the Obama administration has indeed put the United States in a rather favorable strategic position. However, it will be up to President Obama's successor to complete the pivot to the Asia-Pacific. That successor will build on a foundation of solid progress—and will have President Obama to thank for it.

CHALLENGES AND OPPORTUNITIES

While the overall thrust of the Obama administration's foreign policy centered on restructuring America's security engagement in the Middle East and placing greater emphasis on the Asia-Pacific region, it has also been confronted with challenges elsewhere in the world. But it has also taken advantage of opportunities that have emerged to improve America's international standing. Taken together, President Obama has managed to avoid worst-case outcomes while ensuring the United States remains well positioned to deal with the problems of the future.

The Obama administration faced the first of these challenges immediately upon taking office, with the American and global economies reeling from the worst financial crash since the Great Depression. By the time President Obama signed the American Recovery and Reinvestment Act in February 2009—a $787 billion stimulus package—the US economy had already shed some six million out of a total of nine million jobs lost due to the recession. Without the stimulus, job loss would have reached twelve million (Romer 2012). In a poll conducted by the University of

Chicago in 2012, for instance, 80 percent of economic experts surveyed agreed that "the U.S. unemployment rate was lower at the end of 2010 than it would have been without the stimulus bill" (IGM Forum 2012).

It's true that the Recovery Act failed to make up all the economic ground lost during the recession. But as Obama economic adviser Christina Romer put it, the Recovery Act was "a valuable effort that improved the lives of many" and prevented the country from falling into another Great Depression (Romer 2012). At the same time, it made unprecedented investments in infrastructure and clean energy that will serve the United States well into the future (Grunwald 2012).

Indeed, thanks to the Recovery Act and the Federal Reserve's expansionary policies, the United States weathered the recession far better than economies that pursued austerity policies. As slow and halting as America's recovery has been, the European Union's has been anemic by comparison. The US unemployment rate, for instance, fell from a high of 10 percent in October 2009 to 5 percent in November 2015 (Bureau of Labor Statistics 2015), while the EU's unemployment rate has remained steady at around 10 percent since 2010 (Eurostat 2015). European economic growth has also been sluggish in comparison to America's (*Economist* 2015, O'Brien 2013). What's more, austerity may prove disastrously counterproductive in the long run: as Antonio Fatas and Larry Summers argue, "austerity policies not only have caused significant temporary damage to growth but that they might have resulted in exactly the opposite outcome that they were seeking by permanently reducing output" (Fatas and Summers 2015, 5). In other words, President Obama preserved America's economic power over the long term by pursuing stimulus rather than austerity—leaving the United States in a far better strategic position than he found it.

The other major challenge faced by President Obama has been the reemergence of an aggressive, authoritarian Russia. Early on, the Obama administration sought to "reset" America's frayed relations with Moscow. This effort yielded some important results like the New START nuclear arms treaty, a new round of UN sanctions on Iran, and access to supply routes for the war in Afghanistan (White House 2010). But with Vladimir Putin's return to the Russian presidency in 2012, relations began to take a turn for the worse. Major Russian military exercises in 2013 prompted NATO to conduct its own exercises for the first time in eastern Europe (Applebaum 2015).

But worse was yet to come. After popular protests forced Ukrainian President Viktor Yanukovych out of office when he refused to sign an agreement deepening economic ties with the European Union, Putin seized and annexed the Crimea Peninsula in March 2014. He then proceeded to launch a bloody war in eastern Ukraine, claiming in both cases wide authority to intervene to protect ethnic Russian minorities (Marten 2014). In response, the Obama administration launched a series of military deployments and exercises in Europe. Dubbed Operation Atlantic Resolve, this effort included ground, air, and naval deployments to eastern European NATO allies such as Poland, Romania, and the Baltic states (US European Command 2014, US European Command 2015). Moreover, the Pentagon has begun developing contingency plans to deter and, if necessary, repel Russian aggression against America's NATO allies (Ioffe 2015).

The main weapon the United States and its allies in Europe have wielded against Moscow, however, has been economic: sanctions against "individuals and entities responsible for violating the sovereignty and territorial integrity of Ukraine" (US State Department 2014). Combined with low oil prices, sanctions have hit the Russian economy hard. The International Monetary Fund estimated Russia's economy contracted by 3.4 percent in 2015, with sanctions accounting for a reduction of between 1 and 1.5 percent in Russia's real gross domestic product (International Monetary Fund 2015). While sanctions haven't induced Putin to pull back from his Ukrainian adventure, they have imposed significant costs on Moscow for its belligerence—without bringing the United States and Russia into direct military confrontation.

Finally, the Obama administration seized an opportunity to rationalize America's diplomatic relations with Latin America by normalizing relations with Cuba. After some minor adjustments early in his first term, in December 2014 President Obama announced that the United States would restore full diplomatic relations with Cuba—relations that had be cut in 1961 (White House 2014). Both the American embassy in Havana and the Cuban embassy in Washington were opened by July 2015 (Ahmed and Davis 2015), and President Obama met with Cuban dictator Raul Castro at the UN General Assembly the following September to discuss further normalization of ties (Schwartz 2015). Though the economic embargo on Cuba remains in place, the Obama administration deserves credit for removing a cold-war anachronism from America's Latin America policy.

SETBACKS

President Obama's foreign policy has for the most part succeeded in improving America's long-run strategic position. But Obama has largely failed to adequately communicate the broader nature and purposes of his foreign policy approach to the American people, a failure that has allowed his political opponents to inaccurately define his foreign policy as one of retreat. Worse, this failure to communicate threatens to undermine the administration's overall foreign policy, creating an aura of complacency when it comes to immediate problems like the Islamic State.

Nowhere has this disconnect been more apparent than in the Obama administration's approach to Syria—in particular its response to the Assad regime's chemical weapons use and the rise of the Islamic State. President Obama's reluctance to directly intervene in Syria's civil war arose directly from his overall strategic vision. In public and private statements justifying his reluctance to intervene in Syria, Obama repeatedly argued that only "an effort in size and scope similar to what we did in Iraq" would lead to an acceptable outcome (Remnick 2014). But such an effort would be inordinately expensive, with Obama himself estimating in December 2015 that a ground war in Syria would cost the United States $10 billion and one hundred combat deaths a month (Baker and Harris 2015). It would, in short, reverse the hard work done by the Obama administration to reconfigure America's security relationship with the Middle East.

But by failing to make this case directly and instead claiming that, as a result of the drawdowns in Iraq and Afghanistan, "the tide of war is receding" (Obama 2011a), President Obama wound up leaving the false impression that the days of direct American intervention in the Middle East were over. When the Assad regime used chemical weapons on its own people in August 2013, the Obama administration found itself struggling to make the case for American-led retaliation despite public warnings by President Obama himself a year earlier that the use of chemical weapons would change his calculations on intervention (Obama 2012). Already reluctant to use force and wary of crossing public sentiments it had cultivated, the Obama administration agreed to a Russian-brokered deal that saw the Assad regime give up its remaining chemical weapons and accede to the Chemical Weapons Convention.

Worse still was the Obama administration's reaction to the rise of the Islamic State. After the terrorist army seized Fallujah in January 2014, Obama himself minimized the Islamic State as a "jayvee team" that lacked "the capacity and reach of a bin Laden and a network that is actively planning major terrorist plots on the homeland" (Remnick 2014). Born out of an understandable desire to avoid potential demands for an American-led military intervention, this statement sapped the administration's credibility when the Islamic State seized Mosul in a lightning offensive six months later. Having downplayed the threat posed by the Islamic State, the Obama administration reversed course and intervened as the terrorist army closed in on Iraqi Kurdish strongholds and threatened to massacre minorities.

This failure to communicate reached its apotheosis on November 13, 2015. That morning President Obama gave an interview in which he argued—correctly—that the Islamic State had been militarily contained in Iraq and Syria (Saenz 2015). Later that evening, however, Islamic State terrorists would brutally murder 130 innocent people across Paris. While an intensification of the US-led campaign against the Islamic State was already under way, the Paris attack laid bare the gap between the Obama administration's strategic vision and concrete policies on the one hand and its ability to effectively explain them to the American people on the other.

This credibility gap wouldn't be so important if it didn't threaten to undermine the overall strategic shift President Obama's foreign policy aims to achieve over the long term. In the wake of the Paris attacks, more Americans believe a terrorist attack to be very likely in the immediate future than at any point since October 2001 (Martin and Sussman 2015). What's more, a majority of Americans now say the United States should send ground troops to fight the Islamic State (Agiesta 2015). If President Obama has otherwise left the United States in a far better strategic position than he found it, he has also left his successor with an unfinished campaign against the Islamic State and an American public more anxious about terrorism than any time since 9/11.

CONCLUSION

Despite these setbacks and major unresolved problems, President Obama has successfully prepared the United States to face the challenges of the long term. He and his administration have reconfigured America's security relationship with the Middle East, moving from long and costly ground wars to interventions reliant on airpower, special operations, and local partners. This new approach to safeguarding America's security interests in the Middle East has, in turn, allowed the United States to dedicate greater resources to the Asia-Pacific. The Obama administration has forged stronger political, economic, and military ties with the nations of that region, all the while managing an ever-more complex relationship with China. Finally, and perhaps most importantly, the Recovery Act preserved America's economic power while other advanced economies remained stagnant.

Nonetheless, it's still too soon to deliver a wholly positive assessment of the Obama administration's foreign policy. An otherwise commendable focus on America's long-term strategic prospects has let immediate problems like Syria's civil war and the Islamic State fester, and his failure to adequately explain his foreign policy vision to the American people has allowed misconceptions and demagoguery to flourish. Together, these immediate problems and President Obama's inability to put them in an acceptable overall context threaten to undermine his long-term foreign policy objectives.

But these setbacks should not overshadow President Obama's very real foreign policy accomplishments. When he took office, President Obama inherited the worst economic crisis since the Great Depression and two costly wars in Iraq and Afghanistan. His successor—whoever he or she may be—will inherit a country with a comparatively strong economy, more sustainable security engagement in the Middle East, and stronger relations with the nations of the Asia-Pacific region. Thanks to President Obama, the United States is better prepared to meet the challenges of the future when he leaves office in 2017.

WORKS CITED

Agiesta, Jennifer. 2015. "Poll: Most Americans Say Send Ground Troops to Fight ISIS." CNN.com, December 7. www.cnn.com/2015/12/06/politics/isis-obama-poll/.

Ahmed, Azam, and Julie Hirschfeld Davis. 2015. "U.S. and Cuba Reopen Long-Closed Embassies." *New York Times*, July 20. www.nytimes.com/2015/07/21/world/americas/cuba-us-embassy-diplomatic-relations.html.

Applebaum, Anne. 2015. "Obama and Europe: Missed Signals, Renewed Commitments." *Foreign Affairs*, September/October. www.foreignaffairs.com/articles/europe/obama-and-europe.

Bacon, Lance M. 2015. "U.S. Negotiating to Rotate Troops to 8 Philippine Bases." *Navy Times*, April 29. www.navytimes.com/story/military/pentagon/2015/04/28/us-negotiating-troop-rotation-philippines-catapang-china-base-troops/26512301/.

Baker, Peter, and Gardiner Harris. 2015. "Under Fire from G.O.P., Obama Defense Response to Terror Attacks." *New York Times*, December 17. www.nytimes.com/2015/12/18/world/middleeast/president-obama-national-counterterrorism-center.html.

Belasco, Amy. 2014 "The Cost of Iraq, Afghanistan, and Other Global War on Terror Operations Since 9/11." Congressional Research Service, December 8. http://fas.org/sgp/crs/natsec/RL33110.pdf.

Bernstein, Jared. 2015. "Seeing Is Believing." *Democracy* 38. http://democracyjournal.org/magazine/38/seeing-is-believing/.

Bureau of Labor Statistics. 2015. "Labor Force Statistics from the Current Population Survey." Accessed December 19. http://data.bls.gov/timeseries/LNS14000000.

Carter, Ashton B. 2015. "Statement on the Counter-ISIL Campaign before the Senate Armed Services Committee." December 9. www.defense.gov/News/Speeches/Speech-View/Article/633510/statement-on-the-counter-isil-campaign-before-the-senate-armed-services-committ.

Clinton, Hillary. 2011. "America's Pacific Century." *Foreign Policy*, October 11. http://foreignpolicy.com/2011/10/11/americas-pacific-century/.

Davidson, Janine. 2014. "Bob Work Speaks: Out of the Spotlight, the Asia-Pacific Rebalance Continues on Course." Council on Foreign Relations, Defense in Depth, October 1. http://blogs.cfr.org/davidson/2014/10/01/bob-work-speaks-out-of-the-spotlight-the-asia-pacific-rebalance-continues-on-course/.

De Luce, Dan. 2015. "Singapore Approves U.S. Surveillance Flights." *Foreign Policy*, December 7. http://foreignpolicy.com/2015/12/07/singapore-approves-u-s-surveillance-flights/.

The Economist. 2015. "The Euro Area's Uninspiring Recovery." Free Exchange, September 2. www.economist.com/blogs/freeexchange/2015/09/economic-growth-europe.

Eurostat. 2015. "File:Table 2 Unemployment rate, 2003-2014 (%).png." Last modified June 18. http://ec.europa.eu/eurostat/statistics-explained/index.php/File:Table_2_Unemployment_rate,_2003-2014_(%25).png.

Everstine, Brian. 2015. "Inside the B-1 Crew That Pounded ISIS with 1,800 Bombs." *Air Force Times*, August 23. www.airforcetimes.com/story/military/2015/08/23/inside-b-1-crew-pounded-isis-1800-bombs/31166125/.

Fatas, Antonio, and Lawrence H. Summers. 2015. "The Permanent Effects of Fiscal Consolidation." *Centre for Economic Policy Research Discussion Paper No. 10902*, October 14. http://faculty.insead.edu/fatas/CEPR_DP10902.pdf.

Froman, Michael. 2015. "Getting Trade Right." *Democracy* 38. http://democracyjournal.org/magazine/38/getting-trade-right-1/?page=all.

Gordon, Michael R., and Eric Schmitt. 2015. "U.S. Steps Up Attacks on ISIS-Controlled Oil Fields in Syria." *New York Times*, November 12. www.nytimes.com/2015/11/13/us/politics/us-steps-up-its-attacks-on-isis-controlled-oil-fields-in-syria.html.

Gordon, Michael R., and Bernard E. Trainor. 2012. *The Endgame: The Inside Story of the Struggle for Iraq, from George W. Bush to Barack Obama*. New York: Pantheon.

Grunwald, Michael. 2012. "Think Again: Obama's New Deal." *Foreign Policy*, August 13. http://foreignpolicy.com/2012/08/13/think-again-obamas-new-deal/.

iCasualties.org. 2015a. "Operation Iraqi Freedom." Last modified December 17. http://icasualties.org/Iraq/index.aspx.

iCasualties.org. 2015b. "Operation Enduring Freedom." Last modified December 17. http://icasualties.org/OEF/index.aspx.

IGM Forum. 2012. "Economic Stimulus." February 12. www.igmchicago.org/igm-economic-experts-panel/poll-results?SurveyID=SV_cw5O9LNJL1oz4Xi.

International Monetary Fund. 2015. "Cheaper Oil and Sanctions Weigh on Russia's Growth Outlook." August 3. www.imf.org/external/pubs/ft/survey/so/2015/CAR080315B.htm.

Ioffe, Julia. 2015. "Exclusive: The Pentagon Is Preparing New War Plans for a Baltic Battle Against Russia." *Foreign Policy*, September 18. http://foreignpolicy.com/2015/09/18/exclusive-the-pentagon-is-preparing-new-war-plans-for-a-baltic-battle-against-russia/.

Jaffe, Greg, and Thomas Gibbons-Neff. 2015. "Obama Seeks to Intensify Operations in Syria with Special Ops Troops." *Washington Post*, October 30. www.washingtonpost.com/politics/obame-decides-on-small-special-operations-force-for-syria/2015/10/30/a8f69c0e-7f13-11e5-afce-2afd1d3eb896_story.html.

Katzman, Kenneth. 2015. "Iran Sanctions." Congressional Research Service, November 3. www.fas.org/sgp/crs/mideast/RS20871.pdf.

LaGrone, Sam. 2015. "Two Littoral Combat Ships to Deploy to Singapore Next Year, Four by 2017." USNI News, April 24. http://news.usni.org/2015/04/24/two-littoral-combat-ships-to-deploy-to-singapore-next-year-four-by-2017.

Marten, Kimberley. 2014. "Vladimir Putin: Ethnic Russian Nationalist." *Washington Post*, Monkey Cage, March 19. www.washingtonpost.com/news/monkey-cage/wp/2014/03/19/vladimir-putin-ethnic-russian-nationalist/.

Martin, Jonathan, and Dalia Sussman. 2015. "Fear of Terrorism Lifts Donald Trump in New York Times/CBS Poll." *New York Times*, December 10. www.nytimes.com/2015/12/11/us/politics/fear-of-terrorism-lifts-donald-trump-in-new-york-times-cbs-poll.html.

Mead, Walter Russell, and Nicholas M. Gallagher. 2015. "Unexpectedly, the Middle East Meltdown Continues." *The American Interest*, October 12. www.the-american-interest.com/2015/10/12/unexpectedly-the-middle-east-meltdown-continues/.

Mehta, Aaron. 2015. "New US-Vietnam Agreement Shows Growth, Challenges." *Defense News*, June 2. www.defensenews.com/story/defense/policy-budget/budget/2015/06/01/us-vietnam-joint-vision-statement-signed-in-hanoi/28291963/.

Minnick, Wendell. 2015. "Singapore-US Agreement to Boost Defense Cooperation." *Defense News*, December 8. www.defensenews.com/story/defense/policy-budget/leaders/2015/12/08/singapore-us-agreement-boost-defense-cooperation/76980618/.

Naylor, Hugh. 2015. "Islamic State's Moneymaking Streams Take a Hit as It Loses Territory." *Washington Post*, December 4. www.washingtonpost.com/world/middle_east/islamic-states-money-makers-take-a-hit-as-it-loses-territory/2015/12/03/b08910aa-91f6-11e5-befa-99ceebcbb272_story.html.

O'Brien, Matthew. 2013. "That's a 'Depression': Europe's Double-Dip Is Officially Longer Than Its Great Recession." *The Atlantic*, May 16. www.theatlantic.com/business/archive/2013/05/thats-a-depression-europes-double-dip-is-officially-longer-than-its-great-recession/275903/.

Obama, Barack. 2008. "Remarks in Fayetteville, North Carolina: The World Beyond Iraq." The American Presidency Project. March 18. www.presidency.ucsb.edu/ws/index.php?pid=77035.

Obama, Barack. 2009a. "Remarks of President Barack Obama: Responsibly Ending the War in Iraq." February 27. www.whitehouse.gov/the-press-office/remarks-president-barack-obama-ndash-responsibly-ending-war-iraq.

Obama, Barack. 2009b. "Remarks by the President in Address to the Nation on the Way Forward in Afghanistan and Pakistan." December 1. www.whitehouse.gov/the-press-office/remarks-president-address-nation-way-forward-afghanistan-and-pakistan.

Obama, Barack. 2010. "Remarks by the President in Address to the Nation on the End of Combat Operations in Iraq." August 31. www.whitehouse.gov/the-press-office/2010/08/31/remarks-president-address-nation-end-combat-operations-iraq.

Obama, Barack. 2011a. "Remarks by the President on the Way Forward in Afghanistan." June 22. www.whitehouse.gov/the-press-office/2011/06/22/remarks-president-way-forward-afghanistan.

Obama, Barack. 2011b. "Remarks by President Obama to the Australian Parliament." November 17. www.whitehouse.gov/the-press-office/2011/11/17/remarks-president-obama-australian-parliament.

Obama, Barack. 2012. "Remarks by the President to the White House Press Corps." August 20. www.whitehouse.gov/the-press-office/2012/08/20/remarks-president-white-house-press-corps.

Obama, Barack. 2014. "Statement by the President on ISIL." September 10. www.whitehouse.gov/the-press-office/2014/09/10/statement-president-isil-1.

Obama, Barack. 2015. "Address to the Nation by the President." December 6. www.whitehouse.gov/the-press-office/2015/12/06/address-nation-president.

Panda, Ankit. 2014. "Obama: Senkakus Covered Under US-Japan Security Treaty." *The Diplomat*, April 24. http://thediplomat.com/2014/04/obama-senkakus-covered-under-us-japan-security-treaty/.

Remnick, David. 2014. "Going the Distance: On and Off the Road with Barack Obama." *New Yorker*, January 27. www.newyorker.com/magazine/2014/01/27/going-the-distance-david-remnick.

Resolute Support Mission. 2015. "Resolute Support Mission (RSM): Key Facts and Figures." December 10. www.rs.nato.int/images/media/PDFs/RSM/151210_placemat.pdf.

Romer, Christina D. 2012. "The Fiscal Stimulus, Flawed but Valuable." *New York Times*, October 20. www.nytimes.com/2012/10/21/business/how-the-fiscal-stimulus-helped-and-could-have-done-more.html.

Saenz, Arlette. 2015. "President Obama Vows to 'Completely Decapitate' ISIS Operations." ABC News, November 13. http://abcnews.go.com/Politics/president-obama-vows-completely-decapitate-isis-operations/story?id=35173579.

Schwartz, Felicia. 2015. "Raúl Castro, Obama Meet to Further Cuban Normalization Process." *Wall Street Journal*, September 29. www.wsj.com/articles/raul-castro-obama-meet-to-further-cuban-normalization-process-1443562841.

Shane III, Leo, and Joe Gould. 2015. "Budget Deal Gives DOD Stability, Almost All Its Money." *Military Times*, October 27. www.militarytimes.com/story/military/pentagon/2015/10/27/budget-deal-defense/74678048/.

Shear, Michael D., Helene Cooper, and Eric Schmitt. 2015. "Obama Administration Ends Effort to Train Syrians to Combat ISIS." *New York Times*, October 9. www.nytimes.com/2015/10/10/world/middleeast/pentagon-program-islamic-state-syria.html.

Stephens, Bret. 2015. "What Obama Gets Wrong: No Retreat, No Surrender." *Foreign Affairs*, September/October. www.foreignaffairs.com/articles/what-obama-gets-wrong.

Stewart, Phil, and Roberta Rampton. 2014. "Obama to Send 1,500 More Troops to Iraq as Campaign Expands." Reuters, November 7. www.reuters.com/article/us-mideast-crisis-usa-iraq-idUSKBN0IR22I20141108#xFyyUHIE82jCMRiR.97.

Taylor, Rob. 2014. "Australia Embraces Marine Presence in Darwin." *Wall Street Journal*, August 14. www.wsj.com/articles/australia-embraces-u-s-marine-presence-in-darwin-as-nations-gather-for-pitch-black-drills-1408035997.

US Department of Defense. 2015. "Operation Inherent Resolve." Last modified December 16. www.defense.gov/News/Special-Reports/0814_Inherent-Resolve.

US European Command. 2014. "Operation Atlantic Resolve (2014)." January 29. www.defense.gov/Portals/1/features/2014/0514_atlanticresolve/Operation_Atlantic_Resolve_Fact_Sheet_2014.pdf.

US European Command. 2015. "Operation Atlantic Resolve (September 2015)." September 22. www.defense.gov/Portals/1/features/2014/0514_atlanticresolve/docs/Operation_Atlantic_Resolve_Fact_Sheet_22SEP2015.pdf.

US State Department. 2014. "Ukraine and Russia Sanctions." www.state.gov/e/eb/tfs/spi/ukrainerussia/. Accessed December 19, 2015.

White House. 2010. "U.S.-Russia Relations: 'Reset' Fact Sheet." June 24. www.whitehouse.gov/the-press-office/us-russia-relations-reset-fact-sheet.

White House. 2011. "Fact Sheet: East Asia Summit." November 19. www.whitehouse.gov/the-press-office/2011/11/19/fact-sheet-east-asia-summit.

White House. 2014. "Fact Sheet: Charting a New Course on Cuba." December 17. www.whitehouse.gov/the-press-office/2014/12/17/fact-sheet-charting-new-course-cuba.

White House. 2015. "The Iran Nuclear Deal: What You Need to Know About the JCPOA." www.whitehouse.gov/sites/default/files/docs/jcpoa_what_you_need_to_know.pdf. Accessed December 19, 2015.

Woodward, Bob. 2010. *Obama's Wars*. New York: Simon & Schuster.

Zakaria, Fareed. 2015. "Whatever Happened to Obama's Pivot to Asia?" *Washington Post*, April 16. www.washingtonpost.com/opinions/the-forgotten-pivot-to-asia/2015/04/16/529cc5b8-e477-11e4-905f-cc896d379a32_story.html.

6

AMERICA IN DECLINE

Danielle Pletka, American Enterprise Institute

The American people have long debated the proper role of their country in the world. It has become an article of almost conventional, if debatable,[1] wisdom that prior to World War I, the United States preferred to keep to itself, or at least to its own hemisphere. And indeed, even in the wake of a relatively short intervention abroad in 1917–1918, the mood of the nation turned inward, with the Senate rejecting ratification of the treaty creating the League of Nations, and subsequently, the passage of a variety of tariff and neutrality acts that had the effect of deepening America's isolation.

The United States' entry into World War II and the almost immediate transition to the decades-long Cold War, however, put paid to the notion of America's studied indifference. Rather, the notion took hold that the nation and its people have an exceptional role to play on the global stage; one that marries the self-interest of national security and economic prosperity with values-based ideals of commitment to political and economic freedom. To some extent, that remains the America of today, at least in the minds of many Americans.[2]

AMERICA'S PROPER ROLE IN THE WORLD

The election of Barack Obama in 2008 and his two-term tenure have brought change to the air. In part a repudiation of the post-9/11 interventionism, in part the rejection of the utility of the Iraq and even Afghanistan wars, in part a philosophical break with the postwar consensus about American global leadership, in part a growing sense of the complexity of international relations and the rise of regional powers such as the People's Republic of China (PRC), the sum has added up to a perception that the United States has disengaged from the world, a sense of what some have labeled US decline.[3]

Surely, it would be wrong to suggest that military operations are the sole measure of global engagement. Or perhaps, as eminent political scientist Joseph Nye suggests, "decline" is only relative: "The rise of other countries—as well as the increased role of non-state actors—will make it more difficult for anyone to wield influence and organise action."[4] Is decline, therefore, a passive result of the world's reconfiguration in the twenty-first century? Or is it an affirmative decision to do less? As with any such value judgment, the rational path to a decision is to define US interests in the world clearly. So what are America's interests, broadly defined?

The Safety and Security of the American People

Perhaps the clearest constitutional responsibility of the American president, almost an unarguable point, is to "provide for the common defense." As founding father Alexander Hamilton concluded in *Federalist* No. 74, "Of all the cares or concerns of government, the direction of war most peculiarly demands those qualities which distinguish the exercise of power by a single hand. The direction of war implies the direction of the common strength; and the power of directing and employing the common strength, forms a usual and essential part in the definition of the executive authority."[5] Ultimately, this is the rationale for having a robust military capability, for the purpose not simply of defending the homeland in the event of an attack, but for managing threats from abroad as they arise.[6] What follows from an understanding of this responsibility is less clear. Some will argue that providing for the common defense requires a military of sufficient size and lethality to not simply protect the American people at home, or even defeat enemies abroad, but to deter potential enemies from confronting the United States in ways that may be detrimental to the safety and security of the American people.[7] Others contend that the military need only be of a size to counter direct threats to the homeland.[8] Despite ongoing partisan and intra-partisan disagreements, however, modern US history tells the story of broad Democratic and Republican agreement regarding the imperative for a robust national defense capability.

The Economic Systems on which the US Economy Relies and the Global Commons

Prosperity at home, as the United States learned to its detriment in the 1930s, is dependent upon an open system of trading and capital flows. Barriers to commerce are inherently deleterious to the prosperity of the American people (though interest groups take exception to some aspects of this system). More importantly, the United States over many years has acted to ensure the freedom of the global commons—the sea and air lanes through which trade flows. Though some have suggested that the freedom of the commons is not a pillar of American global leadership but rather a system of free riding by others who share our interests, there is a compelling case to be made that only when the United States guarantees such safe passage is there sufficient confidence in the movement of goods, services, and people.

In addition, the global trading system and the rules of the road governing that system—rules that have seen more than a billion people lifted out of poverty in the last half century[9]—were created under American auspices. Bretton Woods, the World Trade Organization, the International Monetary Fund, the World Bank, all are products of US commitments and US resources and have contributed mightily to the prosperity of the American people.

Values of Freedom

The values that underpinned the founding of the United States, and the principles of freedom that have animated American diplomacy and foreign policy, have done more to transform the world than the actions of any analogous power in history. The expansion of political, religious, economic, and civil freedoms globally over the last century has been little short of miraculous. And while some small part of that expansion has been due to US military intervention, the vast majority has been a product of leadership, diplomacy, economic assistance, and a bipartisan commitment to values that the American people hold dear.

Some argue that such a commitment amounts to the "imposition" of US values on others, or suggest that the embrace of freedom is cultural imperialism by another name. Yet there is a persuasive case to be made that the freedom and prosperity of others directly leads to diminished risk to the American homeland, greater prosperity for the American people, and overall, the much-wanted stability that can only spring from classical liberal governance.[10]

More often than not in the US body politic, debate centers less around the pillars of American interests roughly outlined above and more around the nature and extent of actions necessary to defend those pillars and what constitutes the standard of American behavior in recent years. Consider the questions of the proper size, role, and funding for the US military; the debate about the nature of free trade and the protections inherent (or missing) in an agreement such as the Obama-shepherded Trans-Pacific Partnership (TPP); the debate over the nature of assistance to Syrian refugees—which rarely denies the premise of such assistance, merely the mechanisms to provide it (be they asylum, food aid, or other forms of relief).

Some argue that a failure to engage more aggressively militarily in Syria and Iraq in response to the growing danger of the Islamic State (also known as the Islamic State of Iraq and al Sham, the Islamic State of Iraq and the Levant, or by the Arabic acronym "Daesh") is a symptom of US decline. Others, like Steven Simon, a visiting lecturer at Dartmouth College and the former senior director for Middle Eastern and North African Affairs at the White House from 2011 through 2012, and his co-author Jonathan Stevenson, a professor of Strategic Studies at the US Naval War College and the former director for Political-Military Affairs for the Middle East and North Africa on the US National Security Council staff from 2011 to 2013, argue in *Foreign Affairs* that far from an extension of normal, the interventionism during the Bush years was the outlier:

> But the reality is that Washington's post-9/11 interventions in the region—especially the one in Iraq—were anomalous and shaped false perceptions of a "new normal" of American intervention, both at home and in the region. The administration's unwillingness to use ground forces in Iraq or Syria constitutes not so much a withdrawal as a correction—an attempt to restore the stability that had endured for several decades thanks to American restraint, not American aggressiveness.[11]

Simon and Stevenson go on to explain that in fact, continued high-intensity engagement, diplomatic, economic, or political, in the Middle East no longer serves core US interests. Again, there is no argument about the need to engage, were this region still a priority, in their view. Rather, they contend that, with the advent of hydraulic fracturing, the strategic and economic importance of the region to the United States has diminished, and the commitment of US resources to the challenges posed internally and externally is simply no longer vital to the US national interest. In short, they and others[12] make the case that in this instance, it's not decline per se but instead that the Middle East just isn't Washington's problem anymore.

In the same vein, the closing months of 2015 saw a heated argument regarding ratification of the wide-reaching Trans-Pacific Partnership. While there were some opponents of the expansion of free trade itself, the balance of opposition came from Republicans who feared the deal liberalized unevenly and made too many concessions in exchange for benefits.[13] In other words, for those Democrats who supported the deal and those Republicans who opposed on free trade grounds, there is philosophical agreement about the value of free trade, just not on the details of this deal.[14]

BUT WHAT IS DECLINE?

If there remains a relatively stable consensus about the nature of American core interests, but the United States behaves differently than before on the global stage in an effort to secure those interests, then how do we define "decline"?

Clearly, there is a chorus of voices on the left and right who claim that under Barack Obama, the United States has entered a period of decline. For many, the meaning is clear: The United States is no longer leading the world, no longer relied upon by its allies or respected by its adversaries, and no longer defending the interests it has defended over decades. In the resulting vacuum, other powers are rising up that are anathema to US interests.[15]

For others, decline is a matter of the US competition upping its game, whether on infrastructure[16] or military terms;[17] an American economy weakening at its core;[18] or the demise of long-term alliances like the US-

UK relationship or the weakening of the North Atlantic Treaty Organization (NATO). Not all of this is the direct consequence of US action or inaction. As David Rothkopf, the CEO of the *Foreign Policy Group*, points out:

> Perhaps the fact that puts this decline in clearest focus is the steep decline in the size of the British Army. With cuts slated to take it from 102,000 to 82,000 regulars and a recent report suggesting that further cuts could reduce it in size to 50,000 within a few years, we face the prospect that in the not too distant future the military that once conquered the world will be roughly the same size as the New York Police Department.[19]

It's not easy to have a security relationship with a country that has a military that cannot lift even a small percentage of effort required in any operation.

Still, the latter years of the Obama administration are not the first we heard of US decline in the world. Barack Obama came to office on the heels of a wave of national and international condemnation of the George W. Bush administration, vowing to "restore our moral standing so that America is once again that last, best hope for all who are called to the cause of freedom, who long for lives of peace, and who yearn for a better future."[20] Like today, others also panned that administration's dealing with allies (see, for example, the kerfuffle over then Secretary of Defense Donald Rumsfeld's use of the terms "old Europe" and "new Europe" to make what were seen as invidious comparisons between western Europe and the former countries of the Eastern Bloc[21]). In short, decline need not be doing too little: It can also be perceived as doing too much of the wrong thing, or doing what Barack Obama termed "stupid stuff."[22]

Certainly, there was a widespread belief that the United States had lost stature in the world during the Bush years, the result of unpopular wars, perceived "moral" failures such as the terrorist detention facility at Guantanamo Bay, and other much-discussed outgrowths of the terrorist attacks of 9/11 and the ensuing Global War on Terror. In short, decline can take many forms and need not simply be defined as a US retreat from engagement. As such, boosters of Barack Obama believe he has restored American leadership and influence, despite withdrawing from or ignoring many of today's active conflicts.[23]

Setting aside judgment about stature and failures during the Bush years, however, the question still begs as to whether the ensuing decisions to pull back from a variety of theaters constitute an appropriate reaction. Many believe retrenchment was not the answer in the face of a conflict-ridden world. As the bipartisan American Enterprise Institute's *American International Report* frames it:

> The unclear outcomes of recent conflicts on foreign soil that have cost thousands of American lives have led many to question whether the costs of America's foreign policy actions are worth the benefits. But these intense, very visible, and visceral events obscure the broader, longer-term picture. Americans do not stop building firehouses or putting up smoke detectors because some buildings burn down. Neither should they stop trying to put out fires internationally or seeking to prevent them because some have proven hard to extinguish.[24]

Finally, there are others from whom there is little argument that America is a declining power—and who believe that is all to the good. Newly minted Barack Obama famously suggested that while Americans consider themselves "exceptional," so do "Greeks and others,"[25] the clear implication being that America did not have a special role to play on the world stage. Certainly, polls seemed to indicate the president was onto something.[26]

In the years following Obama's election, growing numbers of Americans, suffering under the burdens of one of the worst economic disasters to hit the United States since the Great Depression, were prone to agree with the notion that the world's problems were not theirs. "Nation building here at home"[27] became a mantra with a major following, and the body politic was quick to follow. Constituencies on the left and right for defense spending, diplomacy, and US global leadership collapsed. In other words, decline was real, and it was considered a good thing. Time for someone else to take a turn.

So what does "decline" really mean? Certainly, it does not mean that the United States is not engaged in conflict. Indeed, the United States is still engaged in two wars under Barack Obama, the long war in Afghanistan and the coalition effort to defeat ISIS in the Middle East. Global leadership, in fact, neither means war nor its absence. Rather, a better indicator is to look to the conflicts that do *not* happen as a result of US leadership.

Nor is American decline simply about one man, even if he is the president of the United States. There are generational changes afoot in both the United States and allied nations. The great era of alliances and the cooperation that was the hallmark of World War II is but a distant memory for all but the oldest Americans. And in 2013 the Pew Research Center reported "growing numbers of Americans believe that US global power and prestige are in decline" and that "support for US global engagement, already near a historic low, had fallen further." Not surprisingly, the poll also reported that millennials (ages 18–29) were even less enthusiastic about US global leadership.[28]

Are these numbers real or simply the cyclical ebb and flow of support for US internationalism the United States has seen for more than a century? Or, to put it another way, are these numbers about intrinsic attitudes, are they blowback from the Bush years, or do they go hand in hand with a president who has shied away from rallying Americans to international leadership, giving fewer speeches on national security than most of his predecessors? There are straws in the wind that suggest that Americans are still interested in taking on challenges to global security and are not simply focused on "nation building here at home." As problems proliferated in Obama's second term—Russia's invasion and occupation of Crimea, China's increased aggression in the South China Sea, the spread of ISIS and resurgence of al-Qaeda—a Chicago Council on Global Affairs poll in 2014 reported six in ten Americans wanted an "active" role for the US on the global stage.[29]

Far better than scanning the headlines, poring over polling, or cherry-picking pundits, perhaps the better way to consider the question is to review the evidence.

WHAT DOES AMERICAN GLOBAL LEADERSHIP LOOK LIKE?

Even the simple question of a list of signs of robust American leadership can be contentious. Is American economic primacy such a sign, or is the growing might of other economic powers, such as the PRC, an indicator of relative decline? Are complaints about the American education system or labor laws or environmental standards or infrastructure relevant to the issue, or are the failings (or successes) of the US system dispositive?

Ultimately, there is no objective definition of "decline," and so the reader is forced to judge the evidence and decide for himself or herself. Understanding that any such list could be exhaustive, consider three nonexclusive questions:

Is the United States Enjoying a Period of Relative Peace or Lack of Conflict?

Many historians argue[30] for decisive linkage between the rise of American power in the twentieth century and the decline in great power conflict. For nonhistorians, or those focused more exclusively on the now, the claim that the world is a more peaceful place seems almost absurd, yet it is so. Continental Europe is enjoying the longest stretch of peace in its modern history; Asia is also at relative peace; Central and Latin America are not driven by major conflicts. Yes, there are exceptions, and the Middle East is certainly one, however, prior to the outbreak of the Syrian civil war in 2011, fewer civilians were dying in conflict than at any time in recent memory. And while there are exceptions, many attribute both global economic growth and the decline in conflict-related deaths to the global compact underwritten by the United States over the last seventy years.

Does the United States Enjoy the Confidence and Cooperation of Its Allies?

Former Clinton secretary of state Madeleine Albright famously labeled the United States "the indispensable nation."[31] When faced with a challenge, most nations will indeed turn to the United States for aid of one kind or another. Faced with Russia's invasion, Ukrainian leaders sought out Washington. Troubled by growing threats against Libya's civilian population, the government of France turned to the United States. In the South China Sea, the East China Sea, and even in the Middle East, Asian leaders outside of Beijing fretting about peace and security still look first to America. Nor is this reliance exclusively for security. Looking to ease trade restrictions, both the European Union and Asia's major economic powers believe only Washington can cement global trading alliances that will keep their economies humming.

What Is the Reach of the US Military?

For much of the twentieth century, the US military was nominally positioned for a two-front war, one with the Soviet Union on the European continent, and another in a less defined trouble spot. That deterrent power and the forward deployment of US troops and pre-positioning of US military equipment went a long way toward deterring America's adversaries. Whether protecting the global commons or staring down tyrants, the costs of taking on the US military and the superior fighting power of the US soldier meant that America was in a unique position to lead the world.

The ground has changed substantially since the Cold War, and different adversaries have arisen: Subnational groups such as al-Qaeda and ISIS pose more of a threat than such groups once did. And the proliferation of weapons of mass destruction and the missiles to deliver them have changed the balance of power across the globe. Similarly, cyber warfare is now a commonly used tool, and the abilities of the United States to contend with major cyber attacks is unclear.

Beauty in the Eye of the Beholder—the Partisan View

Partisans of President Barack Obama will argue that the list of the president's accomplishments on the global stage is impressive and that the United States remains not simply an international leader but *the* international leader. They point to a series of foreign policy accomplishments, notable among them:

- The Joint Cooperative Plan of Action, better known as the Iran deal. This deal embraces the relaxation of most sanctions against the Islamic Republic of Iran in return for limited concessions in advancing the nuclear fuel cycle from Tehran.
- The Trans-Pacific Partnership, a historic trade deal between the United States and its Pacific partners (not including the PRC) to lower tariff barriers and smooth the flow of trade.
- The withdrawal of US forces from Iraq. This was a campaign pledge for candidate Obama, and in 2011 the United States withdrew all remaining forces from Iraq and ended all security and

counterterrorism cooperation with the government of Iraq, returning special forces and other troops only after ISIS reared its head.

- Freedom of navigation exercises in the South China Sea. These exercises are in response to China's building and equipping of man-made islands on disputed territory around the Spratly Islands.[32]
- Flybys in China's Air Defense Identification Zone (ADIZ) in the East China Sea around the disputed Senkaku (Diaoyu) Islands. After China's declaration of the ADIZ in 2013, the Obama administration points to push back in a decision to fly two B-52 bombers through the zone without complying with PRC demands for identification.[33]
- Support for allies in the Middle East, particularly Israel. The United States continues to maintain a substantial military presence in the Persian Gulf, extending a security umbrella over the nations of the Gulf Cooperation Council. In addition, the president's allies claim an unprecedented level of security and intelligence cooperation with Israel.[34]
- The death of Osama bin Laden. After a ten-year manhunt, US Special Forces found and killed the man behind the 9/11 attacks.
- Building a coalition to impose sanctions on Russia in the wake of the invasion of Ukraine and the annexation of Crimea.
- The restoration of US relations with Cuba.

A More Jaundiced Eye

Yet many of the president's accomplishments are less gold stars on his record than a small victory in the face of larger failures. Osama bin Laden is dead, but al-Qaeda is flourishing. There is a US embassy in Havana, but the Castro brothers still tyrannize the people of Cuba. China continues to build up in the South China Sea; Russia is now in Syria; and the Iran deal has put Tehran on track to an arsenal of nuclear weapons in ten to fifteen years.[35] More troubling still, there are serious problems that have arisen that are not being addressed.

The Retrenchment and Historic Decline of the US Military

Few military experts of either party disagree with the argument that cuts to the US military have been unprecedented in size and drastic in nature. Obama Secretaries of Defense Leon Panetta[36] and Robert Gates[37] (who also served George W. Bush) have both excoriated the president and the Congress for going too far in cutting the military's budget and end-strength.

And while the Republican Congress deserves some opprobrium for allowing such cuts, even in the mistaken belief that their very scale would deter their implementation, efforts to reverse the cuts have earned numerous veto threats, and an actual veto in 2015, from the White House.[38] But the budget is not the sole indicator of a historic reversal of fortune for the US Armed Forces. The Obama administration explicitly embraced the notion of reducing US capacity to engage in conflict—and concomitantly, to have the resources to deter conflict—in two theaters. Colin Dueck explains:

> In terms of explicit security strategy, the 2012 Defense Strategic Guidance helped clarify key assumptions of retrenchment, abandoning the pretense that the United States be able to fight two major regional contingencies simultaneously. That document de-emphasized heavy-footed counterinsurgency or ground campaigns, stating that the US armed forces would "no longer be sized to conduct large-scale prolonged stability operations." The call instead was for "innovative, low-cost and small-footprint" approaches.[39]

That guidance was written under the shadow of half a billion dollars in defense cuts over a decade. But the real number for the cuts will total $1 trillion.[40]

The President Proclaimed That "The Tide of War Is Receding"

This was announced in 2011–2012 when withdrawing US troops from Iraq and Afghanistan.[41] Secretary of Defense Gates, however, saw this less as a sign of a receding tide, explaining that "for [the president], it's all about getting out."[42] Indeed, it is almost impossible to reconcile that "receding tide" with the rise of ISIS and the spread of al-Qaeda to more than twenty countries.[43]

There are now some 11.8 million refugees and internally displaced persons as a result of the ongoing war in Syria.[44] More than one million have flooded into Europe, and thousands have died trying to get there. ISIS controls substantial territory in Syria, Iraq, and Libya and is spreading into other countries, including along the border with Israel in Egypt's Sinai Peninsula. Two Americans have been beheaded by ISIS in territory under the Islamist extremist group's control, and the United States has responded with limited air strikes. None of these air strikes, however, targeted the Bashar al-Assad regime that the president said for the first time in 2011 must "step aside."[45]

Al-Qaeda too has seen a major resurgence, with its allies in the Taliban now threatening major cities in Afghanistan,[46] other allies controlling large swathes of territory in Syria, al-Qaeda in the Arabian Peninsula operating almost unhindered in Yemen, al-Qaeda ally al-Shabaab claiming territory and lives in Somalia, al-Qaeda in the Islamic Maghrib executing major terrorist operations in Tunisia and Algeria and Burkina Faso,[47] a new al-Qaeda affiliate announced on the Indian subcontinent, and more. Osama bin Laden may be dead, but al-Qaeda lives on and flourishes.

Then there are the terrorist attacks that have marked the last years of the Obama administration. A major ISIS attack in Paris on November 13, 2015, claimed the lives of 130 civilians and marked the first suicide bombings on the European continent.[48] In the weeks that followed, ISIS adherents perpetrated a major terrorist attack in San Bernardino, California, with fourteen killed.[49] Other, smaller attacks have become more regular. Can these all be chalked up to specific policies? There are arguments to be made here about the appropriate policy to combat terror and Islamist extremism. But there is no case to be made that the United States is succeeding in combating the scourge of what Barack Obama prefers to call "violent extremism."[50]

The Iran Deal

Few elements of the Obama presidency have been as contentious. Supporters of the president mark it as one of his greatest achievements.[51] But if the deal itself was an object of controversy[52] (many of the Senate Democrats who backed the deal did so reluctantly. Presidential candidate Sen. Bernie Sanders (I-VT), for example, said of the deal when announcing his support, "This agreement is obviously not all that many of us would have liked."[53]), Iran's behavior since its inking has been even more controversial.

The International Atomic Energy Agency closed its investigation into past Iranian violations of its safeguards agreements on December 15, 2015, under what was reported to be substantial pressure from Washington.[54] But Iran never responded to the IAEA's proven charge that it built a full-fledged covert nuclear weapons program prior to 2003, continued select nuclear weapons research until 2009, and actively obfuscated investigators.[55] Troublingly, particularly because President Obama insisted that such actions would be constrained by relevant UN Security Council resolutions, Iran also tested two ballistic missiles last year on October 10 and November 21.[56] The Security Council failed to act in the intermediate aftermath of those violations, and it took the White House until January 17 to levy desultory sanctions that prevent eleven Iranian entities and individuals linked to the missile program from using the US banking system.[57]

Finally, and contrary to the president's expressed hope that the JCPOA might empower forces of moderation within Iran,[58] Tehran has stepped up its efforts to destabilize the Middle East, escalating technology being supplied to its terrorist proxy, Hezbollah; continuing to support Houthi rebels in Yemen; working aggressively to draw Russia into the Syria conflict; and exacerbating (admittedly with the help of Saudi Arabia[59]) the growing Sunni-Shia divide in the Muslim world; and challenging the United States with the detention and subsequent (negotiated) release of US sailors.[60]

Extremism and Discord within Europe

In 2016 the United Kingdom is poised to vote in a referendum on continued membership in the European Union, the so-called Brexit. The years 2014–2015 both passed by under the shadow of the collapse of successive Greek governments and the collapse of the eurozone. In France, Italy, Germany, Hungary, and Poland, parties hostile to the unity of Europe, to free markets, and immigration grew dramatically, and in some cases rose to power.

Centrifugal forces within Europe are neither the doing of the United States nor the responsibility of the United States to correct. Nonetheless, they have major implications for the alliance and the reach of US power and influence. More than ever before, Europe is now focused on its internal problems, not simply incapable militarily of adhering to its NATO commitment to a floor of 2 percent of GDP in defense spending, but also seemingly incapable of contending with the unbridled flow of refugees onto its territory, massive sovereign debt overhang, chronic unemployment, or lackluster economic growth. The NATO alliance and the US-EU partnership are the backbone of the modern global order, and without

Europe, the United States' ability to preserve the global commons and peace will be markedly more difficult. Or think of it this way: Throughout the Cold War, the United States and western Europe held out hope for the captive nations of the Soviet bloc, and guided those nations to democracy after the collapse of the Soviet Union. Is that still a role that the United States and Europe can or will play for countries hoping to join the community of nations?

Russia. The rise of the revanchist Vladimir Putin is an unmitigated negative, and there are strong arguments to be made that American weakness has created an opening for this czarist nostalgic.[61] The Obama administration began its tenure with the now infamous "reset," which was intended to take the troubled relationship of the Bush years with Moscow back to a more cooperative plane.[62] Instead, and in spite of the reset, there has been a crackdown on Russian civil society of a scope unseen since the days of the USSR, an economic collapse and behavior in Europe and the former Soviet bloc that promises more danger. Under Putin, Russia has invaded neighboring Ukraine, annexing Crimea and occupying two eastern Ukrainian regions. The US response has been to broker, with German help, two peace agreements that have been regularly violated by Moscow.[63]

Less remarked upon, but nonetheless deeply troubling, have been a rising number of Russian air and naval incursions into NATO territory and near misses as a result of those incursions. In 2014 NATO was forced to intercept Russian aircraft 442 times, a level unseen since the Cold War.[64] And in 2015 the number was hardly reassuring: In the Baltics alone, NATO fighters were scrambled 160 times.[65] And of course, as Russia and NATO were flying combat missions in the same air space for the first time in post–World War II history, Turkey shot down a Russian jet that crossed into its territory while flying over Syria.[66]

At the time of the Crimea invasion, many warned that Putin would reach further afield. And sure enough, 2015 saw an Iranian-Russian agreement for Russia to enter Syria, doubling down on Moscow's armament of the beleaguered Assad regime with troops and substantial air strikes. That those air strikes have focused on US allied opposition groups rather than ISIS has come as little surprise to Russia watchers. Subsequently, the former top Russian policy expert at the Pentagon, Evelyn N. Farkas, called on the administration to do more to deter Russia, warning,

"If we don't do so, in an excess of caution, the result could well be that we only embolden Russia."[67]

Trouble in Asia

The increasingly militant regime of Xi Jinping in Beijing has demanded a new approach to Asia, prompting the so-called pivot or rebalancing to Asia in Obama's first term.[68] But that pivot, meant to recast US foreign policy priorities toward the Pacific, has been marred by the rise of conflict in the Middle East and a lack of capacity in the US military to undertake the sort of patrolling and friendly exercises in the region that were anticipated.

The results of America's insufficient presence, and thus influence, in the region—including the ADIZ, Chinese predations in the South China Sea around the Spratlys, growing tension between Japan and China over the identification zone, and an up-tempo of Chinese air and sea operations in Japanese airspace and territorial waters—promise trouble ahead.[69] Finally, China's response to US criticism in the wake of a North Korean nuclear test in early 2016—to blame the United States for Pyongyang's decision—is a harbinger of the difficulties to come, and the failure of the "pivot." The PRC, writes Mark Leonard in "Farewell to the American Century," "is increasingly writing its own rules, and reinventing globalization in its own image, gradually jettisoning many of the norms and conventions used by the United States and Europe throughout their long and hitherto largely unchallenged tutelage of the Third World."[70]

AMERICA IN DECLINE?

Are these signs of decline? If so, are they by choice? Certainly it is difficult to make a coherent argument that the latter years of the Obama administration have seen good news on the world stage. Few regions are without trouble or the promise of trouble ahead. Rapprochement with regimes in Havana and Tehran have borne little fruit in reducing threats or tensions with either. There is widespread intellectual consensus about a United States in retreat, sometimes labeled the "end of the American century" or decline.

As to arguments that stepping back from the problems of the world is a good thing, an argument made by some on both the right and left, the persuasive counterargument to the siren song of neo-isolationism, or the realism that accepts conflicts as an inevitable feature of global interaction, is simply that it is unheard of for the United States to remain insulated from these challenges. Syrians can fight without Washington taking sides, but ISIS has now made it to US shores. Russia can chew up bits of Central Asia and eastern Europe, but at some point it will bite on a NATO ally, and the United States will have treaty obligations. China can lay claim to land and sea throughout Asia, but America has treaty obligations there too. And finally, no one may expect that with the world in tatters, economic growth will be assured or reliable. That too will have substantial knock on effects for the American people.

Too much of what is now taken for granted as the global status quo—free trade, prosperity, unencumbered movement, a sense of security—are the products of a US-led world. The United States can choose not to lead; it can retreat on the pretext of weariness or economic dire straits; it can claim the mantle of superpower but shrink from confronting threats to the values Americans hold dear, as the president did in his last State of the Union address.[71] But to suggest this is not decline, that it is not a danger to the best interests of the American people, is a hard argument to sustain in the face of ample evidence around the world to the contrary.

NOTES

1. Thomas Donnelly, "Empire of Liberty: The Historical Underpinnings of the Bush Doctrine," American Enterprise Institute National Security Outlook (2005), accessed January 1, 2016, www.ciaonet.org/attachments/4990/uploads.

2. Patrick Goodenough, "Poll: Most Americans Reject Isolationism, See U.S. as 'Force for Good in the World,'" CNS News, September 28, 2012, accessed January 1, 2016, http://cnsnews.com/news/article/poll-most-americans-reject-isolationism-see-us-force-good-world; and Pew Research Center, "Most Americans Think the U.S. Is Great, but Fewer Say It's the Greatest," July 2, 2014, accessed January 1, 2016, www.pewresearch.org/fact-tank/2014/07/02/most-americans-think-the-u-s-is-great-but-fewer-say-its-the-greatest/.

3. Christopher Lane, "The End of Pax Americana: How Western Decline Became Inevitable," *The Atlantic*, April 26, 2012, accessed January 1, 2016, www.theatlantic.com/international/archive/2012/04/the-end-of-pax-americana-how-western-decline-became-inevitable/256388/; Colin Dueck, "The Strategy of Retrenchment and Its Consequences," Foreign Policy Research Initiative, April

2015, accessed January 1, 2016, www.fpri.org/articles/2015/04/the-strategy-of-retrenchment-and-its-consequences/; Mark Leonard, "Farewell to the American Century," *New Statesman*, June 25, 2015, accessed January 1, 2016, www.newstatesman.com/politics/2015/06/farewell-american-century; Deroy Murdock, "The United States of Decline," *National Review*, February 17, 2014, accessed January 1, 2016, www.nationalreview.com/article/371248/united-states-decline-deroy-murdock; and David Rothkopf, "National Insecurity," *Foreign Policy*, September 9, 2014, accessed January 1, 2016, http://foreignpolicy.com/2014/09/09/national-insecurity/.

4. Leonard, "Farewell to the American Century."

5. *The Federalist Papers*, No. 74.

6. Debate about the proper size of the US military and its proper responsibilities has gone on for many years. Similarly, there have been changes to the way that observers have characterized American military engagements overseas, recently embracing the construct laid out in Richard Haass's *War of Necessity, War of Choice*, which contrasts so-called wars of choice from wars of necessity. Unfortunately, this construct forces its adherents into invidious choices: For example, was the Arab-Israeli Six Day War a "war of choice" by Israel, which acted preemptively to repulse an imminent invasion? Or was it a preemptive war? Applied, these labels can become misleading. For a lengthy discussion on the constitutional role of American presidents and the intentions of the founders, see Robert Kagan, *The World America Made* (New York: Vintage Books, 2012).

7. Jon Kyl and Joseph Lieberman, *Why American Leadership Still Matters*, American Enterprise Institute, December 3, 2015, accessed January 1, 2016, 29, www.aei.org/publication/why-american-leadership-still-matters/.

8. Doug Bandow, "Hawks Demand More Military Spending Than during Cold War: Stop Squandering 'Defense' Dollars on Other Nations," Huffington Post, October 29, 2014, accessed January 1, 2016, www.huffingtonpost.com/doug-bandow/hawks-demand-more-militar_b_6067600.html; Jonathan Ernst, "What Rand Paul Thinks about Defense Spending," *Newsweek*, April 7, 2015, accessed January 1, 2016, www.newsweek.com/what-rand-paul-thinks-about-defense-spending-320291; and Christopher Preble, "Cut (Really Cut) Defense Spending," CATO Institute, www.cato.org/publications/commentary/cut-really-cut-military-spending.

9. "Towards the End of Poverty," *Economist*, June 1, 2013, accessed January 1, 2016, www.economist.com/news/leaders/21578665-nearly-1-billion-people-have-been-taken-out-extreme-poverty-20-years-world-should-aim.

10. Some will question this assertion, but there is no greater example of the power of freedom than the restoration of Europe after World War II. With US intervention, leadership, assistance, and defense, the European Union has enjoyed an era of sustained prosperity and peace unseen its history.

11. Steven Simon and Jonathan Stevenson, "The End of Pax Americana, " *Foreign Affairs*, November/December 2015, accessed January 1, 2016, www.foreignaffairs.com/articles/middle-east/2015-10-20/end-pax-americana.

12. Ian Bremmer, "The Tragic Decline of American Foreign Policy," *National Interest*, April 16, 2014, accessed January 1, 2016, http://nationalinterest.org/feature/the-tragic-decline-american-foreign-policy-10264.

13. Russell Berman, "Republicans Sour on Obama's Trade Pact," *Atlantic*, October 5, 2015, accessed January 1, 2016, www.theatlantic.com/politics/archive/2015/10/republicans-sour-on-obamas-trade-pact/409054/.

14. At the time of thiis writing, opposition to free trade had not gathered political steam. However, the unusual configuration of the 2016 election resulted in a major shift against trade on both sides of the aisle.

15. Colin Dueck, "The Strategy of Retrenchment and Its Consequences," and David Rothkopf, "The Amazing Decline of America's Special Relationships," *Foreign Policy*, May 8, 2015, accessed January 1, 2016, http://foreignpolicy.com/2015/05/08/decline-of-special-relationships-uk-election-obama-netanyahu/.

16. Stephen Kinzer, "Take a Trip Abroad, See the US in Decline," *Boston Globe*, June 21, 2015, accessed January 1, 2016, www.bostonglobe.com/opinion/2015/06/20/take-trip-abroad-see-decline/OdWqsydaqtHDYaGwfqS3IP/story.html.

17. Peter Harris, "America's Shrinking Military: The End of U.S. Primacy?" *National Interest*, July 14, 2015, accessed January 1, 2016, http://nationalinterest.org/feature/americas-shrinking-military-the-end-us-primacy-13324.

18. Jill Hamburg Coplan, "12 Signs America Is on the Decline," *Fortune*, July 20, 2015, accessed January 1, 2016, http://fortune.com/2015/07/20/united-states-decline-statistics-economic/.

19. Rothkopf, "The Amazing Decline of America's Special Relationships."

20. Barack Obama, "Acceptance Speech" (speech, Democratic National Convention, Denver, CO, August 28, 2008), accessed January 1, 2016, www.nytimes.com/2008/08/28/us/politics/28text-obama.html.

21. Mark Baker, "U.S.: Rumsfeld's 'Old' and 'New' Europe Touches on Uneasy Divide," Radio Free Europe/Radio Liberty, January 24, 2003, accessed January 1, 2016, www.rferl.org/content/article/1102012.html.

22. David Rothkopf, "Obama's 'Don't Do Stupid Shit' Foreign Policy," *Foreign Policy*, June 4, 2014, accessed January 1, 2016, http://foreignpolicy.com/2014/06/04/obamas-dont-do-stupid-shit-foreign-policy/.

23. Susan Rice, "Remarks by National Security Advisor Susan Rice on the 2015 National Security Strategy" (speech, Brookings Institution, Washington, DC, February 6, 2015), accessed January 1, 2016, www.whitehouse.gov/the-

press-office/2015/02/06/remarks-national-security-advisor-susan-rice-2015-national-security-stra.

24. Kyl and Lieberman, *Why American Leadership Still Matters*, 24.

25. Barack Obama (news conference, the White House, Washington, DC, April 4, 2009), accessed January 1, 2016, www.whitehouse.gov/the-press-office/news-conference-president-obama-4042009.

26. Pew Research Center, "Public Sees US Power Declining as Support for Global Engagement Slips: America's Place in the World 2013," December 3, 2013, accessed January 1, 2016, www.people-press.org/2013/12/03/public-sees-u-s-power-declining-as-support-for-global-engagement-slips/.

27. Barack Obama, "Remarks by the President on the Way Forward in Afghanistan" (speech, the White House, Washington, DC, June 22, 2011), accessed January 1, 2016, www.whitehouse.gov/the-press-office/2011/06/22/remarks-president-way-forward-afghanistan.

28. Pew Research Center, *Public Sees US Power Declining*, 4; Dina Smeltz et al., "United in Goals, Divided on Means, Opinion Leaders Results and Survey Breakdowns from the 2014 Chicago Council Survey of American Opinion on US Foreign Policy," June 2015, accessed January 1, 2016, www.thechicagocouncil.org/sites/default/files/2014%20Chicago%20Council%20Opinion%20Leaders%20Survey%20Report_FINAL.pdf; Bruce W. Jentleson, "The Prudent, not Isolationist, Public," *The Hill*, June 3, 2014, accessed January 1, 2016, http://thehill.com/blogs/pundits-blog/international/207987-the-prudent-not-isolationist-public; and Kyl and Lieberman, *Why American Leadership Still Matters*, 11.

29. Chicago Council on Global Affairs, "2014 Chicago Council Survey of American Public Opinion and US Foreign Policy Shows Public Support for 'Active' Role in World Affairs," press release, September 15, 2014, accessed January 1, 2016, www.thechicagocouncil.org/press-release/2014-chicago-council-survey-american-public-opinion-and-us-foreign-policy-shows-public.

30. Kagan, *The World America Made*.

31. Madeleine Albright, interview by Matt Lauer, NBC-TV *Today*, February 19, 1998, accessed January 1, 2016, http://fas.org/news/iraq/1998/02/19/98021907_tpo.html.

32. Helene Cooper and Jane Perlez, "White House Moves to Reassure Allies with South China Sea Patrol, but Quietly," *New York Times*, October 27, 2015, accessed January 1, 2016, www.nytimes.com/2015/10/28/world/asia/south-china-sea-uss-lassen-spratly-islands.html.

33. Thom Shanker, "U.S. Sends Two B-52 Bombers into Air Zone Claimed by China," *New York Times*, November 26, 2013, accessed January 1, 2016, www.nytimes.com/2013/11/27/world/asia/us-flies-b-52s-into-chinas-expanded-air-defense-zone.html.

34. John Kerry to members of Congress, letter, September 2, 2015, accessed January 1, 2016, http://freebeacon.com/wp-content/uploads/2015/09/090215-Iran-Letter-to-House.pdf.

35. Kevin McCarthy's office, "21 Reasons the Iran Deal Is a Bad Deal," press release, July 22, 2015, accessed January 1, 2016, www.majorityleader.gov/2015/07/22/21-reasons-iran-deal-bad-deal/.

36. Leon Panetta, "Sequestration's Self-Inflicted Wounds," *Washington Post*, September 2, 2013, accessed January 1, 2016, www.washingtonpost.com/opinions/leon-panetta-sequestrations-self-inflicted-wounds/2013/09/02/6c186d4a-0e94-11e3-bdf6-e4fc677d94a1_story.html.

37. Joe Gould, "Gates Blasts Lawmakers over Sequestration," Defense News, October 30, 2014, accessed January 1, 2015, http://archive.defensenews.com/article/20141030/DEFREG02/310300041/Gates-Blasts-Lawmakers-Over-Sequestration.

38. Josh Lederman, "Obama Vetoes $612 Billion Defense Bill in Rebuke to GOP," Associated Press, October 22, 2015, accessed January 1, 2015, http://bigstory.ap.org/article/c435017554594341b98f8da93a674547/obama-veto-612-billion-defense-bill-over-funding-cuba.

39. Colin Dueck, "The Strategy of Retrenchment and Its Consequences."

40. Mackenzie Eagle, "Budgeting for Austere Defense," *Strategic Studies Quarterly* 8 (Fall 2015): 69–87, accessed January 1, 2016, www.aei.org/publication/budgeting-for-austere-defense/.

41. Barack Obama, "Remarks by the President on the Way Forward in Afghanistan."

42. The editors, "Obama's Half-Hearted War," *National Review*, January 10, 2014, accessed January 1, 2016, www.nationalreview.com/article/368146/obamas-half-hearted-war-editors.

43. Mary Habeck et al., *A Global Strategy for Combating al Qaeda and the Islamic State*, American Enterprise Institute, December 7, 2015, accessed January 1, 2016, 4, www.aei.org/publication/a-global-strategy-for-combating-al-qaeda-and-the-islamic-state/.

44. "UNHCR: Syrian Arab Republic," The UN Refugee Agency, accessed January 1, 2015, www.unhcr.org/pages/49e486a76.html.

45. Scott Wilson and Joby Warrick, "Assad Must Go, Obama Says," *Washington Post*, August 18, 2011, accessed January 1, 2016, www.washingtonpost.com/politics/assad-must-go-obama-says/2011/08/18/gIQAelheOJ_story.html.

46. Jessica Lewis McFate, Rob Denaburg, and Caitlin Forrest, "Afghanistan Threat Assessment: The Taliban and ISIS," Institute for the Study of War, December 10, 2015, accessed January 1, 2016, 1, www.understandingwar.org/sites/

default/files/Afghani-
stan%20Threat%20Assessment_The%20Taliban%20and%20ISIS_3.pdf.

47. Caleb Weiss, "AQIM Battalion Attacks Tunisian Soldiers in Kasserine," the Long War Journal's Threat Matrix blog, October 13, 2015, accessed January 1, 2016, www.longwarjournal.org/archives/2015/10/aqim-battalion-targets-tunisian-soldiers-in-kasserine.php; Thomas Joscelyn, "Al Qaeda in the Islamic Maghreb Honors Ansar al Sharia's Slain Military Commander," the Long War Journal, October 29, 2015, accessed January 1, 2016, www.longwarjournal.org/archives/2015/10/al-qaeda-in-the-islamic-maghreb-honors-ansar-al-sharias-slain-military-commander.php; and Mathieu Bonkoungou and Nadoun Coulibaly, "Burkina Hotel Retaken from al Qaeda Fighters, but Dozens Dead," Reuters, January 17, 2016, accessed January 19, 2016, www.reuters.com/article/us-burkina-attacks-idUSKCN0UT2HC.

48. "Paris Attacks: Who Were the Victims?" BBC, November 27, 2015, accessed January 1, 2016, www.bbc.com/news/world-europe-34821813.

49. "San Bernardino Shooting Victims: Who They Were," *Los Angeles Times*, December 17, 2015, accessed January 1, 2016, www.latimes.com/local/lanow/la-me-ln-san-bernardino-shooting-victims-htmlstory.html.

50. Dave Boyer, "Obama at Extremist Summit: 'We Are Not at War with Islam,'" *Washington Times*, February 18, 2015, accessed January 1, 2016, www.washingtontimes.com/news/2015/feb/18/wh-defensive-jewish-christian-victims/?page=all.

51. Mike Lillis, "Pelosi: Obama's Agreement with Iran Is a 'Diplomatic Masterpiece,'" *The Hill*, July 30, 2015, accessed January 1, 2016, http://thehill.com/business-a-lobbying/249797-pelosi-dems-will-solidify-iran-deal.

52. Hillary Clinton, "Hillary Clinton Addresses the Iran Nuclear Deal" (lecture, Brookings Institution, Washington, DC, September 9, 2015), accessed January 1, 2016, www.brookings.edu/events/2015/09/09-clinton-iran-nuclear-deal.

53. John Wagner, "Bernie Sanders Announces Support for Iran Nuclear Deal," *Washington Post*, August 7, 2015, accessed January 1, 2016, www.washingtonpost.com/news/post-politics/wp/2015/08/07/bernie-sanders-announces-support-for-iran-nuclear-deal/.

54. "Global Nuclear Watchdog IAEA Ends Iran 'Weapons' Probe," BBC, December 15, 2015, accessed January 1, 2016, www.bbc.com/news/world-middle-east-35104715.

55. Laurence Norman, "IAEA Board Agrees to Close File on Iran's Past Nuclear Activities," *Wall Street Journal*, December 15, 2015, accessed January 1, 2016, www.wsj.com/articles/iaea-board-agrees-to-close-iran-past-nuclear-activities-file-1450195869.

56. "Congress Urges Action on Iran Missile Tests," The United States Institute of Peace: The Iran Primer, January 15, 2016, accessed January 17, 2016, http://iranprimer.usip.org/blog/2015/dec/17/congress-alleged-iran-missile-test.

57. Jay Solomon, "U.S. Lawmakers Blast Delay on Iran Sanctions," *Wall Street Journal*, January 2, 2016, accessed January 5, 2016, www.wsj.com/articles/u-s-lawmakers-blast-delay-on-iran-sanctions-1451694590; and "Iran: US Imposes New Sanctions Over Missile Test," BBC, January 17, 2016, accessed January 19, 2016, www.bbc.com/news/world-us-canada-35338901.

58. Jay Solomon, "Nuclear Deal Fuels Iran's Hard-Liners," *Wall Street Journal*, January 8, 2016, accessed January 10, 2016, www.wsj.com/articles/nuclear-deal-fuels-irans-hard-liners-1452294637.

59. "Saudi Arabia, Iran Face Off as Sectarian Tensions Escalate after Executions," National Public Radio, January 3, 2016, accessed January 5, 2016, www.npr.org/sections/thetwo-way/2016/01/03/461862259/saudi-arabia-iran-face-off-as-sectarian-tensions-escalate-after-executions.

60. Barbara Starr, Tom LoBianco, Holly Yan, and Jim Sciutto, "Video Shows American Sailor Apologizing for Iran Incident," CNN, January 14, 2016, accessed January 15, 2016, http://edition.cnn.com/2016/01/13/politics/iran-us-sailors/index.html?eref=edition.

61. Leon Aron, "Putinology," *American Interest*, July 30, 2015, accessed January 1, 2016, www.aei.org/publication/putinology/.

62. Jill Dougherty, "U.S. Seeks to 'Reset' Relations with Russia," CNN, March 7, 2009, accessed January 1, 2016, www.cnn.com/2009/WORLD/europe/03/07/us.russia/index.html?eref=onion.

63. Andrew Foxall, "The Ceasefire Illusion: An Assessment of the Minsk II Agreement between Ukraine and Russia," Russia Studies Centre Policy Paper, no. 8 (December 2015): 2, accessed January 1, 2015, henryjacksonsociety.org/wp-content/uploads/2015/12/Minsk-II-FINAL-For-Website.pdf.

64. Alberto Nardelli and George Arnett, "Nato Reports Surge in Jet Interceptions as Russia Tensions Increase," *Guardian*, August 3, 2015, accessed January 1, 2016, www.theguardian.com/world/2015/aug/03/military-aircraft-interventions-have-surged-top-gun-but-for-real.

65. "Lithuania Says NATO Jets Scrambled More Often in 2015," *Washington Post*, January 5, 2016, accessed January 10, 2016, www.washingtonpost.com/world/europe/lithuania-says-nato-jets-scrambled-more-often-in-2015/2016/01/05/21b67074-b3b2-11e5-8abc-d09392edc612_story.html.

66. Denis Dyomkin, "Putin Says Turkey Shot Down Russian Plane to Defend IS Oil Supplies," Reuters, November 30, 2015, accessed January 1, 2016, www.reuters.com/article/us-mideast-crisis-syria-russia-turkey-idUSKBN0TJ2EQ20151130.

67. Evelyn Farkas, "Putin Is Testing Our Resolve," *Politico*, November 24, 2015, accessed January 1, 2016, www.politico.com/magazine/story/2015/11/isil-syria-putin-nato-airspace-213393.

68. Hillary Clinton, "America's Pacific Century," *Foreign Policy*, October 11, 2011, accessed January 1, 2016, http://foreignpolicy.com/2011/10/11/americas-pacific-century/.

69. Chris Buckley, "China Claims Air Rights Over Disputed Islands," *New York Times*, November 23, 2013, accessed January 1, 2016, www.nytimes.com/2013/11/24/world/asia/china-warns-of-action-against-aircraft-over-disputed-seas.html.

70. Leonard, "Farewell to the American Century."

71. Barack Obama, "State of the Union Address as Delivered" (speech, Capitol Hill, Washington, DC, January 12, 2016), accessed January 15, 2016, www.whitehouse.gov/the-press-office/2016/01/12/remarks-president-barack-obama-%E2%80%93-prepared-delivery-state-union-address.

7

PROGRESS AND GOOD GOVERNANCE IN DOMESTIC POLICY

Ruth O'Brien, City University of New York Graduate Center

Beyond his specific achievements and failures, beyond all the legislation and executive orders and programs and regulations, beyond his status as the first African American president, Barack Obama's most significant accomplishment in domestic policy has been to establish a new tradition of American governance.

Setting aside the two previous models—the "nanny state," in which an active government provides and prescribes for a citizenry facing a complicated and dangerous world, and the "night-watchman state," in which a passive government enforces order and safety when violations come to its attention—Obama envisioned a third tradition: an interactive, multilateral, participatory government in which citizens, stakeholders, and different levels and departments of government, acting on their own and in ever-shifting coalitions, combine to establish laws, rules, and practices that recognize and accommodate difference while enforcing equality. This chapter will examine how Barack Obama followed this third tradition of good governance during his presidency, first with a friendly and then with a hostile Congress, and in so doing made fundamental changes in American life that will be problematic to reverse.

TWEAKING DOMESTIC POLICY?

Part one of this chapter emphasizes the noneconomic domestic policy behind President Obama's two signatory laws, both passed in 2010—Obamacare (the Patient Protection and Affordable Care Act) and the Dodd-Frank Wall Street Reform and Consumer Protection Act. Obamacare and Dodd-Frank created important political institutions governing health care and consumer care on the federal, state, local, and municipal levels, and these will account for a great part of his positive legacy as a president.

Obamacare, having cleared two critical Supreme Court hurdles after its passage, is more likely to be eroded than repealed, even if a united Republican government takes office in 2017. Dodd-Frank's central institution, the Consumer Financial Protection Bureau, is more vulnerable to change, though it has gained more power and authority, and more of a political constituency with the middle class, than was first predicted.

Obamacare and Dodd-Frank do not fit into Theodore Lowi's public-policy boxes (redistributive, distributive, and regulatory) (Lowi 1964), nor do they generate clear political-coalition beneficiaries or a national constituency, like the one Franklin D. Roosevelt formed with the New Deal (Chambers and Burnham 1975, Skowronek 1997). The institutions that these two laws created accomplish all three domestic-policy functions, being simultaneously distributive (by giving benefits to constituents), redistributive (by taking benefits from one constituency to give to another in a zero-sum equation), and regulatory (since federal, state, and local agencies execute and implement the laws, dictated by federal regulations issued by the executive branch).

Part two of this chapter reviews what used to be called social policy but is more accurately characterized as cultural policy. It covers the real stuff of Obama's domestic legacy: cultural public policies that, like his signatory laws, are overlapping in their distributive, redistributive, and regulatory aspects, such as the faith-based initiative or LGBTQ identity politics (since discrimination has an economic impact). Unlike the signatory laws, however, these cultural policies reflect epochal shifts in national public opinion. While not entirely instigated by Obama, they constituted a wave that this Hawaiian president caught, and that should carry his legacy into the next presidency and beyond.

Obama's domestic policies constantly call to mind a multiplicity of factors connoting difference in identity, including class, race, gender, age, disability, geographic origin, sexual orientation, artistic talent, and athletic ability. Few Americans have a single identity or one factor. Difference is best described as multiple or intersectional and must be framed as value added, not subtracted. As much feminist work on male privilege and critical race theory, including the theory of whiteness, reveals, belonging to a dominant group distorts both one's moral ontology and one's moral epistemology (Clemmitt 2010; Stavrou 2009; Watson 2007, 107). Obama himself embodies intersectionality by being half African and half white, in addition to having spent part of his childhood in Indonesia. Not surprisingly, given this lineage and experience, Obama has long sought to define himself as something other than a traditional legal liberal who supports assimilation or equal treatment versus difference (Sugrue 2010, O'Brien, 2013).

KEY TERMS IN DOMESTIC POLICY

Neotribalism and the Social Sphere

Lowi's tripartite scheme, always criticized by political scientists as overlapping, is inherently so under Obama's presidency no matter what the domestic policy is, since the distinction between the public, private, and social spheres has little meaning to him. Most domestic public policies are a public-private hybrid—the question is, what is the public-private equation? The short answer is that it varies, but what does not vary for Obama is that his governance is better described for all domestic-policy implementation as part of the newly enlarged social sphere that subsumes the public and private spheres (O'Brien 2013).

When Obama married the public, private, and social spheres, he focused not on production but on consumption. And, to be sure, he recognized the perils associated with an interconnected and interdependent state, market, and society. What happens when people—deliberative citizens—do not participate in politics at home?

The Big Three, Obama's Faith, and Civic Religion

Obama supported the twin principles of "faith and work" as a community organizer after graduating from Columbia University. Obama's interpretation of the separation of church and state is that freedom of religion applies solely to "groups whose primary purpose is the inculcation of religious values and who primarily serve their own members." This interpretation has outraged many religious organizations, since they do "far more than simply teach their tenets or minister to the faithful" (Crabtree 2012).

Three religious traditions exist in the United States: liberal secularism, religious nationalism, and civic religion. Liberal secularism envisions a clean separation between church and state, whereas religious nationalism seeks their reunification. Yet until Ronald Reagan in 1981, no president spoke the language of religious nationalism. Most referred to Christianity, and to God, but it was a unitarian God. Then, in 2001 George W. Bush introduced "God talk," marking a new turn in politics toward evangelicalism or a Christian nation (Lincoln 2004, 22–29; Gutterman 2001).

Before taking office Obama made it clear that he rejected the idea of a Christian nation, opting instead for civic religion informed by Alexis de Tocqueville (O'Brien 2013). Obama's vision of civic religion relies heavily on "the sacred responsibility for others"—the responsibility of the individual, the state, and society. Indeed, this was what attracted Obama to the church in the first place (Gorski 2011, Bellah 1967, Obama 2007a, Gerson 2007, Goodstein 2007, Pew Research Center 2009, Brooks 2007).

Obama has a complex understanding of responsibility about the roles of the church and state. The only religious values that belong in a democracy, in his view, are those that can be translated *not* into a universally appealing set of Christian values but into a *plurality* of religious values (O'Brien 2013). Obama renounces *one* truth. He speaks of truths. To him, religion is about becoming, striving, or a person's quest for perfectibility (Frank 2004, Frank 2011, Fish 2009, Obama 2007b, Robinson 2015).

Neotribalism

When comparing various types of fundamentalism—Christian, Islamic, and Judaic—most people focus on the differences among them. Yet while such differences in kind can be stark, this chapter appropriates the term *neotribalism* as a means of concentrating on the primary assumption that religious fundamentalisms share: patriarchal rule performed in a re-enlarged private sphere in opposition to Obama's domestic policies, particularly the cultural ones, such as LGBTQ rights, women's rights, and his definition of Tocqueville's notion of civic religion (O'Brien 2013). The term *neotribalism* comes from the postmodern Left, though I return it to historical roots by highlighting the global religious resurgence (Kepel 1993, O'Brien 2013).

Getting the public sphere to limit a woman's autonomy regarding her reproductive capacity and killing her for sullying the family's name are both the results of neotribalism. The extended family—the tribe—reestablishes the primacy of the patriarch. In the United States, religious organizations, primarily Christian ones such as conservative Catholic dioceses and evangelical churches, declared the war on women, hoping to push reproductive health back into the private domain once Obamacare was on the horizon (O'Brien 2013, Dionne 2012).

Why call this tribal? It is tribal because the resurgence of religion in the 1970s and 1980s, and the subsequent culture wars in the 1990s, fostered a political culture that transcends borders. And by accepting an expanded definition of religious freedom under the conservatives' interpretation of the Religious Freedom Restoration Act of 1993, the United States promoted patriarchal rule. If a Catholic hospital refuses to give contraception to women or perform abortions with federal government funding, a central tenet of this religious belief—patriarchal rule—has become public (Davidson 2012; Failinger 2012, 137; *Los Angeles Times* 2012; O'Brien 2013, 73–75).

Obama's domestic public policies aimed to provide safety for all "others," including women and children. They do not allow a Christian priest, an Islamic mullah, or a Jewish rabbi to deprive them of their dignity, rights, or autonomy (O'Brien 2013). To put it positively, Obama's domestic policies expand the social sphere as a means of curbing patriarchal or heterosexual masculinity with reproductive rights, and by extending civil rights to gays, lesbians, and transgender people, most prominently in the Affordable Care Act. (For pluralities see Benhabib 2009, Scott 2007, Norton 2013, Endsjø 2011).

Health Care

Obama was swept into office in 2008 with large majorities in both houses of Congress, including (at first) a filibuster-proof 60–40 margin in the Senate. He needed these majorities to enact health-care legislation, since the Republicans made clear from the start that on this legislation, they would not cooperate in any way. Not a single Republican member of Congress voted for the final version of the Affordable Care Act, which was passed on March 21, 2010.

The United States spends more than any other industrialized nation on health care. The cost adds up to a full 16 percent of the nation's GDP, and even this amount does not cover everyone. Elizabeth Warren, while still a Harvard professor, observed that 62 percent of all personal bankruptcy cases involved medical debt (Himmelstein et al. 2009).

With health care accounting for one-sixth of the US economy, crafting a system that would be acceptable to providers, payers, and patients alike, against a background of Republicans issuing lurid portrayals of "rationing," "death panels," and "socialized medicine" at every opportunity, took a lot more work than just sitting down with congressional leaders and hashing out a deal (eHealth 2010, Ferrara 2009, Goldhill 2009).

The ACA did not permit insurance companies to discriminate against people with preexisting conditions; they had to insure anyone who applied. Insurance exchanges were established for individuals and small businesses, and tax credits were extended to those who would have trouble paying the premiums. Finally, to identify fraud, abuse, and waste, the law created independent commissions. It dictated that 85 cents of every premium dollar be spent on medical care in small-group markets and by Medicare Advantage insurers; for large-group markets the figure was 80 cents of every premium dollar (eHealth 2010).

Insurance companies still make money, of course, but they do so in the manner of public utilities, by offering a tightly regulated and essentially identical product to a captive market. The ACA expanded the insurance industry's pool of customers, reduced competition, and insured the insurers against excessive losses in their uncharted new economic environment, even as it left fewer Americans uninsured due to poverty or illness. This was a classic Obama win-win (Wolffe 2010, 17). And Obama's health-care reform had another function: redistributing wealth "through hard-fought steps to place new charges on businesses and the well-to-do" (Skocpol and Jacobs 2010, 36).

Obamacare and Good Governance

The ACA also furthered Obama's notion of federalism, making state and federal responsibilities "interwoven, interdependent, and varied," as one expert noted. The success of the plan depends on how well they coordinate with one another (Gais 2010).

When applied to government, Obama's stakeholder idea is based on collaborative governance. It encourages participation and partnership, collaboration, diversity, and competition. It promotes an integration of policy domains while remaining decentralized. And the implementation problems that the ACA has faced reveal a weakness of this style of governance: It depends on parties to respond to incentives to cooperate, but a party who is dead-set against participating for political reasons will sometimes act against their own interest (and those of their constituents).

A Renew Deal regime (to use Orly Lobel's term) practices civic republicanism and pragmatism simultaneously. When Congress and the president draft legislation in an indeterminate way, their avoidance of conflict and controversy gives the deliberating publics more power. Public-interest groups have more input into the policy-making process, and new groups demand more access (Lobel 2004, 372–74).

Obama's ideas on government resemble those of the seventeenth-century philosopher Baruch Spinoza. Spinoza said that in a well-run or ethical society, people act in concert with one another not out of altruism but because it is in their self-interest to do so in order to survive. (A similar example from American history would be, not rugged pioneers fending for themselves, but the wagon train, whose members stick together, share resources, and cooperate for the common benefit.) The task of government is to design institutions that encourage interaction and cooperation. It is behavioral economics writ large, a system in which our differences drive us together (O'Brien 2013, 35–40).

As might be expected from an African American who won the presidency with widespread support across all demographics, Obama avoids the language of identity politics in favor of a politics of real, universal equality of opportunity and difference that reflects ever-changing norms. If African American children constitute the majority of children in poverty without health care, Obama believes in universalizing health care for *all* children in poverty. It's their lack of health care, not their identity, that creates the problem.

Yet this is not to say that Obama accepts all norms. He does not believe in universal social services, and he spurns most entitlements. For this reason, he did not support universal health care in the manner of Britain's National Health Service. No one should have a right to health care; rather, they should have a realistic opportunity to purchase it. And the ACA's structure carries Obama's outlook down to the level of the individual patient: It is a system that emphasizes prevention, and prevention works only when patients listen and take a role in their own health care.

The ACA's genesis was an example of Obama's governance, as its designers gathered ideas from across the political spectrum. In 1989 Stuart Butler of the conservative Heritage Foundation wrote a report called "Assuring Affordable Health Care for All Americans," which came up with the concept of the individual mandate. (He renounced it in 2012.) This idea was modeled after the way many states "require passengers in automobiles to wear seat-belts for their own protection" (Butler 1990).

Mitt Romney, a future Republican presidential nominee, had made the individual mandate the centerpiece of his health-care plan as governor of Massachusetts. During the 2008 Democratic primary campaign, John Edwards and Hillary Clinton made the individual mandate one of the legislative linchpins underlying their proposals for health-care reform. In fact, "the main Democratic holdout," reports Ezra Klein, "was Senator Barack Obama," who started supporting the individual mandate in office to pass the ACA (Klein 2012, Obama 2009). The mandate that made it into the final version of the ACA could be avoided if the individual chose to pay a penalty instead; this feature saved the law, since the Supreme Court ruled in *National Federation of Independent Business v. Sebelius*, 132 S.Ct. 2566 (2012), that this made it a tax rather than a mandatory purchase, which might have been unconstitutional.

As the end of Obama's presidency approached, the ACA's continuance seemed likely, though its popularity was shaky and Republicans still vowed to repeal it. After a rocky start with a poorly designed Internet presence, it was unclear whether the number of participants Obamacare attracted would be enough to keep the system going. Features that drew criticism included its cost (young, healthy people overpay to defray the costs of caring for the older and sicker), the too-frequent need to switch doctors and networks, and the failure of some state-run exchanges.

Yet the system brought insurance to ten million Americans who had not been insured before, and its other popular features, including mandatory coverage for children on their parents' insurance up to age twenty-six and guaranteed issue (applicants who complete the process cannot be turned down, regardless of preexisting conditions), are so popular that they are unlikely to be repealed. These features of the ACA are most characteristic of Obama's style of government: They make care available to all on an equal basis, but individuals have options even if they choose not to participate in the exchanges. The ACA's more traditionally top-down aspects, such as its rigid cost controls, restructuring of hospitals, and mandatory national database, have encountered more resistance.

Banking, Finance, and Consumer Reform

On July 21, 2010, President Obama signed into law the Dodd-Frank Wall Street Reform and Consumer Protection Act. It had been precipitated by the economic crisis of 2008, so the "Wall Street" part included leverage limits, new capital requirements, restrictions on proprietary trading, a wholesale reform of the securities-rating industry, and new rules for derivatives trading. It established a Financial Stability Oversight Council (FSOC), charged with identifying and responding to any risks that endanger the financial system's stability. And it gave federal regulators resolution authority for "systemically important firms in danger of defaulting."

The act was also motivated by a desire to end predatory corporate lending to consumers, so it had a "Consumer Protection" part as well: steps to prevent deceptively high interest rates and severe payment terms, increase consumers' financial literacy, handle complaints expeditiously, and protect members of the armed forces from financial exploitation. But the president made sure the act was designed to facilitate a stakeholder society; he stressed the importance of ending a "culture of irresponsibility that encompasses banks *and* borrowers" (Appelbaum 2009; emphasis added). The act's centerpiece was a consumer-finance regulatory agency that would "give consumer protection an independent seat at the table" (US Department of the Treasury, 2009).

A century earlier Theodore Roosevelt had softened capitalism with the creation of the Bureau of Labor Statistics, the Workers' Compensation

Program, and other progressive reforms (Sklar 1988). In his most anti–Wall Street speech, delivered in Osawatomie, Kansas, in December 2011 to introduce economic themes on which he would run for reelection the following year, Obama made direct references to Theodore Roosevelt and the rules of capitalism (Obama 2011b).

But instead of Progressive Era–style top-down federal regulation, Obama's financial reform brought a whole new dimension—a consumer dimension—to capitalism, something that Elizabeth Warren, then a law professor and later a senator, had long advocated applying to the financial sector. She made clear the connections between the excesses and abuses of Wall Street and the crisis of the American middle class. In a 2007 article called "Unsafe at Any Rate," Warren argued in favor of an administrative agency dedicated to protecting consumers of financial products. The very health and well-being of capitalism and democracy depended on it, she wrote. The article's title intentionally invoked Ralph Nader's 1965 book *Unsafe at Any Speed*, as Warren argued that the state should regulate credit products for the same reasons it regulates automobiles and other consumer goods: They too are dangerous if those who purchase them are not fully informed and if the state creates no guidelines and standards (Warren 2007, 9–10).

Representatives of the financial industry, such as the American Bankers Association, opposed the plan to create a new oversight agency, and while they lost that fight, critical proposals of the Consumer Protection Act were watered down through lobbying. Still, the stakeholder-state-and-society perspective was clear, and this shift in thinking arguably constituted the largest transformation brought about by the act (Skocpol and Jacobs 2010, 176).

The Consumer Protection Act is an example of horizontal federalism. The act took a modest approach toward preemption, providing that only inconsistent state laws would be preempted. As with the Clean Air Act, state laws offering greater protection to consumers are permitted; here the Obama administration embraced a states' rights movement that a liberal or progressive could love.

The states even gained involvement in federal regulatory rulemaking: "The Bureau shall issue a notice of proposed rulemaking whenever a majority of the States has enacted a resolution in support of the establishment or modification of a consumer protection regulation by the Bureau" (Section 1041). The states' continuing involvement has entrenched consumer financial protection in a way that will be difficult for subsequent presidents to undo. Finally, Dodd-Frank created the Consumer Financial Protection Bureau (CFPB). It has extensive jurisdiction over the extension of credit and the sale of financial products to consumers, with the intent of ensuring that lenders act fairly and that consumers understand what they are signing.

Consumerism constitutes a full-information critique of capitalism. It accepts the basic principles of private property and profit that underlie capitalism but argues that certain parts of the market do not work. This type of economic reform recognizes that suppliers of credit products have an unfair advantage over consumers, who lack access to full information about products that are potentially dangerous to their financial health (Cohen 2003, 408; Whitman 2007, 349; *New York Times* 2012b).

Reformers had long identified consumerism as a way out of class conflict. In 1912 Walter Weyl wrote that "to think of Americans as 'consumers' was thus to think of them as members of a kind of universal class, with a single common interest—an interest in buying things that were both 'cheap' and 'good.' The key to creating justice and social peace in democratic America lay in making consumers understand that they all shared this common interest." Dodd-Frank was the federal government's first serious attempt at achieving this century-old goal (Weyl 1912).

K–12's Race to the Top

The Education Department's "Race to the Top" grant competition was another example of Obama's interactive governance. It allotted $4.35 billion of the 2009 stimulus package for competitive grants to states whose public schools took specified steps to improve standards and assessments, upgrade data systems, and strengthen the recruitment and training of teachers. This "race" led dozens of states to lift their caps on charter schools and institute rigorous teacher-evaluation programs, though almost every teachers' union (normally among the Democrats' most loyal supporters) took issue with these measures. The federal money and the competition proved effective at breaking the political logjams that had frustrated reformers, providing the momentum to move their packages through state legislatures. And even when states failed to secure federal funding (only twelve received grants), the Obama administration succeeded in getting them to reexamine their policies. The best thing about the Race to the Top money, administration officials said, was that it proved so highly leveraged.

The politics of education are notorious in that the strongest interest groups—teachers' unions and school management—both oppose change. The presidencies of Lyndon B. Johnson and George W. Bush showed Obama that education could change in significant ways only through a national initiative (Grunwald 2011). Obama insists that the programs seeking funding create a "shared expectation" of desired outcomes. The state then acts as a facilitator, promoting and standardizing innovations that start out small, local, and private.

The federal government's role is less one of direct action than one of providing financial support, strategic direction, and leadership for other governmental actors. In keeping with this process of refinement and revision, in late 2015 the Republican Congress passed and Obama signed the Every Student Succeeds Act, which largely undid these reforms by returning to the states significant areas that had been under federal control since the No Child Left Behind Act of 2002 (Layton 2015).

Stakeholders and Norm Generators

Under the traditional regulatory model, industries and private individuals are the objects of regulation. The EPA targets companies that pollute; the National Labor Relations Board seeks out employers who violate laws governing wages or hours. By contrast, the stakeholder model does not have fixed targets. All individuals are "norm-generating subjects," in constant flux, creating norms and changing them. The company doing the polluting and the citizen ingesting the pollution are on an equal footing, and this parity extends even to citizens who do not live in the polluted area but value clean air or water. Feminist, critical race, and gay legal theorists who earlier rejected "the law as a means of effecting social change" have come aboard the stakeholder regulatory ideal. With the principle that there is no homogeneity of norms, they see how existing laws can promote change (Lobel 2007).

Negotiated rulemaking underscores how intertwined and interdependent each player or actor is with all the others. When it works, win-win language rather than zero-sum discourse is heard around the table. It matches means to ends by involving all stakeholders, yet still offers choices or policy options on the basis of competition rooted in difference, as people interact with their neighbors and see their relationships: as sellers and consumers, employers and employees, property owners and tenants, planners and citizens, and administrators and service recipients (Parlow 2008).

In a stakeholder society, difference is the key (just as it is in diversifying one's financial portfolio). Diversity creates competition, and competition creates pluralities—pluralities of beliefs, values, and ideas, which in turn generate more agendas, norms, and solutions, which perpetually evolve or change. It's the journey, not the destination, that counts. This type of thinking forms the backbone of Obama's philosophy of government.

The participation of all major players gives the government legitimacy. The state must safeguard the process, ensuring that no group or party receives special treatment. "For procedural legitimacy to be meaningful," writes Orly Lobel, "there must be a commitment to public values, such as political equality, which is endangered when power and wealth are deeply imbalanced" (Lobel 2004, 389, 467, 469).

CULTURAL POLITICS AND POLICY

After his first two years in office, Obama faced a considerably different situation in Congress. The Tea Party rebellion and hostility to the ACA had led to a large Republican wave in the 2010 midterm elections. Now the House was under comfortable Republican control (242–193), and the Democrats' margin in the Senate was thin enough (53–47) that the Republicans could easily filibuster bills and nominations they disliked. The Democrats would gain a few seats back with Obama's reelection in 2012, then lose control of the Senate in 2014, but never again could Obama count on a friendly Congress to pass the legislation he wanted.

Fortunately for Obama, the multilateral, multilevel nature of his brand of governance gave him numerous other ways besides congressional action to effect change. Executive orders could influence public opinion and set strong examples for other levels of government; federal agencies could interpret old and new laws in ways that furthered a progressive agenda, or could reach agreements with public-interest groups that cemented Obama's goals as public policy; and judicial appointments and nuanced defenses of problematic laws could achieve results through the courts.

LGBTQ and LGTBQers

Perhaps the greatest revolution in domestic policy during Obama's presidency was the great advance in both civil rights and social acceptance of lesbian, gay, bisexual, transsexual, and queer (LGBTQ) Americans, a shift that transformed the political and cultural landscape. When Obama ran for president in 2008, same-sex marriage was a surefire vote loser, having been voted down in eighteen statewide referenda and never approved by a popular vote. As a presidential candidate, Obama said his Christian faith told him that marriage was between a man and a woman, though his views were "evolving." By his last year in office, same-sex marriage was legal everywhere in the United States, gays were serving openly in the military, and even transsexuals—a group rarely even mentioned in political discourse when Obama first ran for president—were becoming accepted (Wallsten and Wilson 2012).

Perhaps most surprising of all, Obama was able to play a major role in effecting these changes even though he faced a Republican majority in the House from 2011 on (and marriage was generally understood to be a responsibility of the states). He used all the weapons at his disposal: executive orders, his role as commander in chief, his Justice Department's discretion in deciding which laws to defend, and even the bully pulpit. LGBTQ policy is an example of good multilateral governance, as states enacted their own same-sex-marriage laws, courts and the media got into the act, and different federal policy areas (e.g., Social Security, the military, family law) interacted to further acceptance. Within a few years, the Supreme Court had no choice but to ratify the shift in sentiment.

As early as the spring of 2010, Obama instructed his administration to reinterpret the Family Medical Leave Act (FMLA) so that same-sex partners would have the same rights as opposite-sex partners. Obama also supported equal adoption rights for members of the LGBTQ community and urged states to treat same-sex couples with "full equality in their family and adoption laws" (Huffington Post 2011, Gerstel 2011, Pear 2010, Schacter 2010, Human Rights Campaign 2015).

The anti-Democratic wave in 2010 reduced Obama's influence over Congress but also liberated him to express his policy preferences more openly. He started before the new Congress assembled, when a lame-duck session of the 112th Congress repealed the Don't Ask, Don't Tell policy in the armed forces. This Clinton-era compromise had softened the military's traditional antipathy toward gays by forbidding the armed services to discharge members for homosexuality unless they openly revealed their preference. Its repeal, at Obama's instigation, ended military discharges for sexual preference and allowed gays to serve openly. (In 2015 Obama ordered that women could serve in the armed forces in full equality with men, even in combat roles.)

Next to fall was the Defense of Marriage Act (DOMA). This law, passed by wide majorities and signed by President Bill Clinton in 1996, did not ban states from allowing same-sex marriages but did prevent the federal government from recognizing such marriages for purposes such as taxation, federal pensions, Social Security, and immigration. In February 2011 Obama instructed Attorney General Eric Holder not to enforce DOMA because it was unconstitutional. The House of Representatives appointed a team of lawyers to defend the law in court, but the administration's refusal had sent a powerful signal (Markon and Somashekhar 2011; *Massachusetts v. U.S. Dept. of Health and Human Services*, F.3d 1, 2010).

In May 2012 Obama took the symbolic step of announcing his support for same-sex marriage. (The president actually lagged behind popular sentiment; in 2011 a journalist wrote that five years earlier "support for gay marriage barely topped a third of all Americans. Now, 53 percent say gay marriage should be legal") (Somashekhar and Craighill 2011). In his January 2013 inaugural address, the president renewed his call for marriage equality, and in June of that year, in *U.S. v. Windsor*, 133 S.Ct. 2675, the US Supreme Court affirmed a lower court's decision to strike down DOMA, though it stopped short of asserting that there is a fundamental right for gays to marry. In *Obergefell v. Hodges*, 135 S.Ct. 2071 (2015), the Supreme Court finished the job, ruling that states could not discriminate against same-sex couples in their marriage laws (Landler 2011, Barnes 2012b, Savage 2012).

The court's decisions in these two cases were made easier by numerous states' adoption of same-sex marriage on their own, sometimes under compulsion from state courts and other times by legislative initiative or popular referendums, and by numerous local gay rights ordinances. Politicians and the court had changed with the culture.

As for the T in LGBTQ, here again Obama took whatever steps he could, given the nation's federalist structure, to improve the legal rights and social acceptance of transgender individuals, again with surprisingly positive results. In a controversial move, in June 2010 Obama's State Department started issuing passports to transgendered people without requiring them to specify a gender (*Washington Times* 2010).

While the passport decision was the first major policy change that expanded transgender rights, it was far from the only one. Over the next few years, at least a dozen federal agencies, at Obama's instigation, announced actions that created, expanded, or protected equal rights for the transgendered. Some were expansion of eligibility rules, some technical procedures for recording gender, some reductions of paperwork, but all of them furthered the principle of equality and, just as important, required coworkers, bankers, teachers, employers, and many others to treat individuals as the gender that they identified with (Obama Administration 2015).

By the end of his term, without any significant legislation or court decision, acceptance of the transgendered—a group so marginal when Obama took office that they were barely even mentioned in equal rights rhetoric—had spread to the point where a former Olympic men's decathlon champion who was transitioning to female appeared on the cover of *Vanity Fair* as a woman, to great acclaim; women's colleges were routinely accepting students who had been born male but identified as female; and the very idea of gender as a fixed biological fact was being widely discarded.

Obama explained his concept of universality in October 2011: "Every single American—gay, straight, lesbian, bisexual, transgender—every single American deserves to be treated equally in the eyes of the law and in the eyes of our society. It's a pretty simple proposition." By playing a weak hand masterfully, Obama may have done more than anyone else toward making that proposition a reality (Obama 2011a).

Criminal-Justice Reforms and #BlackLivesMatter

Another Obama success in shifting social attitudes came with his scaling back of the "War on Drugs" and with criminal-justice reform more generally. Here too he had the benefit of a developing consensus, as the pendulum was swinging back after the lock-'em-up consensus of the 1980s and 1990s; and here too he found a solution in crafting universal rules (equalizing punishment for different forms of cocaine, for example) instead of targeting particular identity groups. Unlike with most of his policy initiatives, he had broad ideological support, as conservatives and liberals agreed that too many people were being imprisoned for too long (though they did not always agree on the causes).

The United States has 5 percent of the world population but 25 percent of its prisoners. Moreover, 48 percent of the U.S. prison population is black, nearly four times their proportion in the population. Michelle Alexander, a former ACLU lawyer who clerked for Supreme Court Justice Harry Blackman, expands upon these statistics in *The New Jim Crow: Mass Incarceration in the Age of Colorblindness*: "The United States imprisons a larger percentage of its black population than South Africa did at the height of apartheid" (el-Khoury 2009, 63, 72; Garland 2001; Sheridan 2009; Alexander 2012).

Mass incarceration began in earnest with California's trend-setting 1994 "three strikes, you're out" law, under which anyone convicted of a third felony is imprisoned for life (Dzur 2010, Bottoms 1995). This trend resulted from the forty-year so-called war on drugs. President Richard Nixon declared it a war in the early 1970s, and every president thereafter supported it, with Ronald Reagan and George W. Bush stepping it up. In the process, crime became racialized (Clark, Capuzzi, and Fick, 2011; el-Khoury 2009, 64).

To begin addressing the racial injustices underlying the criminal-justice system, Obama signed the Fair Sentencing Act into law. Long needed, it reduced the 100-to-1 sentencing disparity between powder cocaine (sold mainly by whites) and crack cocaine (sold mainly by African Americans). The Obama administration's new emphasis on drug enforcement focused on white, middle-class drug abusers and prescription-drug abuse.

Rather than criminalizing drug abusers, the Obama administration emphasized treatment. Of the approximately twenty-five million substance abusers in the United States, only approximately two million were receiving any form of treatment. The Obama administration hoped to triple that number, making drug-addiction treatment part of the primary health-care system. As Obama's term neared its end, he hinted at possible support for federal legalization of marijuana, while reiterating his endorsement of reduced criminal penalties and directing his Justice Department not to prosecute users in states where marijuana was legal (whether medical or recreational).

Dismantling the War on Drugs was part of a larger attempt to reform criminal justice. In this attempt Obama found rare common ground with a significant sector of conservatives. As early as 1996, William F. Buckley Jr., founder of right-wing *National Review* magazine, had proposed making narcotics legal, and the movement's libertarian wing joined small-government conservatives dismayed at prison overcrowding and the related overspending (Dzur 2010; Braithwaite and Pettit 1990; Gillman 2009; Atkins 2011; *Dorsey v. United States*, 132 S.Ct. 2321 (2012); Barnes 2012a; *New York Times* 2012a; Katel 2009; Nano 2011; *National Review* 1996). To Obama, mass incarceration is wrong because it disproportionately harms African Americans; to libertarians, drug prohibition infringes on their personal freedom; to mainstream conservatives, data shows that long sentences are ineffective at reducing crime. Here too Obama managed to unite diverse groups with disparate interests around a common set of goals.

Diversity and Inclusivity Trump Truth(s) in Affirmative Action and Civil Rights

Obama's preference for diversity as inclusivity could best be seen when Sonia Sotomayor caught Obama's eye after Supreme Court Justice John Paul Stevens announced his retirement, effective at the end of the 2009–2010 term. Sotomayor, an appeals-court judge, was neither a law professor nor a legal theorist who would fall prey to accusations of being too radical or too ethnic. Her style of judicial rendering was conservative. With a few exceptions, Jeffrey Toobin wrote, her opinions "stuck closely to the facts of each case" (Toobin 2009). Nonetheless, critics of Obama's judicial appointments saw the selection of Sotomayor as "reverse racism" (Buchanan 2009, Baker 2009).

The high-water mark for Supreme Court support of civil rights, especially equality of outcomes or results, had come in 1971, nearly forty years earlier, when the Burger Court transformed the *negative* idea of affirmative action into the *positive* notion of diversity based on inclusion. Even better, diversity could be universalized and extended to all other cultures in the United States—for example, Latinos and Latinas, Asians—all articulated by historian David Hollinger's notion of a "Post-ethnic America" (Hollinger 1995).

Obama captures the complexity of racial progress and regress in the United States. His postracial narrative is considered a whitewashing by many in the African American community. Liberals and progressive Democrats remain disappointed with his record on building the big social-welfare state that, like Franklin D. Roosevelt's, did not in the end serve African Americans very well. And after Johnson's Great Society, liberal Democrats did little to help African Americans left in decaying urban areas who faced eroding tax bases and white flight (Slessarev 1997).

On civil rights and race relations, Obama saw many important issues raised during his term, including police killings, structural and systemic societal racism, and discrimination and marginalization in educational institutions. Early in his term, when the distinguished historian Henry Louis Gates, an African American, was mistaken for an intruder in his own Cambridge, Massachusetts, house by a white policeman, Obama brought the two men together at the White House and worked out their differences. Yet by the middle of his second term, events had gotten ahead of Obama to the point that, when it came to racial issues, on which he had spoken so eloquently during the 2008 campaign, he was essentially a bystander. Police shooting incidents and racial attacks on college campuses had so greatly multiplied that Obama's aspiration to be a healer on racial matters rang hollow, since he had little influence or jurisdiction on the local level.

On race Obama was trapped by the differing public perceptions of his identity. Had he campaigned on his identity—as a civil rights leader—it is unlikely he would have been elected. He would have been seen as an "us against them" politician or simply as a partisan for African Americans. Had he gotten into office and pursued big-state solutions, he would have lost his individuality as a distinctive type of liberal who preached interdependence rather than a zero-sum state that promotes either the individual or society. Yet, ironically, his longest legacy may well be attributable to his intersectional perspective, particularly when it comes to decking the federal bureaucracies' halls.

Fully Inclusive Federal Institutions

Obama's approach to diversity first remedies systemic discrimination. He does not explain discrimination from a left-right perspective; rather, he argues for privileging diversity and inclusivity in terms of "empathy." One can assume, he points out, that a judge from a historically excluded group has struggled in life. By including groups symbolized by their exclusion in the past, he ensures that all voices are heard (Scherer 2011).

Months before his 2008 election, Obama began working on a plan to transform the federal government through diversification. By 2014 hundreds of openly gay, lesbian, bisexual, and transgender appointees populated the federal government. Of Obama's two hundred most important appointees, 53.5 percent confirmed by the Senate were not straight white men. By contrast, Bill Clinton put forth 37.5 percent, and George W. Bush only 25.6 percent (Burke 2009). As for the courts, only 29 percent of the federal judges Obama appointed in his first two years in office were white, presumably straight, men. By mid-2015 42 percent of his judicial nominees had been women and 36 percent had been nonwhite, both figures easily outdoing any previous president (Tobias 2010, Eilperin 2015).

Faith-Based Initiative

To Obama, religious groups, secular grassroots community groups, and public-interest advocacy groups all represent avenues for practicing deliberative democracy. Rather than disbanding the Office of Faith-Based Initiatives (OFBI), he expanded it and made it more inclusive (Bradley 2012). Obama flipped the original intent of the OFBI on its head by adopting a very narrow interpretation of religious freedom in the United States. Like governmental contractors, both secular and religious groups and organizations must follow national laws if they accept governmental funding (*New Zealand Herald* 2012, *Christian Science Monitor* 2012, Crabtree 2012).

By 2011 the Obama administration had shifted the burden of compliance back to these religious organizations, rendering a very narrow definition of religion. "[The] works of Florence Nightingale, Mother Teresa," an editorial complained, "the Salvation Army, or any modern-day good

Samaritan would not be religious" under this definition (*Christian Science Monitor* 2012).

The only religious values that belong in a democracy, in his view, are those that can be translated not into a universally appealing set of Christian values but into a *plurality* of religious values. What is more, the only type of religion that should influence governance is that which is founded on reason and argumentation, not on blind faith. Obama advances a cosmopolitan version of civic religion (Henneberger 2012, Frank 2011).

The Obama administration knew that the Supreme Court would, and will continue to, employ a very expansive definition of the role of religion in the United States. In October 2011, for example, a unanimous court reinforced the so-called ministerial exception permitting religious organizations the freedom to hire and fire ministers, or those who perform ministerial duties, without having to follow federal employment laws, such as antidiscrimination laws (*Hosanna-Tabor v. EEOC*, 143 S.Ct. 694, 2012). And in 2014 a divided court allowed Hobby Lobby Stores to exclude contraceptives from its employees' health-care coverage to accommodate the religious beliefs of the company's owners (*Burwell v. Hobby Lobby Stores, Inc.*, 134 S.Ct. 2751, 2014).

Climate, Immigration, and Other Cultural Issues

To be sure, not all of Obama's reform initiatives were successful. He did his best to advocate for gun control, and a distressing number of multiple shootings during his presidency, often in schools, provided frequent opportunities to do so. Yet Congress passed no major legislation, and public opinion did not shift noticeably. The 2010 case of *McDonald v. Chicago*, 561 U.S. 742 (2010), in which an activist Supreme Court ruled that the Second Amendment prevents states and localities from banning individuals from owning firearms, seemed to invigorate gun owners and demoralize opponents, who were reduced to advocating such things as gun-owner registries and waiting periods for buyers.

Climate change was important enough for Obama to mention it in his victory speech at the end of the 2008 primaries: "This was the moment when the rise of the oceans began to slow and our planet began to heal." His administration allocated billions of dollars in grants, loan guarantees, and other forms of aid to companies researching green-energy projects, and his EPA worked hard, with at least partial success, to put coal-burning power plants out of business and boost automotive gasoline mileage. Yet even with large majorities in Congress during 2009–2010, his cap-and-trade plan for carbon emissions went nowhere, and he failed to secure Senate ratification of the Kyoto Protocols on carbon pollution, or meaningful commitments from foreign polluters (China chief among them) to reduce their own emissions. The 2015 Paris climate conference yielded commitments from nearly every nation to reduce carbon emissions (eventually), with the United States' cuts being among the most ambitious. But since the agreement was not submitted for Senate approval as a treaty, there is no guarantee that good governance will result and future administrations will enforce it.

On immigration, Obama benefited from a fractured opposition, as Republican anti-immigration activists fought an intra-party battle against businesspeople who welcomed cheap labor. Indeed, since the number of new arrivals, especially from Mexico, dipped dramatically after the 2008 crisis, the greatest area of controversy during Obama's presidency was not immigration but immigrants—the eleven million or so undocumented ones already in the United States. With Democrats in Congress skittish and Republicans unable to unify, there was no chance for Obama to see the comprehensive immigration reform he hoped for, in which the undocumented would be given a path to citizenship in return for stronger controls and enforcement on those who came after.

Short of that, Obama did his best to help the undocumented with programs like Deferred Action for Childhood Arrivals, citizenship for those who served in the armed forces, toleration or encouragement of sanctuary cities, opposition to Arizona's punitive program for reporting undocumented migrants, easing and expansion of asylum rules, and the nondeportation of migrants convicted of minor crimes. Here again Obama used his executive powers to encourage and entrench a social change (acceptance of the undocumented) in hopes of encouraging its eventual formal acceptance. The process was still incomplete as the end of his term approached.

OBAMA'S ANTI-IDENTITY IDENTITY LEGACY

When Obama was elected, supporters hoped that he would bring something new to the presidency in more than just the obvious way. He largely managed to achieve that goal, and the irony is that while he is completely identified in law and social policy by identity politics, this is what he tried to eschew the most. He was boxed in not by racism but by identity—which is different because it is personal, not demographic or statistical.

Obama shuns identity politics because it interferes with our societal pursuit of the common good and with our individual attempts at self-perfection. Obama's governance depends on shifting alliances, fluid coalitions, and flexible interactions; group identities interfere with this. Identity politics worked well in the past, when identity groups tended to be homogeneous and clannish but needed help in uniting politically. Nowadays, when most people have multiple or mixed identities and associate freely with people worldwide, identity politics can be more of a barrier than a blessing. In the 2012 presidential campaign, Obama's team used "big data" and advanced analytics to craft specific appeals to individual voters and thereby assemble a majority. His style of governance runs along similar lines. To Obama, identity marketing and identity politics are both relics of the twentieth century, on the way to becoming outdated. Neotribalism is the opposite of this trend, as it seeks to multiply and harden identities fostered by millennia-old religions.

Paradoxically, Obama's early failures gave birth to further success. The loss of a majority in Congress meant he had to work through other channels, and this demonstrated the potency of his multilateral, intersectional methods in getting things done. Once in power, the Republicans had to actually govern instead of simply posturing; House speaker John Boehner had to make numerous compromises to get legislation passed, to the point where it eventually cost him his job. Obama's strength has always been as a moderator or conciliator who finds common ground; and, like many deciders, he knows that decisions can be easier to make when there are constraints than when you have an open field (such as large majorities in both houses of Congress).

For cooperative methods to work, some common ground must exist. Obama's governance works best when a cultural consensus is already starting to develop behind his proposed reforms and when the changes are not expensive and won't greatly or directly impair most individuals' rights. It is less effective when lots of money is involved, the reform will directly affects lots of Americans' lives, and it addresses no strongly perceived need or desire on the part of the public.

If a large constituency is adamantly opposed, whether because it stands to lose something, because of partisan politics (just as no military plan survives contact with the enemy, no political philosophy survives contact with the party system), or because they are extremely angry (such as campus radicals), it's hard to be conciliatory. Gun control, for example, is usually not the most important issue for its advocates, but for gun owners it is; and a strongly determined opposition, however ill-informed, can undercut even a genuinely nonpartisan effort, such as Common Core.

When asked in the 1970s whether the American Revolution had been a success, longtime Chinese premier Chou En-lai famously replied: "It's too early to tell." It probably won't take two centuries to evaluate Barack Obama's revolution in American governance, but the early returns look more promising than Obama's few supporters and many detractors foretell.

WORKS CITED

Alexander, Michelle. 2012. *The New Jim Crow: Mass Incarceration in the Age of Colorblindness*. New York: The New Press.

Appelbaum, Binyamin. 2009. "Obama Defends Financial Overhaul." *Washington Post*, June 18.

Atkins, Kimberly. 2011. "U.S. DOJ Backs Retroactive Reduction of Crack Sentences." *Lawyers Weekly USA*, June 7.

Baker, Peter. 2009. "Court Choice Pushes Issue of 'Identity Politics' Back to Forefront." *New York Times*, May 31.

Barnes, Robert. 2012a. "Justices Weigh Cocaine Sentencing Law." *Washington Post*, April 18.

Barnes, Robert. 2012b. "Same-Sex Marriage Headed to High Court." *Washington Post*, June 6.

Bellah, Robert N. 1967. "Civil Religion in America." *Journal of the American Academy of Arts and Sciences* 96: 1–21.

Benhabib, Seyla. 2009. "Claiming Rights across Borders: International Human Rights and Democratic Sovereignty." *American Political Science Review* 103: 691–704.

Bottoms, A. 1995. "The Philosophy and Politics of Punishment and Sentencing." Iin *The Politics of Sentencing Reform*, ed. C. Clarkson and R. Morgan. Oxford: Clarendon Press, 40.

Bradley, Gerard V. 2012. "The Audacity of Faith." *Public Discourse*, May 18.

Braithwaite, John, and Philippe Pettit. 1990. *Not Just Deserts: A Republican Theory of Criminal Justice*. Oxford: Oxford University Press, 35.

Brooks, David. 2007. "Obama, Gospel and Verse." *New York Times*, April 26.

Buchanan, Pat. 2009. "A Quota Queen for the Court." *Creators Syndicate*, June 1.

Burke, John R. 2009. "The Contemporary Presidency: The Obama Presidential Transition, an Early Assessment." *Presidential Studies Quarterly* 39(3): 574–604.

Burwell v. Hobby Lobby Stores, Inc. 2014. 134 S.Ct. 2751.

Butler, Stuart M. 1990. "Assuring Affordable Health Care for All Americans." *Journal of Health Care for the Poor and Underserved* 1(1): 63–73.

Chambers, Nisbet, and Walter Dean Burnham, eds. 1975. *The American Party Systems: Stages of Political Development*. New York: Oxford University Press.

Christian Science Monitor. 2012. "Obama and the Contraception Mandate." May 23.

Clark, Peter, Kevin Capuzzi, and Cameron Fick. 2011. "Medical Marijuana: Medical Necessity versus Political Agenda." *Medical Science Monitor* 17: 249–61.

Clemmitt, Marcia. 2010. "Teen Pregnancy: Does Comprehensive Sex-Education Reduce Pregnancies?" *CQ Researcher* 20, no. 12 (March 26).

Cohen, Lizabeth. 2003. *A Consumers' Republic: The Politics of Mass Consumption in Postwar America*. New York: Vintage.

Crabtree, Susan. 2012. "Catholics' Mandate Suit Draws Dividing Line for Obama." *Washington Times*, May 28.

Davidson, Amy. 2012. "The War on Nuns: Two Women Go to Rome." *New Yorker*, June 1.

Dionne, E. J., Jr. 2012. "A Catholic Spring?" *Washington Post*, May 24.

Dorsey v. United States. 2012. 132 S.Ct. 2321.

Dzur, Albert W. 2010. "The Myth of Penal Populism: Democracy, Citizen Participation, and American Hyperincarceration." *Journal of Speculative Philosophy* 24: 355–59.

eHealth. 2010. "Rejuvenating US Healthcare System—President Obama Creates History." April 1, http://ehealth.eletsonline.com/2010/04/11385/.

Eilperin, Juliet. 2015. "Obama Has Vastly Changed the Face of the Federal Bureaucracy." *Washington Post*, September 20.

el-Khoury, Laura J. 2009. "Racial Profiling as Dressage: A Social Control Regime!" *African Identities* 7: 64.

Endsjø, Dag Ølstein. 2011. *Sex and Religion: Teachings and Taboos in the History of World Faiths*. Chicago: University of Chicago Press.

Failinger, Marie A. 2012. "Finding a Voice of Challenge: The State Responds to Religious Women and Their Communities." *University of Southern California Review of Law and Social Justice* 21: 137.

Ferrara, Peter. 2009. "Repeal Health Care Fascism." *American Spectator*, February 25. http://spectator.org/archives/2009/02/25/repeal-health-care-fascism/.

Fish, Stanley. 2009. "Barack Obama's Prose Style." *New York Times*, January 22.

Frank, D. A. 2004. "Arguing with God, Talmudic Discourse, and the Jewish Countermodel: Implications for the Study of Argumentation." *Argumentation and Advocacy* 41: 71–86.

Frank, D. A. 2011. "Obama's Rhetorical Signature: Cosmopolitan Civil Religion in the Presidential Inaugural Address, January 20, 2009." *Rhetoric & Public Affairs* 14: 605–30.

Gais, Thomas L. 2010. "Federalism during the Obama Administration." Rockefeller Institute of Government, presented at 27th Annual Conference of the National Federation of Municipal Analysts, Santa Ana Pueblo, NM, May 7. www.rockinst.org/pdf/federalism/2010-05-07-federalism_during_obama_administration.pdf.

Garland, David. 2001. *The Culture of Control: Crime and Social Order in Contemporary Society*. Chicago: University of Chicago.

Gerson, Michael. 2007. "The Gospel of Obama." *Washington Post*, June 29.

Gerstel, Naomi. 2011. "Rethinking Families and Community: The Color, Class, and Centrality of Extended Kin Ties." *Sociological Forum* 26: 1–20.

Gillman, Todd J. 2009. "It's No Longer a 'War' on Drugs, So to Speak." *Dallas Morning News*, March 16.

Goldhill, David. 2009. "How American Health Care Killed My Father." *The Atlantic*, September: 38, 40.

Goodstein, Laurie. 2007. "Faith Has Role in Politics, Obama Tells Church." *New York Times*, June 24.

Gorski, Philip S. 2011. "Barack Obama and Civil Religion." In *Rethinking Obama*, ed. Julian Go, *Political Power and Social Theory*, no. 22. Bingley, UK: Emerald Group, 179–214.

Grunwald, Michael. 2011. "The Stimulus Turns Two: How Obama Quietly Changed Washington." *Time*, February 17.

Gutterman, David S. 2001. "Presidential Testimony: Listening to the Heart of George W. Bush." Johns Hopkins University Press, *Theory & Event* 5(2).

Henneberger, Melinda. 2012. "Is Catholic Church Taking on Obama?" *Washington Post*, June 8.

Himmelstein, David U., Deborah Thorne, Elizabeth Warren, and Steffie Woolhandler. 2009. "Medical Bankruptcy in the United States, 2007: Results of a National Study." *American Journal of Medicine* 122:8 (August), 741–46.

Hollinger, David A. 1995. *Postethnic America—Beyond Multiculturalism*. New York: Basic Books.

Hosanna-Tabor Evangelical Lutheran Church and School v. Equal Employment Opportunity Commission. 2012. 143 S.Ct. 694.

Huffington Post. 2011. "Obama on Gay Marriage Position: 'I'm Still Working on It.'" October 3.

Human Rights Campaign. 2015. Obama Administration Policy Advancements on behalf of LGBT Americans. www.hrc.org/resources/obama-administration-policy-legislative-and-other-advancements-on-behalf-of.

Katel, Peter. 2009. "Legalizing Marijuana: Should Pot Be Treated Like Alcohol and Taxed?" *CQ Researcher* 19, no. 22, June 12.

Kepel, Gilles. 1993. *The Revenge of God: The Resurgence of Islam, Christianity, and Judaism in the Modern World*. University Park, PA: Penn State University Press.

Klein, Ezra. 2012. "Unpopular Mandate." *New Yorker*, June 25.

Landler, Mark. 2011. "Obama Still Lets Surrogates Take the Lead as Gay Rights Momentum Builds." *New York Times*, December 31.

Layton, Lyndsey. 2015. "Obama Signs New K–12 Education Law That Ends No Child Left Behind." *Washington Post*, December 10.

Lincoln, Bruce. 2004. "Bush's God Talk." *The Christian Century*, October 5, 22–29. www.religion-online.org/showarticle.asp?title=3135.

Lobel, Orly. 2004. "The Renew Deal: The Fall of Regulation and the Rise of Governance in Contemporary Legal Thought." *Minnesota Law Review*, vol. 89, November; San Diego Legal Studies Paper No. 07-27.

Lobel, Orly. 2007. "The Paradox of Extralegal Activism: Critical Legal Consciousness and Transformative Politics." *Harvard Law Review* 120(4): 937–88.

Los Angeles Times. 2012. "For Contraceptives, a Catholic Exception?" May 30.

Lowi, Theodore J. 1964. "American Business, Public Policy, Case-Studies, and Political Theory." *World Politics* 16(4): 677–715.

Markon, Jerry, and Sandhya Somashekhar. 2011. "In Gay Rights Victory, Obama Administration Won't Defend Defense of Marriage Act." *Washington Post*, February 23.

Massachusetts v. U.S. Dept. of Health and Human Services. 2010. F.3d 1. *McDonald v. Chicago*. 2010. 561 U.S. 742.

Nano, Stephanie. 2011. "Number of Prescription Drug Deaths Has Tripled." *Washington Post*, November 2.

National Federation of Independent Business v. Sebelius. 2012. 132 S.Ct. 2566.

National Review. 1996. "The War on Drugs Is Lost." February 12. www.nationalreview.com/article/383913/war-drugs-lost-nro-staff.

New York Times. 2012a. "Abiding by the Fair Sentencing Act." April 18.

New York Times. 2012b. "The Phony Regulation Debate." May 27.

New Zealand Herald. 2012. "Catholics Sue Obama over Birth Control Mandate." May 22.

Norton, Anne. 2013. *On the Muslim Question*. Princeton, NJ: Princeton University Press.

Obama, Barack. 2007a. "A Politics of Conscience." Speech delivered at the United Church of Christ General Synod, Hartford, CT, June 23, 2007. www.ucc.org/news/significant-speeches/a-politics-of-conscience.html.

Obama, Barack. 2007b. "The Fiery Urgency of Now." Speech delivered November 10, 2007, at Des Moines, IA, Jefferson-Jackson Dinner. www.discoverthenetworks.org/viewSubCategory.asp?id=1642.

Obama, Barack. 2009. Interview with CBS News, July 16. www.cbsnews.com/news/my-interview-with-president-obama/.

Obama, Barack. 2011a. Remarks at the Human Rights Campaign's Annual National Dinner, October 1. www.whitehouse.gov/the-press-office/2011/10/01/remarks-president-human-rights-campaigns-annual-national-dinner.

Obama, Barack. 2011b. Remarks by the President on the Economy in Osawatomie, Kansas, December 6. www.whitehouse.gov/the-press-office/2011/12/06/remarks-president-economy-osawatomie-kansas.

Obergefell v. Hodges. 2015. 135 S.Ct. 2071.

O'Brien, Ruth. 2013. *Out of Many, One: Obama & the Third American Political Tradition*. Chicago: University of Chicago Press.

Parlow, Matthew J. 2008. "Civic Republicanism, Public Choice Theory, and Neighborhood Councils: A New Model for Civic Engagement." *University of Colorado Law Review* 79: 137.

Pear, Robert. 2010. "Gay Workers Will Get Time to Care for Partner's Sick Child." *New York Times*, June 22.

Pew Research Center. 2009. "Obama's Favorite Theologian? A Short Course on Reinhold Niebuhr." Pew Forum on Religion & Public Life, June 26. http://pewresearch.org/pubs/1268/reinhold-niehbuhr-obama-favorite-theologians.

Robinson, Marilynne. 2015. Interview with Barack Obama, *New York Review of Books*, November 5.

Savage, David G. 2012. "Key Part of Marriage Act Ruled Invalid." *Los Angeles Times*, June 1.

Schacter, Jane S. 2010. "The Early Obama Administration: Capacity and Context: LGBTQ Rights and the Obama Administration's First Year." *Stanford Journal of Civil Rights & Civil Liberties* 6: 147.

Scherer, Nancy. 2011. "Diversifying the Federal Bench: Is Universal Legitimacy for the U.S. Justice System Possible?" *Northwestern University Law Review* 105: 590.

Scott, Joan Wallach. 2007. *The Politics of the Veil*. Princeton, NJ: Princeton University Press.

Sheridan, Mary Beth. 2009. "On Mexico Trip, Clinton Criticizes U.S. Drug Policy; She Says Her Country Shares Blame for Violence." *Washington Post*, March 26.

Sklar, Martin J. 1988. *The Corporate Reconstruction of American Capitalism, 1890–1916: The Market, the Law, and Politics*. Cambridge: Cambridge University Press.

Skocpol, Theda, and Lawrence R. Jacobs. 2010. *Reaching for a New Deal: Ambitious Governance, Economic Meltdown, and Polarized Politics in Obama's First Two Years*. New York: Russell Sage Foundation.

Skowronek, Stephen. 1997. *The Politics Presidents Make: Leadership from John Adams to Bill Clinton*. Boston: Belknap Press.

Slessarev, Helene. 1997. *Betrayal of the Urban Poor*. Philadelphia: Temple University Press.

Somashekhar, Sandhya, and Peyton Craighill. 2011. "Slim Majority Back Gay Marriage, Post ABC Poll Says." *Washington Post*, March 18.

Stavrou, Nikolaos A. 2009. "The Obama Presidency in Philosophical and Historical Context." *Mediterranean Quarterly* 20(4): 1–9.

Sugrue, Thomas J. 2010. *Not Even Past: Barack Obama and the Burden of Race*. Princeton, NJ: Princeton University Press.

Tobias, Carl. 2010. "Diversity and the Federal Bench." *Washington University Law Review* 87(5): 1197–1211.

Toobin, Jeffrey. 2009. "Bench Press." *New Yorker*, September 21.

United States v. Windsor. 2013. 133 S.Ct. 2675.

US Department of the Treasury. 2009. "Financial Regulatory Reform—a New Foundation: Rebuilding Financial Supervision and Regulation." www.treasury.gov/initiatives/Documents/FinalReport_web.pdf.

Wallsten, Peter, and Scott Wilson. 2012. "Obama Endorses Gay Marriage, Says Same-Sex Couples Should Have Right to Wed." *Washington Post*, May 9.

Warren, Elizabeth. 2007. "Unsafe at Any Rate: If It's Good Enough for Microwaves, It's Good Enough for Mortgages: Why We Need a Financial Product Safety Commission." *Democracy: A Journal of Ideas*. December 8.

Washington Times. 2010. "Obama's War on the Traditional Family; Radical Groups Dictate Administration." July 1.

Watson, Lori. 2007. "Constituting Politics: Power, Reciprocity, and Identity." *Hypatia* 22(4): 96–112.

Weyl, Walter E. 1912. *The New Democracy: An Essay on Certain Political and Economic Tendencies in the United States*. New York: Harper & Row, reprinted 1964.

Whitman, James Q. 2007. "Consumerism versus Producerism: A Study in Comparative Law." *Yale Law Journal* 117: 340–406.

Wolffe, Richard. 2010. *Revival: The Struggle for Survival Inside the Obama White House*. New York: Crown.

8

THE LIMITS OF GOVERNMENTAL ACCOMPLISHMENT

Obama's Domestic Policies

Andrew E. Busch, Claremont McKenna College

Barack Obama entered the presidency with hefty domestic policy goals. Those goals could be summarized in the following way: Restore activist government, prove that it works, and—most ambitious—ultimately transform America along social-democratic lines. "We are a few days away from fundamentally transforming the United States of America," Obama proclaimed to a campaign crowd in November 2008, and in retrospect it was clear that he was serious. When, early in the campaign for the Democratic nomination, Obama expressed some admiration for Ronald Reagan, less astute Democrats condemned him. He was not, however, praising Reagan's policies or philosophy but declaring his intention to be the Reagan of the left.

Many other Americans, from ordinary voters to exalted pundits, had other domestic goals for him, goals that they sketched onto the largely blank slate that he supplied. One was the hope cherished by many that Obama would serve as a racial bridge builder. Another, that he would serve as a partisan bridge builder, in keeping with his prime-time declaration at the 2004 Democratic National Convention that "there's not a liberal America and a conservative America—there's the United States of America."

From the very beginning of his presidency, his domestic policy goals were in tension with both the projected goals of others and certain objective realities. In areas including economic policy, health care, education, crime, and social issues, Obama's domestic policy was consistent with his activist liberal approach, but it also consistently fell short of the promised outcomes. Consequently, it is far from clear that his presidency will be transformational rather than transitional.

ECONOMIC POLICY

Even Barack Obama's detractors must acknowledge that he inherited a terrible economic situation. The housing bubble had burst, the financial system had, it seemed, narrowly avoided collapse in the fall of 2008, GDP was shrinking, and companies and governments were shedding millions of jobs. From the beginning, Obama's response was built around a major expansion of federal power. The key elements of the Obama economic policy were the American Recovery and Reinvestment Act of 2009 (the "stimulus" package), the Dodd-Frank financial regulation act, and increased overall levels of domestic spending, redistributionism, and regulation.

Stimulus Package

Within weeks of Obama's inauguration, the Democratic Congress passed and the president signed his first legislative priority, an unprecedented $787 billion stimulus package that sought to provide a Keynesian surge in consumer demand. Funds were divided between tax rebates, transportation projects, aid to state and local governments, a variety of welfare programs, and green-energy subsidies. Obama set the tone for the rest of his presidency when he worked exclusively with Democratic leaders to fashion the bill and responded to Republican concerns by telling House Republican Whip Eric Cantor, "Elections have consequences . . . and Eric, I won" (Ryan, Cantor, and McCarthy 2010, 52).

The president contended that funds were going to "shovel-ready" public works projects around the country, and the incoming chair of the Council of Economic Advisors estimated that the unemployment rate one year later would be nearly 2 percentage points lower if the package passed than if it did not. In actuality, unemployment by mid-2010 was a full percentage point higher than she had estimated it would be if the bill *did not* pass (Adams 2011). Obama was forced to concede that "it turns out there is no such thing as 'shovel-ready' projects," and the administration was reduced to claiming that the stimulus had created *or saved* three million jobs, a slippery standard that could hardly be disproved. It was also a figure that was never indicative of a count of actual jobs, but was the result of computer modeling based on particular (optimistic) assumptions (Renshon 2012, 241–43). Even if true, critics noted that each job would have cost the federal government over $260,000. An alternative analysis by economists Timothy Conley and Bill Dupor estimated that the ARRA created or saved between 156,000 and 563,000 public-sector jobs, but may have even reduced net private-sector jobs by redirecting resources, not implausible given actual rates of joblessness (Conley and Dupor 2013).

As doubts about the economic benefits of the stimulus grew, more attention was paid to the degree to which the program disproportionately benefited Democratic-leaning interest groups. On balance, by late 2010 68 percent of respondents told a *Washington Post* survey that they believed most stimulus funds were wasted (*Washington Post*/ABC News Poll 2010). By 2012 President Obama hardly mentioned the stimulus on the campaign trail.

Dodd-Frank

The proximate cause of the financial crisis and recession was the collapse of the housing bubble of the early 2000s. Economists are still debating the chain of cause-and-effect, though plausible culprits include Federal Reserve policies that maintained very low interest rates for too long, federal subsidies that undergirded two-thirds of the subprime loans in America through Fannie Mae and Freddie Mac, federal pressure on lenders to loosen lending practices for low-income borrowers, irresponsible financial institutions, and (though hardly anyone in politics dared say it) the borrowers themselves, who often tried to buy houses they could not really afford (Wallison 2011).

In theory, the crisis might have been avoided with three rules: that home loan borrowers had to verify their incomes, that borrowers had to make a significant down payment, and that lenders had to keep a significant portion of each loan they made so they shared the risk. Instead, the Obama administration responded by providing billions of dollars of mortgage relief to homeowners facing foreclosure (angering many homeowners who had not overextended themselves); endorsing and prolonging the Fed's loose monetary policy; stifling any serious reform of Fannie Mae, Freddie Mac, or the Community Reinvestment Act; and supporting a 2,300-page-long financial regulation bill whose two prime sponsors (Sen. Chris Dodd, D-Conn. and Rep. Barney Frank, D-Mass.) were deeply implicated in the original fiasco. (Dodd was entangled in a financial relationship with Angelo Mozilo, the disgraced head of Countrywide Mortgage, while Frank had publicly expressed a willingness to "roll the dice a little bit more" with loose borrowing requirements.)

The Dodd-Frank Act, or Wall Street Reform and Consumer Protection Act, established three new regulatory agencies, altered five more, and required 243 rules, sixty-seven studies, and twenty-two periodic reports in pursuit of greater financial stability. By one estimate, it has spawned more regulations than all other laws passed during the Obama administration combined (McLaughlin and Sherous 2015). To implement these regulations, J.P. Morgan Chase alone had to hire ten thousand additional compliance officers in 2013–2014, at a time when it was cutting its overall payroll by five thousand (Wallison 2014). Not least, Dodd-Frank's Consumer Financial Protection Bureau was deliberately designed to evade democratic accountability, endowed with a budget that was untouchable by Congress and rule-making authority that could not be easily checked by Congress or the courts.

Yet more than five years after its passage on another near-party-line vote (only three Republicans voted for it in the Senate, and none in the House), many analysts reported that Dodd-Frank had not established conditions that made a repeat of the 2008 financial collapse less likely—because most of its provisions had little to do with the actual causes of the crisis. Like the stimulus, Dodd-Frank was largely an exercise in using a genuine crisis as an opportunity to do unrelated things that liberals had long wanted to do anyway. The act may also have slowed the economic recovery by making credit flows more difficult, and certainly led to the consolidation of the banking industry, as an average of one community bank or credit union was closing per day by 2015 (Hensaerling 2015). Critics have reason to complain that Dodd-Frank is "taking the power to allocate capital—the lifeblood of the U.S. economy—away from the free market and delivering it to political actors in Washington" (Hensaerling 2015).

Overall Spending and Regulation

In keeping with the spirit of the ARRA, federal spending grew from \$2.98 trillion in fiscal year 2008 to \$3.60 trillion in 2011, an inflation-adjusted increase of 17 percent in just three years. Both discretionary domestic spending and entitlement spending grew nearly twice as fast as defense from 2008 to 2011 (Federal Budget 2016). As a proportion of the nation's economy, federal spending increased from 20.2 percent of GDP in 2008 to 24.4 percent just a year later, and it was still 23.4 percent in 2011. The growth of the deficit was even more alarming, rising from 1.1 percent of GDP in 2007 to 3.1 percent in 2008 to 9.8 percent in 2009. When it slipped back to 8.5 percent of GDP in 2011, it was still almost half again higher than at any time since World War II (Federal Budget 2016). As a result, the national debt ballooned from \$10 trillion in 2008 to nearly \$18 trillion in 2014.

The seemingly unconstrained spending, deficit, debt, and domestic ambition of the Obama agenda nurtured a political backlash—already sparked in the waning days of the Bush administration by passage of the Troubled Assets Relief Program (TARP)—that took the form of the Tea Party movement. When the backlash led to the loss of sixty-three Democratic House seats in the 2010 midterm election, Republicans gained the House majority, which they held for the remainder of the Obama presidency. The two forces—Obama, unchastened and still committed to a program of activist government and Keynesian economics, and House Republicans, emboldened and backed by a vigorous new movement in no mood for compromise—collided frequently over the next few years. The Republicans forced numerous concessions from Obama, most importantly an agreement in 2011 to match an increase in the debt limit with an equal amount of spending reduction, with budget caps enforced by sequestration. This countervailing force led to a significantly different fiscal policy. Spending stabilized and then fell back from its 2011 peak, and the deficit fell to 2.8 percent of GDP in 2014. Obama and his allies in the media (such as economist Paul Krugman) even complained that "austerity" had taken hold—and in comparison with the open spigot of 2009–2011, it had. However, the overall spending increase since 2008 was mostly locked into place, as was an \$8 trillion increase in the national debt, permanent consequences of a temporary crisis. That the concessions the Republicans wrung from Obama were too little rather than too great was given credence by Standard & Poor's, which downgraded the US credit rating for the first time ever after it judged that the 2011 budget fight had not made enough of a dent in the nation's dismal fiscal picture.

That fight highlighted two consistent and unfortunate features of Obama's fiscal approach throughout his presidency. He was pulled only with great reluctance into any effort to address the short-term deficit through spending restraint. And he steadfastly declined to exert any real leadership to address the looming entitlement crisis for the long term—such as Social Security's $10.6 trillion unfunded liability over the next seventy-five years—a pattern he laid down early in his presidency when he appointed the Simpson-Bowles Commission to recommend bipartisan solutions to the nation's deficit and debt crises, then made no serious effort to salvage its proposals when it actually did so. Altogether, Obama consistently treated the willingness of the House of Representatives to exercise its constitutional power of the purse as the equivalent of domestic terrorism, though it was Obama himself who broke a bipartisan precedent in late 2015 by holding the annual defense authorization hostage to force Congress to ease budget caps on domestic spending.

If the ARRA foreshadowed the overall trend of federal spending under Obama, Dodd-Frank exemplified the overall trend in regard to regulation. In total, the Obama administration created 22 percent more economically significant rules from 2009 to 2014 than had been initiated in the previous six years. This was a result of (among other things) Dodd-Frank itself, the Patient Protection and Affordable Care Act, and environmental initiatives aimed to make production and consumption of fossil fuels more expensive (Carey 2015, 11–12). For example, in 2009 Obama backed, and the House approved, a "cap-and-trade" bill that would have given the federal government the power to control carbon usage throughout the economy, but the Senate demurred. Failing to achieve the objective through the legislative process, Obama turned to the Environmental Protection Agency to propose regulations that critics said would destroy the coal industry. He delayed construction of the Keystone XL oil pipeline from Canada for six years before finally killing it in 2015, and substantially cut oil and natural gas drilling permits both offshore and on federal land (FactCheck.org 2012).

The Obama administration also proposed a bevy of new labor regulations that would negatively impact jobs in the private sector, especially in small business. These included a $10.10 minimum wage, which the Congressional Budget Office estimated could cost half a million jobs; new rules expanding the number of people eligible for overtime compensation; edicts on indirect ownership and contracting that could make unviable the entire franchise model of small-business ownership; and direct attacks on the "gig economy" (such as Uber) that promised growth outside the confines of existing bureaucratic control (Caldiera 2015, CBO 2014, CBO 2015). By one estimate, regulations imposed by the Obama administration in 2014 alone carried a cost of $200 billion per year (Newman 2014). Of untold future cost would be the momentous decision by Obama's Federal Communications Commission to place the Internet under increased federal regulation.

Redistributionism

Obama's economic policy was ultimately encapsulated in a rhetoric emphasizing redistribution over growth, with policies to match. On the campaign trail in 2008, Obama famously told "Joe the Plumber" that "when you spread the wealth around, it's good for everybody." Throughout his presidency Obama showed little appreciation of the role of entrepreneurs in the American economy, instead disparaging their contributions by saying, "If you've got a business—you didn't build that. Somebody else made that happen." His primary objective in tax policy was not to untangle the complexity of the US tax code, which many economists believe hampers economic growth, nor to make the US economy more competitive by lowering the corporate tax rate, which is now among the highest in the industrial world. It was to rescind the 2001 tax cuts for joint earners making above $250,000 in the name of fairness. The Republican House forced him to compromise shortly after his reelection; the tax increase began at $450,000, while the rest of the 2001 tax cuts were made permanent. At the same time, Social Security Disability and Food Stamps (now called SNAP) exploded in cost, and Obama used waivers to free states from the strict work requirements of the 1996 welfare reform.

Overall, in a global index of economic freedom, the United States fell from sixth in the world in 2008 to sixteenth in 2015 (Bedard 2015). The poor results of this return to big-government Keynesianism were not surprising to anyone who had noticed the failure of such policies to reignite economic growth in 1930s America or 1990s Japan, or the theoretical limitations of Keynesianism exposed by the stagflation of the 1970s. On the positive side of the ledger, the recession ended in mid-2009, the stock market rebounded (largely due to near–0 percent interest rates that gave investors few options), and unemployment rates gradually drifted lower after peaking in 2010. A cheap-energy boom was a bright spot in the American economy.

But how should we assess Obama's part in recovery? Every recession in US history has eventually ended, including recessions and depressions in the 1800s and early 1900s when federal economic intervention was minimal or nonexistent. Even if government intervention was important to stabilization, the decisive intervention may have come before Obama was elected, in the form of the TARP program. And the energy boom was achieved in spite of Obama's policies rather than because of them. Consequently, it is arguably more relevant to assess the quality of the recovery under Obama:

- The economic recovery that started in 2009 was by far the weakest recovery since World War II. Economic growth averaged around 2 percent a year, far below the postwar norm of 3.5 to 4 percent.
- Job growth lagged far behind that of the normal recovery as well. The reduction in unemployment rates was the result of modest job creation combined with a decline in the labor force participation rate from 65.7 percent in January 2009 to 62.4 percent in October 2015, the lowest labor participation rate since 1977 (US Labor Department 2015). Some economists noted that rates of "involuntary" part-time work were historically high for a recovery and estimated that the "real" unemployment rate—those who were officially counted as unemployed plus those who wanted a job but had given up looking—may have been as much as twice the official figure (10 percent rather than 5 percent in October 2015) (Moore 2015a). By one calculation, the economy through mid-2015 created twelve million fewer jobs under Obama than the average postwar recovery would have to that point (Gramm 2015).
- Incomes stagnated for the average American. Real median household income was 8 percent lower in 2013 than it had been in 2007, the year before the financial crisis. Most of that decline occurred after the recession ended in mid-2009, and through 2013 there had been not even a partial recovery of incomes (US Census Bureau 2014). Had the Obama recovery matched the average postwar re-

covery, middle-income families would have been nearly $12,000 a year better off than they actually were by mid-2015 (Gramm 2015).

- In the first three years of the recovery, despite Obama's egalitarian rhetoric, 95 percent of economic gains were captured by the top 1 percent of earners (O'Brien 2014). Low-income workers experienced the biggest drop in pay from 2009 to 2015 (Schwartz 2015), while the poverty rate in 2013 was still 14.5 percent, higher than the 14.3 percent of Obama's first year in office (US Census Bureau 2014, Table B-1). Obama's redistributionism not only proved incompatible with growth, it did not even lead to increased equality.

The contrast between the Obama recovery and the Reagan recovery, built on very different limited-government principles, is instructive. On almost every measure—not just economic growth and job creation but middle-class incomes and poverty—Reagan's economy beat Obama's handily. For his part, Bill Clinton, who reformed welfare, balanced the budget, and declared "the era of big government is over" in conjunction with the Republican Congress of that time, also led an economy that outshone Obama's. By the sixth year in each recovery, the US economy had grown by more than 30 percent under Reagan, more than 20 percent under Clinton, nearly 20 percent under George W. Bush—and just a bit more than 10 percent under Obama (Davidson 2015).

HEALTH CARE

Although a focus on economic policy was forced on Obama by circumstance, it was in the area of health care that he hoped to build his greatest domestic policy legacy. From the beginning Obama made clear his affinity for centralizing big-government solutions. To be sure, Obama did not attempt to drive immediately to the fullest degree of government control, a "single-payer" system in which government was the sole insurer, though his comments indicated that he saw his own plan as a step on the road to single payer. Obama relented when the Senate removed the public option—in which a government insurance plan would compete with private insurance—but the bill that ultimately passed included about $1 trillion in taxes and spending over the following decade, as well as myriad federal boards, regulations, and programs. Medicaid, the federal program for the poor, was to be expanded significantly to cover many in the middle class; health-care exchanges were to be set up by states or the federal government with subsidies available for many applicants; all Americans were required by law to purchase health insurance (the "individual mandate"); all businesses with fifty or more full-time employees (those who worked thirty hours a week or more) were required to supply insurance to them; federal rules would dictate what services insurance policies must cover; and an Independent Payments Advisory Board was established to define what treatments were acceptable in what circumstances, perhaps as a step toward imposing health rationing. All of this was to be paid for by cutbacks in Medicare spending for the elderly, largely achieved in the private-sector-oriented Medicare Advantage program, taxes on high-end insurance policies and on medical devices, a Medicare tax surcharge on upper-income taxpayers, and reduced flexible-spending accounts. An enormous amount of power would be placed in the hands of the Internal Revenue Service and the Department of Health and Human Services to craft the hundreds of regulations that would be necessary to effectuate the law. Taking into account the volume and character of the regulations, taxes, and mandates of the ACA, it is not unreasonable to conclude that it was the most authoritarian legislation passed by Congress since the National Industrial Recovery Act of 1933.

From the summer of 2009 on, a plurality or majority of Americans said they disapproved of Obama's health-care reform package (though some minor provisions had majority support), and it only passed Congress by the barest of margins, propelled by a stream of unsavory congressional deal making and what can only be called public deception. Perhaps the biggest deception was uttered by Obama when he repeatedly assured Americans that "If you like your insurance, you can keep it." (PolitiFact later declared this statement "Lie of the Year" in 2013.) Supporters bragged that the trillion-dollar entitlement program would reduce the federal deficit in the next ten years, but they seldom mentioned that this claim was based on a calculation that included ten years of revenue but only six years of spending. The president promised a small but pivotal band of pro-life Democrats that the bill would not promote abortion. And so on. Later, Jonathan Gruber, the MIT professor who helped design the Affordable Care Act, admitted that the administration had relied on taking advantage of "the stupidity of the American voter." In actuality, Obama ultimately secured passage not by persuading the public—which remained unpersuaded despite an estimated fifty-four presidential speeches on the subject (Knoller 2010)—but by winning the support of the national interest groups representing hospitals, insurance companies, and the pharmaceutical industry with the promise of thirty million new involuntary customers delivered by the individual mandate.

During the battle over the Affordable Care Act, critics argued that Americans would not really be able to keep their insurance if they liked it, that premiums would be driven up, that insurance choices would be diminished, that the federal deficit would balloon, that the measure would cost jobs, that abortion would be subsidized, and that, in general, the health-care system would be thrown into disarray. They also complained that Americans would be made even more dangerously dependent on the largesse of the federal government and that government itself would break loose from any remaining sense of constitutional limits. By 2015 it could be said that the critics, though not entirely vindicated, had by far the better of the argument.

This did not become clear all at once, largely because the law turned out to be so poorly crafted or so practically problematic that the president had to authorize dozens of delays or revisions, so that even in late 2015 not all of its provisions had been fully implemented. Nevertheless, Americans formed a judgment framed by the disastrous initial rollout of the exchanges in October 2013, which served as a powerful symbol of the gap between Obamacare's promises and results.

The facts that they had to weigh included the following:

- In October 2015 the administration estimated that enrollment in Obamacare policies in 2016 would be less than half what the Congressional Budget Office had predicted just the previous March, with only one in seven people eligible for Obamacare—a total of ten million—actually signing up (McCoughey 2015). Moreover, many of those who signed up to an Obamacare exchange, including 90 percent in 2013, already had other coverage (Pipes 2015).
- Contrary to the president's core promise, approximately five million people lost their insurance in 2013 because it did not meet Obamacare requirements. Facing a backlash, Obama signed another ad hoc executive order providing a short-term fix, but millions more will be forced off in future years.

- Rather than saving the average family $2,500 as Obama had promised in 2008, his program cost many families a great deal. The National Bureau of Economic Research reported in 2014 that insurance rates in the individual market were 24.4 percent higher than they would have been without Obamacare, and insurers asked for alarmingly large rate increases in 2015 (Pipes 2015, Demko 2015, McArdle 2015).
- The dynamic created by Obamacare led directly to a wave of consolidation among insurance companies, and in 2015 the nation's largest insurer, United Health, indicated it was easing out of Obamacare exchanges due to financial unsustainability. These developments reduced consumer choice and will likely lead to even higher prices in years to come.
- As of mid-2015 nearly half of the seventeen state health exchanges were struggling financially, while all but one of the twenty-three experimental health "cooperatives" favored by many liberals as the next best thing to the public option were operating at a financial loss (Sun and Chokshi 2015, Turner and Miller 2015). By the end of the year, twelve cooperatives had closed altogether, leaving hundreds of thousands of people looking for new insurance (Owens 2015).
- In a Physicians Foundation 2014 survey of twenty thousand American doctors, fully half judged that Obamacare deserved a grade of "D" or "F," while only a quarter said "A" or "B." Obamacare, the strong plurality argued, was harming patients by disrupting the doctor-patient relationship (Singer 2014). In other surveys, around 60 percent of doctors said they intended to retire early, finding the new health-care system not at all to their liking (Pipes 2015).
- Estimates from the Congressional Budget Office indicated at best a mixed fiscal and economic picture for Obamacare. In mid-2015 the CBO estimated that full repeal of Obamacare would reduce the deficit by $109 billion over five years and would boost GDP by nearly a percentage point, though longer-term (and hence less certain) effects might increase the deficit after 2020 (CBO 2015). The federal government was not alone in its fiscal predicament. Those states that accepted Medicaid expansion were destined to face in-

creasing fiscal pressures as the federal government stops covering the full cost of the expansion in the near future.

- In anticipation of the onset of the employer mandate, large businesses around the country began cutting work of employees to below the magic number of thirty hours a week required to trigger the mandate, a process stalled only by the issuance of another presidential delay. Obamacare compliance costs posed a particular drain on small businesses, with an average annual cost of $15,000 (Rosenberg 2015).
- Despite the president's assurances, HHS regulations mandated that employers provide not only common contraceptives but products widely seen as abortifacients. In the *Burwell v. Hobby Lobby Stores* case in 2014, a majority on the Supreme Court ruled against the administration, holding that closely held companies whose owners have religious objections cannot be forced to violate their consciences in that way.
- In other Supreme Court cases, key provisions of the ACA barely survived judicial scrutiny, and then only as a sort of favor to the administration. In 2012 in *National Federation of Independent Business v. Sebelius*, the court upheld the individual mandate, but in doing so it rejected as a dangerously expansive reading of federal power the administration's own argument that Congress could use the Commerce Clause to compel Americans to engage in commerce; it substituted its own justification grounded in the power to tax. In *Burwell v. King*, the Supreme Court ruled in 2015 that the IRS could issue insurance subsidies to those in both state and federal exchanges despite the fact that the plain language of the ACA said that only those in state exchanges were eligible.

Altogether, by late 2015 there had been a modest (and significantly smaller than expected) net increase in the number of insured—but no one who opposed the ACA in 2010 argued that there would be *no* increase in the number of insured. The question was always what price would be paid by the 85 percent of the American people who were already insured and by the nation as a whole—in terms of the cost, availability, and choice of care, in terms of negative impact on jobs and wages, in terms of burden on the nation's budget and economy, and in terms of individual liberty and constitutional integrity. From 2010 through 2015, the majority of

Americans has consistently concluded in polls that those costs have not been worth it—a verdict reinforced by the voters in 2010 and 2014—and given the picture outlined above, it is not hard to see why.

EDUCATION

As in economic and health policy, Obama's drive in education has been for centralization, homogenization, and federal control. In higher education Obama has sought to fight tuition increases by increasing subsidies to students. However, there is good evidence that subsidies have themselves been a major contributor to rising college tuition, which may be one reason that four-year public university tuition experienced a 37 percent spike during the Obama years (Moore 2015b).

Another notable initiative in higher education involved a major intrusion into local college administration when a federal Department of Education official penned a "Dear Colleague" letter to colleges and universities indicating that their federal aid would be imperiled if they did not abandon the "clear and convincing evidence" standard in favor of a "preponderance of evidence" standard when adjudicating sex discrimination and sexual assault allegations. In other words, institutions of higher education were required by federal mandate to find the accused guilty—with expulsion or firing a possible consequence—even if only 50.1 percent of the evidence seemed to point that way. This change, which was imposed without the government's required comment and review period for new regulations (and was hence of debatable legality), was justified by reference to a widely contested claim that one in five college women were victims of sexual assault. The change in federal policy contributed to higher college costs as institutions hired more lawyers and Title IX specialists at six-figure salaries. (Vanderbilt University revealed that it spent $150 million, or 11 percent of its 2013–2014 budget, on total federal regulatory compliance [Moran 2015]). It also led to concerns that important procedural protections had been trampled in order to satisfy the ideological agenda of radical feminists, concerns reinforced by lawsuits from defendants around the country who alleged they had been railroaded. The backlash reached Harvard Law School, where twenty-eight faculty members signed a letter condemning the change as injurious to due process ("Rethink . . ." 2014).

Arguably the most dangerous trend in higher education came from the intersection of an intolerant political orthodoxy and the tender sensitivities of students who were increasingly likely to demand the creation of antiseptic learning environments free from controversy. From New England to Southern California, a wave of episodes demonstrated the fragility of freedom of speech and the power of a new complex of campus bullies, almost always abetted by compliant administrators (and sometimes taking advantage of the helpful tools offered by Education Department decrees). The president's philosophical soul mates were at the forefront of this development, and he showed no inclination to call them off. Indeed, there was evidence that his nationwide political organization was central to the movement (Sperry 2015).

At the K–12 level, Obama's Department of Education helped facilitate creation and promotion of the "Common Core" standards. While these standards were defended as the result of a voluntary process among state governors, the federal government played an important role in coordinating the governors and in using federal money and waivers of No Child Left Behind requirements as levers to encourage (or coerce) state adoption. One of the standard arguments made by advocates of federal involvement in K–12 education since 1965 was that, whatever else the federal government was doing, it was not trying to take over curricular decisions from states and local communities. Common Core threatened that longstanding barrier to centralized education. Moreover, the standards themselves, and much of the curriculum they engendered, quickly came under severe criticism from across the political spectrum for methodological or substantive flaws. Indeed, Common Core managed to perform the incredible feat of bringing together social conservatives, libertarians, and teachers unions, all of whom voiced their opposition. By 2015 four of the original forty-six states had rescinded their earlier decision to join the national movement, others threatened to, and Common Core's momentum (at least for the time being) was stalled.

At all levels the Obama administration showed, on balance, hostility to educational diversity and student choice. In higher education the administration launched a push against for-profit universities, a segment of American higher education that, whatever its shortcomings, was innovating, providing alternatives, and giving students a reprieve from stultifying politicization. Obama also worked to entirely replace private federally guaranteed student loans with direct government loans, even though more than a decade after the advent of government loans, families still preferred private loans 80 percent of the time (Spruiell 2009).

At lower levels the administration supported charter schools to a degree but fought against school vouchers in Louisiana, the District of Columbia, and elsewhere. The District's school system exemplifies the very definition of educational failure, spending more dollars per student than every state in America with very low outcomes of academic performance and student safety. Obama nevertheless sought to zero out appropriations for the DC voucher program, which would have consigned 1,400 children (most of whom are poor and 97 percent of whom are black or Hispanic) to a substandard education had House Speaker John Boehner not successfully insisted on preserving the funding.

CRIME

Barack Obama took office at a time when crime rates in the United States were at their lowest levels in fifty years. Obama could have quietly worked to reinforce law-enforcement strategies that had aggressively policed neighborhoods and kept thousands of hardened repeat offenders off the streets, making large swaths of urban America much safer. Instead, he focused on three ideologically driven objectives: gun control, reduced sentencing, and racially tinged criticism of the police.

The first focus was merely ineffective, as Congress would not budge on the administration's package of gun control measures in the wake of the Sandy Hook Elementary School shooting. Later, Obama would show more radical colors by praising Australia's mandatory gun buyback, an anti-constitutional idea even less likely to gain traction.

The second focus led to the release of approximately thirty thousand illegal alien felons a year in 2014 and 2015, including one every twelve days who went on to commit a murder (Hanson 2015). As the administration neared its end, it announced plans to release another forty thousand felons, including six thousand in 2015. Rhetorically, Obama was consistently critical of high rates of incarceration, lending his support to federal and state attempts to weaken sentencing laws, frequently based on exaggerated assertions about rates of incarceration of nonviolent drug offenders (MacDonald 2015).

The third focus may have been the most damaging. Obama's problematic record began in the summer of 2009 when his friend, black Harvard professor Louis Gates, was arrested during an altercation with a white policeman, and Obama declared the arresting officer had "acted stupidly." On at least two other critical occasions, Obama threw gasoline on racial fires that desperately needed a calming influence from the White House. In one case, black teenager Trayvon Martin was shot in Florida by neighborhood watch captain George Zimmerman, bringing commentary by Obama that Martin looked like his son would have looked if he had one. In another case, unarmed black teenager Michael Brown was shot in Ferguson, Missouri, by police officer Darren Wilson. Reports, later proven false, quickly spread that Brown had been shot, possibly in the back, while trying to surrender. To show support, Obama sent administration officials to Brown's funeral. However, the evidence ultimately exonerated both Zimmerman and Wilson.

In all of these instances, the cause of racial peace and lawfulness would have been well served by Obama reminding concerned communities to refrain from judgments until all the facts were known. Instead, Obama made bad situations worse. Indeed, he continued referencing "Ferguson" as an example of racist policing long after his own Justice Department had cleared Darren Wilson of wrongdoing. None of this is to say there were no genuinely troubling racial episodes during the Obama years. There were, and they would have provided sufficient opportunity for the president to take a moral stand for racial justice. Yet the president and his allies—which he has made clear include the radical Black Lives Matter movement—frequently seemed less interested in weighing the facts than in forcing every case into a simple and politically convenient narrative.

Whatever the chain of cause-and-effect, the outcome of this policy stew was disturbing. By late 2015 murder rates in Baltimore, New York City, Chicago, Milwaukee, New Orleans, Washington, DC, St. Louis, and at least two dozen other cities had exploded, a trend that threatened to take the United States back to the rampant crime of the 1970s. As usual, the victims were disproportionately poor minorities (Davey and Smith 2015). FBI Director James B. Comey ventured his considered opinion that officially nurtured hostility toward law enforcement (what some analysts called the "Ferguson Effect") had caused the police to become more cautious and less effective (Comey 2015). On this score, no one could blame Obama alone, as mayors such as Bill de Blasio of New York City and Stephanie Rawlings-Blake of Baltimore went out of their way to attack their own police forces. But no one could doubt that Obama helped set the tone nationally.

SOCIAL POLICY

Finally, Barack Obama's policies on social issues were immoderate, often disingenuous, and threatened to drive the country further apart. One may take as examples two particularly divisive issues: abortion and same-sex marriage. Unlike Bill Clinton, who promised to make abortion "safe, legal, and rare," Obama "adopted a more militant approach in which no abortion is beyond the pale" (McGurn 2015). Obama was consistently uninterested in bridging the social gap on this issue, even rhetorically, instead choosing to become inarguably the most pro-abortion president in American history.

On same-sex marriage, Obama ran in 2008 on a platform of opposition to gay marriage. According to his key campaign aide David Axelrod, it was all an act (Axelrod 2015). When running for reelection he changed his position, reflecting the growing support for gay marriage in his party as voiced by Vice President Joe Biden before the president himself switched positions. Here too Obama jettisoned Clinton's moderate approach and gave legal support to the ultimately successful court challenges that led a 5–4 majority on the Supreme Court to discover that the Constitution contained a right to gay marriage. In so doing, he endorsed the court short-circuiting the democratic process just as *Roe v. Wade* had done four decades before and on constitutional grounds that were no firmer. Supporters of the president's (true) position argued they were advancing marriage equality, but to others the judicial imposition of gay marriage served as the exclamation point on a five-decade-long project of judicially deconstructing the moral foundations of American society.

Leaving aside the merits of Obama's positions, on which there is no consensus, two things were obvious. First, Obama's policy was deeply polarizing—whether on abortion or pushing for a radical redefinition of the nation's most important social institution the moment there were five votes on the Supreme Court favoring it. Second, it became increasingly apparent that Obama's defense of abortion and same-sex marriage were hardly libertarian exercises in live-and-let-live, but were rather part of a movement intent on using social and governmental power to suppress alternative views by everyone from high-flying tech executives and television stars down to lowly bakers, wedding photographers, small-town pizzeria owners, and nuns.

Indeed, the administration's policies on social issues were frequently intertwined with a broader disrespect for freedom of religion and conscience. Obama's attempt to compel those morally opposed to abortion, ranging from large companies like Hobby Lobby to small Catholic charities like Little Sisters of the Poor, to provide abortifacients to their employees, was a policy denying freedom of conscience to both the employer and the pro-life employee who might want the opportunity to work for a company that reflects his or her values. His administration simultaneously aligned itself with the theory that a constitutional right to same-sex marriage could carry with it the right of the state to punish churches that do not accept the new order by removing their tax-exempt status. On neither issue would Obama allow one to be a conscientious objector in the ongoing progressive campaign against traditional Judeo-Christian morality. At the pinnacle of this approach, the administration advocated a conception of freedom of religion that would have deprived religious organizations of the right to define who was a minister of their faith—an interpretation novel enough that it was rebuked by a 9–0 decision of the Supreme Court (*Hosanna-Tabor v. EEOC*) as a violation of the First Amendment. Altogether, there was no major issue involving freedom of religion in which the Obama administration did not take the side of less religious freedom and less protection for individual conscience.

DOMESTIC POLICY AND OBAMA AS "BRIDGE BUILDER": PARTY AND RACE

Contrary to hopes that Obama stirred in 2008, partisan polarization clearly grew during his presidency. Although some scholars like Thomas Mann and Norman Ornstein blamed a conservative drift among Republicans (Mann and Ornstein 2014), it is clear that Obama's domestic policies were a (if not the) major contributor. His three most notable legislative achievements—the stimulus, health-care reform, and financial reform—were passed with virtually no Republican votes after a process in which

Obama and Congressional Democrats were by design the only major players. Gay marriage was imposed judicially after a presidential bait-and-switch, while Obama adhered to the most extreme possible defense of abortion. Obama himself frequently treated opposition as if it were a personal affront.

If one asked the question whether it was Congressional Republicans or Obama who had moved further from the positions of their 1990s predecessors, the answer was clear: Obama. Republicans barely budged from the positions Newt Gingrich had advanced in the 104th Congress. Obama, as we have seen, shifted well to the left of Bill Clinton's policies on the budget, welfare dependency, business regulation, law enforcement, abortion, and gay marriage. Much of this move was owed to changes in the Democratic Party as a whole, and some to broader changes in America (Swanson 2015). None of this alters the fact that Obama had traveled much further than his opponents, widening the gap between the parties. In the end, surveys showed that Obama was the most polarizing president since polling began. Seeking "fundamental transformation" is inherently polarizing. One should not then be surprised when polarization increases.

Similarly, almost from the beginning, Obama and his first attorney general, Eric Holder, disappointed hopes for racial reconciliation with policies and rhetoric that did not heal but inflamed. Obama's conduct in controversial law-enforcement cases reinforced the generally divisive thrust of his civil rights policies, which favored racial preferences in college admissions, dismissed supporters of voter identification laws as racists trying to disenfranchise blacks, and even pushed local school districts to discipline students differently based on race (Riley 2015). Overarching this entire polarizing scene was the tendency of Obama to accept, if not tacitly promote, a concept that damaged both his claim to bipartisanship and his potential as a racial bridge builder. The concept was that opposition to Obama and his agenda was motivated primarily, if not wholly, by racism—as if Republicans and conservative independents would otherwise have embraced a $1.4 trillion annual deficit, a government takeover of health care, a nationalized education curriculum, and aggressively redistributionist rhetoric.

With more than three-fourths of the president's term spent, a consensus had emerged that race relations in America were at a low point in recent history. A July 2015 *New York Times*/CBS News poll revealed "that nearly six in ten Americans, including heavy majorities of both whites and blacks, think race relations are generally bad, and that nearly four in ten think the situation is getting worse." By comparison, in early 2009 about two-thirds of Americans called race relations "generally good." Twice as many respondents said Obama had driven the races further apart than said he had made things better (Sack and Thee-Brenan 2015).

CONCLUSION

Barack Obama began with three major domestic policy objectives: to restore activist government, prove that it works, and thereby permanently transform the United States into a different country than the one he inherited, more to the liking of progressive intellectuals and European social democrats. He will end his presidency with a mixed and uncertain record in respect to those objectives.

On one hand, there is no question that he restored activist government within the parameters of what was possible, although the national backlash against the effort eventually constricted those parameters to the walls of the White House and Executive Office Building, sometimes abetted by the Supreme Court. Working with a Democratic Congress in the first two years of his presidency, he added half a trillion dollars of domestic spending to the annual federal budget, restored Keynesian economics to a place of dominance in federal economic policy, gained enactment of the closest approximation of national health care yet achieved as well as a major top-down overhaul of the nation's financial system, and established a new pro-regulation baseline.

After 2010 he dug in to defend his gains. Sometimes he fell short, as when cap-and-trade legislation and gun control were derailed in Congress, or when his administration's more extreme anti–religious freedom positions were set aside by the court. He was also forced to compromise when the Senate passed a health-care bill without the public option and when Republicans in Congress forced limits on spending after 2011 that Obama found highly objectionable (and which also cut the deficit by two-thirds as a proportion of GDP). At varying points Obama made a priority of policies that endangered the First and Second Amendments, separation of powers, federalism, due process, and the rule of law. Consistently, whether on offense or on defense, Obama's domestic policies expressed the progressives' de facto constitutional doctrine that the federal government can permissibly do almost anything and everything that the activist imagination can conjure.

But did he prove that it works? Far from it, either objectively or in the eyes of public opinion. The economy stabilized but produced the weakest recovery since World War II, with mediocre economic growth, job creation, and wages. Obama's fiscal policies ballooned the national debt with no appreciable payoff and with no apparent plan or intent to contain the damage. Though some Americans were covered, the results of health-care reform oscillated between serious underperformance and shambolic wreck, producing what one could have called multiple negative unanticipated consequences—if they had not actually been anticipated and decried by the plan's opponents throughout the long debate preceding passage. In both health care and finance, Obama's regulatory policies had the perverse effect of concentrating economic power among a smaller and smaller number of bigger and bigger companies. The centerpiece of his K–12 education approach, the Common Core standards, was harshly criticized across the political spectrum and lost momentum. Violent crime surged, as proven crime-control strategies were denounced and set aside in favor of liberal nostrums. Racial tensions surged hand in hand with presidential policies that promoted balkanization.

Friedrich Hayek, author of the 1944 classic *The Road to Serfdom*, would have explained these outcomes with a simple observation: The notion that a diverse and complex country of 320 million people can be successfully governed from the top down by the wisdom of enlightened bureaucrats is delusional. He would have added that no attempt to do so can be made without a constant application of state coercion, which threatens not only prosperity but liberty.

Americans were not oblivious to these failings. Polls consistently showed that majorities—often large majorities—disapproved of the state of the economy, Obamacare, the fiscal stimulus, and the overall direction of the country. Americans also told pollsters that they thought the federal government under Obama had come to pose a substantial threat to their rights, and only one in five said the country still operates on consent of the governed ("19% Think . . ." 2014). Obama's average job-approval rating on the Real Clear Politics website was below 50 percent for almost the entire time from mid-November 2009 through mid-June 2016. For most of that time, including almost all of the first three years of his second term, his average approval level was not only below 50 percent but was "underwater," below his average disapproval level. Many factors contributed to these anemic numbers, including scandals and foreign policy failings (especially in the second term), but domestic policy clearly played a major role.

Even when he was reelected, domestic policy represented a drag on his appeal, as exit polls showed that a plurality of the 2012 electorate rejected Obamacare and a majority said they preferred a government that did less to one that did more by a 51-to-43 percent margin, thus repudiating the central philosophical presumption holding together the sum of Obama's domestic policies. Nearly three in five voters identified the economy as their number-one issue, on which they trusted Mitt Romney more by 4 percentage points; another 15 percent of voters cared most about the deficit and trusted Romney more on that issue by 34 percentage points (CNN 2012). The hopes pinned on Obama by others fared no better. Partisan polarization increased during the Obama years, driven largely by the president's own domestic policies and his typically rigid approach to dealing with opposition. Those who saw in Obama someone who would heal the racial divide were also deeply disappointed.

So did Obama succeed in transforming America? That remains to be seen. Some of his domestic policy innovations will be hard to undo, or to undo completely, and the nation will also have irretrievably lost eight years during which it might have made some progress toward confronting its inevitable entitlement spending crisis. On the other hand, especially after his first two years, many of Obama's gains were limited to executive actions and bureaucratic rule making, making them vulnerable to a change in administration. Whatever happens in the 2016 elections, it is unlikely that Obama will leave his party in as strong a position to influence policy as he found it; and it is very possible that he will leave it in much worse shape. It is hard to say how much of Obama's winning coalition can be held together in the absence of Obama himself.

As importantly, transformation, if achieved, is not necessarily equivalent to improvement. Our health system may well be transformed in the direction of higher costs, less competition, worse quality, and less individual choice; our economy may be transformed in the direction of greater centralization, greater welfare dependency, and less economic freedom; our social norms and institutions may be transformed in the direction of a rootless hedonism and rampaging political correctness combined with correspondingly less freedom of thought; our Constitution may be transformed in the direction of limitless federal (and particularly presidential) power, ambiguous rights, only the shadow of consent of the governed, and less liberty as the Founders would have recognized it; indeed, our entire polity may be transformed in the direction of a soft totalitarianism hidden under the mask of an unchanged formal structure, Tocqueville's "democratic despotism" realized.

All of these would represent transformation, none of them improvement. Barack Obama might leave any or all of them as his legacy. But none is preordained. It is possible instead that Obama's domestic project will someday be seen as the apogee of the arc of American progressivism, one of the last gasps of a centralizing doctrine struggling to impose itself upon a decentralizing world. Americans have previewed this transformation and for the most part have declared it unsatisfactory. Ultimately, they will decide the question of whether the transformation is consummated, contained, or rejected.

WORKS CITED

Adams, Becket. 2011. "The Chart That Shows Just How Wrong Obama's Stimulus Projections Were." www.theblaze.com/stories/2011/10/10/the-chart-that-shows-just-how-wrong-obamas-stimulus-projections-were/.

Axelrod, David. 2015. *Believer: My Forty Years in Politics*. New York: Penguin.

Bedard, Paul. 2015. "U.S. Drops to 16th on 'Economic Freedom' List, Behind Canada, Chile." *Washington Examiner*, September 14.

Caldiera, Steven. 2015. "Labor Department Edicts Will Cost Jobs." Real Clear Politics, July 28, www.realclearpolitics.com/articles/2015/07/28/labor_department_mandates_will_cost_jobs.html.

Carey, Maeve P. 2015. "Counting Regulations: An Overview of Rulemaking, Types of Federal Regulations, and Pages in the Federal Register." Congressional Research Service, July 14. https://fas.org/sgp/crs/misc/R43056.pdf.

CNN, 2012. "President: Full Results: Exit Polls." www.cnn.com/election/2012/results/race/president/#exit-polls.

Comey, James B. 2015. "Something Deeply Disturbing Is Happening All Across America." *Wall Street Journal*, October 28, 2015.

Congressional Budget Office. 2014. "The Effects of a Minimum Wage Increase on Employment and Family Income." February.

Congressional Budget Office. 2015. "Budgetary and Economic Effects of Repealing the Affordable Care Act." June.

Conley, Timothy, and Bill Dupor. 2013. "The American Recovery and Reinvestment Act: Solely a Government Jobs Program?" *Journal of Monetary Economics*, vol. 60, no. 5, pp. 535–49.

Davey, Monica, and Mitch Smith. 2015. "Murder Rates Rising Sharply in Many Cities." *New York Times*, August 31.

Davidson, Kate. 2015. "Economy Picks Up but Stays in Its Rut." *Wall Street Journal*, July 31, p. A1, 2.

Demko, Paul. 2015. "Experts See Big Price Hikes for Obamacare." *Politico*, May 30.
FactCheck.org. 2012. "Obama's Drilling Denials." October 19. www.factcheck.org/2012/10/obamas-drilling-denials/.
Federal Budget Fiscal Year 2016. www.whitehouse.gov/omb/budget/Historicals.
Fox, Justin. 2015. "Full-Time Work Is Harder to Find." *Bloomberg View*, September 4.
Gramm, Phil. 2015. "What's Wrong with the Golden Goose?" *Wall Street Journal*, April 21, p. A19.
Hanson, Victor Davis. 2015. "A Tale of Two Shootings." PJ Media, November 9. http://pjmedia.com/victordavishanson/tale-of-two-shootings/?print=1.
Hensaerling, Jeb. 2015. "After Five Years, Dodd-Frank Is a Failure." *Wall Street Journal*, July 20, p. A15.
Knoller, Mark. 2010. "Obama Has Given 54 Speeches on Health Care." CBS News, March 9, 2010. www.cbsnews.com/8301-503544_162-200000825-503544.html.
MacDonald, Heather. 2015. "The Decriminalization Delusion." *The City Journal*, July. www.city-journal.org/2015/25_4_decriminalization.html.
Mann, Thomas E., and Norman J. Ornstein. 2014. *It's Even Worse Than It Looks: How the American Constitutional System Collided with the New Politics of Extremism*. New York: Basic Books.
McArdle, Megan. 2015. "Sticker Shock for Some Obamacare Customers." Bloomberg View, May 25.
McCoughey, Betsy. 2015. "ObamaCare Is Entering Its Dreaded 'Death Spiral.'" *New York Post*, October 19. http://nypost.com/2015/10/19/obamacare-is-entering-its-dreaded-death-spiral/.
McGurn, William. 2015. "The Political 'Science' of Planned Parenthood." *Wall Street Journal*, July 28, p. A11.
McLaughlin, Patrick, and Oliver Sherous. 2015. "The Dodd-Frank Wall Street Reform and Consumer Protection Act May Be the Biggest Law Ever." Mercatus Center, July 20, http://mercatus.org/publication/dodd-frank-wall-street-reform-and-consumer-protection-act-may-be-biggest-law-ever.
Moore, Stephen. 2015a. "Obama Earns a 'D' on Handling Economy." *Orange County Register*, November 8.
Moore, Stephen. 2015b. "The Demise of the Small American Bank." *Wall Street Journal*, July 31.
Moran, Melanie. 2015. "Assessment Estimates Cost of Federal Regulation Compliance at Vanderbilt." Vanderbilt News, July 31. http://news.vanderbilt.edu/2015/07/assessment-estimates-cost-of-federal-regulation-compliance-at-vanderbilt/.
Newman, Alex. 2014. "Obama Imposed 75,000 Pages of New Regulations in 2014." December 30, *New American*. www.thenewamerican.com/usnews/constitution/item/19803-obama-imposed-75-000-pages-of-new-regulations-in-2014.
"19% Think Federal Government Has Consent of the Governed." 2014. Rasmussen Reports, April 11. www.rasmussenreports.com/public_content/politics/general_politics/april_2014/19_think_federal_government_has_consent_of_the_governed.
O'Brien, Matt. 2014. "The Middle Class Is Poorer than It Was in 1989." *Washington Post*, October 1, 2014. www.washingtonpost.com/news/wonkblog/wp/2014/10/01/the-middle-class-is-poorer-today-than-it-was-in-1989/.
Owens, Caitlin. 2015. "Even if You Like Your Obamacare Co-Op Insurance, You Probably Can't Keep It." *National Journal*, November 15.
Pipes, Sally. 2015. "Unhappy Birthday, Obamacare: Five Years after Its Signing, the Affordable Care Act Is Failing to Live Up to Its Promise." *New York Daily News*, March 23. http://www.nydailynews.com/opinion/sally-pipes-unhappy-birthday-obamacare-article-1.2157297.
Renshon, Stanley A. 2012. *Barack Obama and the Politics of Redemption*. New York: Routledge.
"Rethink Harvard's Sexual Harassment Policy." 2014. *Boston Globe*, October 15.
Riley, Jason. 2015. "The Wages of Racial Discord." *Wall Street Journal*, August 5, p. A11.

Rosenberg, Joyce M. 2015. "Small Businesses Struggle with Health Care Law." Associated Press, March 22. www.usatoday.com/story/money/2015/03/22/affordable-care-act-small-business/24959177/.

Ryan, Paul, Eric Cantor, and Kevin McCarthy. 2010. *Young Guns: A New Generation of Conservative Leaders*. New York: Simon & Schuster, Threshold Editions.

Sack, Kevin, and Megan Thee-Brenan. 2015. "Poll Finds Most in U.S. Hold Dim View of Race Relations." *New York Times*, July 23.

Schwartz, Nelson D. 2015. "Low-Income Workers See Biggest Drop in Paychecks." *New York Times*, September 2.

Singer, Jeffrey A. 2014. "Why Doctors Give Obamacare a Failing Grade." *The Hill*, October 5. http://thehill.com/blogs/congress-blog/healthcare/220715-why-doctors-give-obamacare-a-failing-grade.

Sperry, Paul. 2015. "How Obama Is Bankrolling Non-stop Protest Against Invented Outrage." *New York Post*, November 14. http://nypost.com/2015/11/14/how-obama-is-bankrolling-a-non-stop-protest-against-invented-outrage/.

Spruiell, Stephen. 2009. "Today Student Loans, Tomorrow Health Care." *National Review*, July 17. www.nationalreview.com/article/227896/today-student-loans-tomorrow-health-care-stephen-spruiell.

Sun, Lena H., and Niraj Chokshi. 2015. "Health Care and Policy." *Washington Post*, May 1.

Swanson, Ana. 2015. "These Political Scientists May Have Just Discovered Why U.S. Politics Are a Disaster." *Washington Post*, October 7. www.washingtonpost.com/news/wonk/wp/2015/10/07/these-political-scientists-may-have-discovered-the-real-reason-u-s-politics-are-a-disaster/.

Turner, Grace-Marie, and Thomas P. Miller. 2015. "Another Obamacare Dream Goes Bust." *Wall Street Journal*, June 23.

US Census Bureau. 2014. "Incomes and Poverty in the United States." Table B-1, September, p. 5.

US Labor Department. 2015. Bureau of Labor Statistics. http://data.bls.gov/timeseries/LNS11300000.

Wallison, Peter. 2011. "Hey Barney Frank: The Government Did Cause the Financial Crisis." *The Atlantic*, December 13. www.theatlantic.com/business/archive/2011/12/hey-barney-frank-the-government-did-cause-the-housing-crisis/249903/.

Wallison, Peter. 2014. "Four Years of Dodd-Frank Damage." *Wall Street Journal*, July 20. www.wsj.com/articles/peter-wallison-four-years-of-dodd-frank-damage-1405893333.

Washington Post/ABC News Poll. 2010. October 3, 2010. www.washingtonpost.com/wp-srv/politics/polls/postpoll_10052010.html.

9

BACK FROM THE BRINK

Obama's Economic Record

Daniel E. Ponder, Drury University

In August 1928, President Calvin Coolidge visited the Hull Rust Mine, the deepest iron-ore pit on the planet, located on Minnesota's desolate Iron Range. There to dedicate a new viewing stand, he watched the machines and shovels dig deeper, and though some expected him to give a speech, he simply turned around and said, "That's a pretty big hole" (Brown 2011).

When Barack Obama looked out at the throng of nearly two million people who gathered on the National Mall to hear his inaugural address on January 20, 2009, he likely felt much the same way, though instead of a vast mine, he looked out over the American economy, which had fallen into a deep, deep hole. An expanding housing bubble had burst toward the end of 2007 and into 2008, setting the American economy on a downward spiral that included the near collapse of the financial system, jobs hemorrhaged at an average of a quarter million per month during 2008 (though the actual figures late in that year were much higher), the failure of financial giants such as the investment bank Bear Stearns (as well as the failure or near failure of many others), and an American automobile industry, once a symbol of American economic strength and resilience, teetering on the verge of collapse. It was indeed a "big hole," the worst economy inherited by any president since Franklin Delano Roosevelt took over from Herbert Hoover in 1933. And since there is nothing magical about noon on January 20, Obama did not even inherit an economy whose decline was complete. Inertia is hard to counteract, and at the appointed hour for George W. Bush (on whose watch most of the damage had been done) to give way to the forty-fourth president, the economy was nowhere near hitting rock bottom.

This analogy illustrates the way President Obama's economic legacy should be judged. Political scientist James Campbell (2011) argues that isolating analysis on a president's term without considering inherited economic conditions leads to wrong or misleading conclusions about that president, or of party differences in economic legacies. In Obama's case the economy had fallen into a big hole, and while he was left with a near-historic mess, it was Obama's job to try to clean it up. The economy is fickle, and many things affect it. But by any metric, economic improvement has been impressive under Obama's stewardship. In many instances Obama's economic policies, coupled with help from the Federal Reserve, and against Congressional Republicans set on making him a failed, one-term president, brought the country out of the hole and onto solid ground. Not only are many indicators (e.g., the unemployment rate, job creation, the deficit, to name a few) in better shape than they have been in years, in some cases decades, but they turned around more quickly than many analysts and pundits thought possible.

In a cross-national comparison spanning more than eight centuries, Reinhart and Rogoff (2009) show that recessions that begin with housing crises last longer than other economic downturns. That economic decline began with a bursting housing bubble. Obama had no time to waste, given that the hole was not only deep but likely to get deeper. I argue in this chapter that while it has taken time to turn the tide, *it did not take as long as many expected*, in large part due to Obama's policies, which from time to time were driven by Democrats (albeit with some defections) with almost no Republican support, though there were fleeting instances of bipartisanship.

In this chapter I briefly describe how the economy went so bad, survey the most prominent policies Obama pursued to attack the crisis, and the effects of those policies. Presidents are elected to do a job over a four- or eight-year period, so my analysis focuses on the trends in the economy over Obama's two terms. I examine average change, locating those changes in the context of the dozen presidents who have served since the end of World War II and the Great Depression. I conclude by arguing that President Obama did indeed play a pivotal role in bringing the American economy back from the brink, out of the deep hole, and onto solid ground. While more work needs to be done (e.g., in dealing with inequality), Obama can stake a claim that his was one of the more successful economic legacies of any president since World War II.

THE PRESIDENTIAL CONTEXT

The economy is of primary importance to presidents, and much of what they do affects the economy even if the measures they push do not fall into the category of "economic policy." The state of the economy has political implications for presidents. The general shape of the economy, consumer confidence, and other economic factors are all important for a president's approval ratings; when the economy is good, so usually are the president's approval ratings (Erikson, MacKuen, and Stimson 2002). Wood (2007) demonstrates that presidents can influence the economy through rhetoric. Still, presidents are, to some degree, hamstrung because they are often at the mercy of factors outside their control; for example, the Federal Reserve has a lot of sway over the economy and public reactions to it, as does the market.[1]

The economy is often used as a benchmark for assessing presidential legacies in general and, more immediately, prospects for reelection in particular. Jimmy Carter was hurt by stagflation, (i.e., simultaneously high levels of unemployment and inflation), which until then was something that Keynesian economic theory held to be nearly impossible. Persistently high levels of stagflation, high interest rates, and other factors largely beyond his control (such as the Iranian hostage crisis) doomed Carter at the polls in 1980. His successor, Ronald Regan, endured an economic recession early in his first term, and by the time reelection came around in 1984, he harvested the fruits of a robust recovery and cruised to victory. The lesson is simple: The economy has profound implications for a president's political capital, prospects for reelection, and his legacy.[2]

Presidents can use their unique position in American politics to address the economy and are sometimes successful (Wood 2007), though they have to rely on Congress to pass their initiatives. Much of Franklin D. Roosevelt's storied success in dealing with the crisis of the Great Depression in the first one hundred days of his administration was due not only to his efforts (e.g., FDR declared a bank holiday and he and his staff crafted a banking bill in one day's time), but he had to rely on Congress to pass the enabling legislation. Conversely, President Obama had to deal with a hostile Congress reluctant to pass his initiatives. Others in this volume have demonstrated that Obama had nearly intransigent opposition in Congress, whose opposition deepened further after the passage of the Affordable Care Act in March 2010.

So Obama had to act swiftly, and he did. The record of Obama's two terms demonstrates that he presided over one of the most impressive economic recoveries of any presidency since World War II, and indeed one of the most impressive in history. To be sure, the economy was in such a sorry state that any recovery would be seen as some improvement. But there is nothing that says the economy would not have fallen further. Herbert Hoover, an engineer by training, did little to arrest the declining economic situation in the aftermath of the stock market crash in October 1929, relying instead on the perceived self-corrective capacities of the market. On his watch the market, and therefore the economy, never corrected and the economy slid into the Great Depression, marking the failure, at least in this instance, of the laissez-faire approach. Relying on the market sometimes works, but government exists in part to step in when the market fails. And as Election Day 2008 approached, failure was on the horizon.

THE ECONOMIC CONTEXT

When George W. Bush took the oath of office on January 20, 2001, he inherited from President Clinton a robust economy and a budget surplus. Partly because of this economic situation, Bush was able to secure a large tax cut. Then, in the aftermath of the September 11 terror attacks, Bush took the United States to war in Iraq and Afghanistan, the former on the basis of faulty information that Iraq had weapons of mass destruction, and the latter to try to ferret out Osama bin Laden and others responsible for the attacks. This put enormous pressure on the budget as spending increased dramatically and revenues declined because of the tax cuts. As a result, the budget surplus was soon a memory and there was little slack with which to deal with an economic crisis should one arise.

That crisis came in the form of an economic collapse, hastened by a financial crisis, culminating in what some economists call the "Second Great Contraction" (the first being the Great Depression of the 1930s). Two prominent economists have argued that "'contraction' is an apt description of the wholesale collapse of credit markets and asset prices that has marked the depth of these traumatic events, along with . . . contracting employment and output" (Reinhart and Rogoff 2009, 393, n7), caused mainly by massive borrowing by the United States.

The financial crisis originated in the subprime mortgage housing bubble in 2007 and 2008, which featured a robust and some thought healthy increase in housing prices as a result of unprecedented current account and trade imbalances. Additionally, there were new financial instruments being developed such as "securitization mortgages," which combined pools of loans into more "standardized" loans, credit default swaps, derivatives, and other creative financing tools. As Rogoff and Reinhart write, "To the extent that the U.S. current account was being driven by superior U.S. financial innovation, there was also nothing to worry about. Or so top U.S. financial regulators maintained" (Rogoff and Reinhart 2009, 404 n13).

The regulatory regime that oversaw these new and incredibly complex financial tools was increasingly lax and permissive, largely because elected officials stripped regulators of tools with which to conduct oversight. This slack dates back to the 1990s when the Glass-Steagall Act, which required banks to separate traditional banking services from high-risk insurance and investment activities, was partially repealed. Banks could now mix the two activities, which put debtors at risk, many of whom are wage earners. The stage was set for a catastrophic crash if anything were to give.

The first cracks in the system emerged in late 2007. Foreign countries flooded the U.S. market with investment dollars, which led to cheap money in the form of low interest rates as banks and other financial institutions made it easy for earners of almost any income to obtain housing loans. This was dangerous because the temporarily low introductory rates allowed many borrowers to purchase houses they otherwise could not afford. When those rates expired and the new higher rates took effect, many were unable to pay their monthly mortgages, which had sometimes quadrupled. With no way to refinance those loans, many had no recourse but bankruptcy (Reinhart and Rogoff 2009, 207–8). The dramatic increase in bankruptcies fueled a global panic, and the nightmare scenario was in place, leading to the largest downturn in the American economy since the Great Depression. Not only was the downturn severe, it was almost immediate and left policymakers little time to formulate an effective response.

This occurred in 2007 and 2008, and it is no exaggeration to observe that the economy was in free-fall just before the 2008 election. On September 15, the day that 158-year-old financial giant Lehman Brothers went bankrupt, Republican presidential nominee John McCain uttered the incredible statement that the "fundamentals" of the economy were "strong." In the uproar caused by these words, McCain's campaign hit crisis mode. It tried to clarify that he was referring to the "American worker" and not the economy. But less than two days later, McCain reversed course entirely and said that the economy was in "total crisis" and targeted "greed" on Wall Street (Cooper 2008). McCain called for the two candidates to suspend their campaigns and attend a White House summit on the economic crisis. Obama refused to suspend his campaign but took a day to meet with Bush, McCain, and others, including Treasury Secretary Henry Paulson. McCain seemed lost, lacking a basic grasp of the situation and even less of an idea of how to deal with it. Obama, on the other hand, impressed even his Republican adversaries by not only mastering the intricacies of the crisis but coming up with concrete ideas to improve it. When word spread, McCain's prospects for winning the Oval Office shrank even further. When Obama won the presidential election on November 8, 2008, the results suggested a mandate for Obama and not simply a referendum on an unpopular president (Weatherford 2012).

FIRST THINGS FIRST: DEALING WITH THE RECESSION[3]

After Obama took the oath as the first African American president of the United States, there was little time for fanfare and celebration. The forty-seven-year-old president faced the "big hole" that was the economy, and two interrelated things needed to be dealt with immediately: the recession and the financial crisis (see also Weatherford 2012).

By the time Obama came to office, Bush had asked for and Congress had passed a mammoth bailout of toxic assets (the Toxic Assets Relief

Program, or TARP), and Bush signed it on October 3, 2008, a month before the presidential election. This did not endear him to many in his party, who lambasted him as lacking conservative credentials because he used government to intervene so dramatically with market economics.

In mid-December, just five weeks after his election, Obama and his team met to hammer out solutions to the crisis. The first was to propose a mammoth stimulus package that they hoped would jump-start a badly flagging economy. Incoming chair of the Council of Economic Advisers (CEA) Christina Romer proposed $1.2 trillion, a staggering number. Knowing the political realities of Republicans in Congress and many fiscally conservative "Blue Dog" Democrats, Obama knew that number, whether necessary or not, was out of reach. Instead they pushed for a more "modest" $800 billion stimulus.

On February 13, Congressional Democrats, with virtually no support from Republicans (zero in the House), passed HR-1-PL 111-5, which provided nearly $800 billion in stimulus money in a package of programmatic spending cuts and tax reduction. The sum of $575.3 billion came in the form of new funding over eleven years to save existing jobs and create new ones, and to cut taxes by $211.8 billion over the same time frame.

Obama needed an extremely large stimulus in order to pack the kind of punch the economy needed to turn around and get moving in the right direction. He wanted a more expansive bill than the nearly $800 billion he got. But in order to secure even that much, he had to pare it down to attract enough conservative and moderate votes on both sides of the aisle (particularly Democrats, since he could not count on many Republicans to support the bill). Overall, the final bill mirrored the Senate's version because it was able to attract three Republicans, and the bill cleared the Senate 60–38, barely enough to stave off a filibuster.

When President Obama signed the stimulus into law on February 17, 2009, it was easily the largest stimulus project in American history. By way of comparison, Bill Clinton had proposed a $16 billion stimulus (nearly $24 billion in 2009 dollars) when facing an economic downturn in the 1990s. Obama, facing a far bigger economic mess, signed a bill more than thirty times the size Clinton had proposed. Obama also fought for and won the bill's passage, which touched nearly every part of American life. As noted above, the bill combined spending and tax-cut provisions. the following are just a few examples.

Spending

Education and Training: The largest item called for a massive investment in education and job training totaling $53.6 billion, including $15.6 billion to increase Pell Grants to help pay for college tuition, $13 billion for Title I schools (those whose primary student population is from economically disadvantaged families), $12.2 billion for special education, and $4 billion for job-training programs.

Transportation: $45.2 billion to upgrade the nation's transportation infrastructure, including highway construction, Amtrak/high-speed rail, and mass transportation.

Assistance for the Poor: While the crisis hit nearly everyone, the poorest were hit hardest because they were most unlikely to have access to savings and educational opportunities and were most vulnerable to losing jobs. Consequently, Obama targeted $24.1 billion for low-income assistance. Most of that went to increasing nutrition programs by $20 billion, with another $2 billion going to support child-care programs for some three hundred thousand low-income households, and $2.1 billion for Head Start, a program of early childhood education for economically disadvantaged families.

Public Housing: The bill also targeted $8 billion for public housing, including increasing energy efficiency in older buildings to allow for cheaper rent because landlords would save on utility bills, and a $4 billion increase in rent assistance and other projects.

Environment: $7.2 billion was set aside for the environment, including programs for clean water and Superfund cleanup.

Energy: $38.2 billion was targeted at modernizing the electric grid, supporting energy efficiency, and for weatherization assistance.

Miscellaneous: Finally, the bill included $24 billion for other programs such as extending broadband access to rural areas to increase educational programs and enhanced economic activity, law enforcement, and programs for the departments of Homeland Security and Defense.

Tax Cuts

While the bulk of the stimulus package emphasized new spending, more than a quarter of the cost of the program came from $211 billion in tax cuts. These were a political necessity to attract enough support to pass the bill, but also to provide incentives for spending and investment at all levels of the income spectrum in a series of both short- and long-term cuts.

Individual tax cuts included increasing the Earned Income Tax Credit, a refundable tax credit, a one-year increase in the amount of income not counted toward the Alternative Minimum Tax (AMT), assistance for retirees, increasing the child tax credit, and credits for tuition and home buyers.

Business also benefited from several tax write-offs. For example, the bill extended a program allowing companies to claim 50 percent depreciation on equipment and land in the first year, as well as providing energy production credits, and incentives for health-care providers to use electronic record keeping. Tax-exempt bonds were issued for school construction and economic-recovery zones.

Finally, a series of mandatory programs benefited from tax cuts. Unemployment benefits were extended, including a 65 percent increase in subsidies on health-care premiums, allowing workers who lost their jobs to temporarily keep their employer-provided health insurance. Also included was an expansion of aid to displaced workers, and a temporary increase in state Medicaid reimbursements.

While not part of the stimulus per se, three other programs helped to sustain the effort to improve the economy. First, Obama signed a "Cash for Clunkers" bill that gave consumers rebates of up to $4,500 when trading in their gas-guzzling cars for fuel-efficient ones. The program lasted until mid-August.

Second, Obama threatened to veto a bill that would have cancelled the second installment of TARP. The Senate acquiesced, allowing the installment to go through, although it was later reduced as part of the Dodd-Frank legislation.

Third, as a matter of political necessity, Obama signed an end-of-year measure to extend the Bush tax cuts. The decision was part of a tradeoff to secure the extension of unemployment benefits when the economy continued to hemorrhage jobs throughout 2009. Obama originally wanted cuts on all annual incomes above $200,000 to expire, but that proved intractable, especially in the Senate. He negotiated a deal to extend unemployment benefits for thirteen months, as well as a one-time, one-year reduction in payroll taxes, particularly on Social Security, that was expected to boost the economy by nearly $200 billion. The hope was that those receiving the money would increase their spending, which in turn would stimulate the economy. For this display of bipartisanship, Obama paid a political price when dissension came from furious House Democrats, who felt that he had given in to the Republicans too easily (*Congressional Quarterly Almanac* 2009, 14-3). He got less than he wanted but more than he could have by standing firm on the more limited expiration of the Bush tax cuts. John Gilmour (1995) calls this type of politics "getting half-a-loaf," meaning you get something rather than nothing.[4] In this case Obama got much of what he wanted but had to forego lost revenue from fewer taxes in the wake of the tax cut extension. Still, the fact that the long-term unemployed could count on more than an additional year of support, and those who were still getting a paycheck would see a hike in their take-home pay, helped the recession-battered economy begin to improve.

The Auto Bailout

In addition, Obama had to deal with the aftermath of the auto bailout. After the election but before Obama took office, the Bush administration used TARP to provide more than $13 billion in loans to keep General Motors and Chrysler, the bulk of Detroit's auto industry, solvent.[5] Less than four months after taking office, the administration expanded GM's bailout by adding some $6 billion to the loan, and on June 1 GM filed for bankruptcy reorganization and cut costs by, among other things, selling off brands such as Saturn, Saab, and Hummer. As part of that filing, the administration provided another $30 billion in debtor-in-possession (DIP) loans, which took precedent over all other debts incurred by GM.

Across the ideological spectrum, the auto bailout was largely unpopular. It was seen as either the least bad of many terrible options or as a giant government power grab, even though it was wildly successful. Many agreed that something had to be done because the auto industry was the backbone of many industries, and if it had been allowed to fail, not only would they fail, but it would have a large splash with ripple effects pulsating throughout the economy. Many industries, from car dealers to suppliers to parts makers, trucking companies, and others, would be at risk. This would have even greater effects as the price of commodities would certainly rise given the costs of getting them to market.

But it worked, and more quickly than virtually anyone expected. In April 2010 GM made its final repayment on its loan, reducing government's stock share to just over 60 percent. By July 2010, barely thirteen months after filing, GM emerged from bankruptcy and in short order repaid most of its loans and further reduced the government's stake in the company to 33 percent. Over the next three years, well ahead of schedule, GM repurchased all of its common stock, the government sold all of its stocks, and by December 2013, less than five years after nearly collapsing, GM was once again on solid ground and the government owned no more stock in the car giant. Chrysler's move from near bankruptcy to solvency, while not quite as successful, was nearly as fast, though it moved from government-held debt to cheaper institutionally held debt by 2011, even though the terms of the agreement did not require repayment until 2017. All in all, Chrysler's bankruptcy protection cost the government just over $1 billion, but far less than it would have cost the economy had it been allowed to fail and had Obama not expanded the terms of the bailout.

Assessing Obama's Recovery Policies

In what became a common refrain directed at many aspects of the Obama presidency, the stimulus was criticized from both sides of the partisan divide. On the left, former President Bill Clinton argued that while the stimulus bill was well conceived, it was not large enough to fully help the economy (Mak 2011). On the right, Republicans, even years later, argued that it did little but load debt on future taxpayers (Lauter 2014).

Economists and pundits will debate the effects for years to come, but on a number of different fronts, Obama's stimulus was a clear success. Even a report from the conservative American Enterprise Institute conceded as much, albeit grudgingly (Pethokoukis 2013).

Recall that while the bill phases in various programs between 2009 and 2019, it was imperative that most of the effects be felt in a relatively short period of time. Protracted woes would continue to drag down the economy and perhaps require even more government spending and revenue loss. In a summary of the early assessments, a *Washington Post* analysis found that of the nine initial studies conducted by economists across the ideological spectrum, no fewer than six showed unambiguous evidence that Obama's stimulus package had indeed worked, while none of the other three found that it had not worked, but that the impacts were either small or impossible to detect (Matthews 2011). In terms of the massive amount of lost income due to the downturn, the stimulus had erased fully 90 percent of the lost income due to job losses, and did so in less than three years (CBO 2014, Burtless 2014). With the combination of the TARP program, which Obama protected via a veto threat, the Federal Reserve's quantitative easing (briefly described below), and especially the Obama stimulus, the effects showed the economy turning around, albeit in fits and starts, and the recovery began to accelerate.

FIXING A HOLE: DEALING WITH THE FINANCIAL CRISIS

I have described above the administration's response to the recession caused by the subprime crisis. Once the Obama administration dealt with the recession, it turned its attention to fixing the problem in the financial system that caused all the trouble (Reinhart and Rogoff 2009, 207). Though Wall Street was widely blamed as the cause of the painful downturn, it would be difficult to find political support for a financial system overhaul, in part because Obama had just won a hard-fought victory on health-care reform, which used up a lot of his political capital.

Although keenly aware that the opposition of financial interests to his banking reforms would only grow stronger as the post-election honeymoon faded into the past, Obama set aside financial regulation to focus on health-care reform as the great initiative of his first year. When he unveiled his proposal for banking regulation, it faced the opposition of a financial sector that—aided by the government bailout—had returned to profitability much faster than the economy as a whole and was prepared to mount a well-coordinated lobbying blitz (Weatherford 2012, 306).

Obama knew that he needed to mobilize political action to rein in a serious regulatory lapse that had, at minimum, allowed the sequence of events leading to the financial crisis to occur. In a succession of policy moves designed as much to quell the fears of a panicked public as addressing serious flaws in the regulatory environment, Obama culminated a long battle by signing the Dodd-Frank Wall Street Reform and Consumer Protection Act, commonly referred to as Dodd-Frank. The signing ceremony was rife with symbolism, as he signed the bill in the Ronald Regan Building and International Trade Center in Washington, DC, harkening back to a time when bipartisanship was more the norm, a none-too-subtle reminder that this bill had passed almost entirely along party lines (only three Senate Republicans and three House Republicans voted for the bill, while nineteen House Democrats voted no).

Ironically, though most of the public feared another meltdown, many politicians had to tread lightly in addressing issues of the financial system. The public was tired of bailouts. A *USA Today* poll taken just days before the House passed Dodd-Frank showed the country was basically split. While a clear majority favored stepping up regulation of the financial industry, a nontrivial minority (44 percent) opposed it (*USA Today* 2010). Because of these mixed signals, there was little incentive for Republicans to support the president's program. In April, while the bill was being debated, 52 percent trusted Obama to handle the financial crisis while only 35 percent trusted congressional Republicans; but in the same poll the country was split on whether they approved of his handling of the issue (48 percent approved, 47 percent disapproved) (ABC-*Washington Post* 2010a). In July, just before the final Senate action was taken, 50 percent disapproved of Obama's handling of the financial crisis and 44 percent approved (ABC-*Washington Post* 2010b).

The Bill[6]

On that hot July day in Washington, Obama signed the Dodd-Frank bill, easily the most extensive regulatory legislation overseeing Wall Street since the Great Depression. The bill was broad and touched or revised virtually every twentieth-century financial law. Part of the legislation was designed to alleviate the idea that government would step in when a company was "too big to fail" or when banks, securities trading, and so forth might collapse, even if doing so would threaten domestic and international financial systems.

Further, it required transparency in financial markets. The bill's namesakes, Senator Christopher Dodd (D-CT) and Representative Barney Frank (D-MA), shepherded the bill through the labyrinth that is the congressional process. Dodd was chairman of the Senate Committee on Banking, Housing, and Urban Affairs, and Frank chaired the House Financial Services Committee. The bill placed derivatives and credit default swaps under federal control and required greater transparency of these incredibly complex financial tools.

The administration insisted the bill ease systemic risks that threatened to destabilize the financial system. The federal government was given responsibility to identify and monitor financial institutions that are "too big to fail." It created a Financial Stability Oversight Council consisting of existing regulators and the Secretary of the Treasury. It limited banks' trading and investing in private equity funds. The FDIC was charged with discharging failed financial institutions if the president, Secretary of the Treasury, and two regulators acquiesced and only as a last resort.

Consumers were sheltered by a Bureau of Consumer Financial Protection located within the Fed. It was required to enforce consumer protection laws, regulate large lending institutions, mortgage-related business, and pay-day lenders, cutting down on predatory lending. It also protected consumers from purchasing or borrowing more than they could handle, with an eye toward reducing the number of bankruptcies and defaults. And the Fed was given new power with some restrictions. For example, its ability to make certain kinds of loans to individual institutions in deep trouble was curtailed. This had allowed the Fed to bail out insurance giant AIG when, some argued, it should not have been saved.

The federal government asserted new powers by requiring derivatives to be traded on an open, regulated exchange. And for the first time since Glass-Steagall was neutered in the late Clinton administration, banks were required to spin off their riskiest derivatives so that failure would not affect other parts of the system. Finally, Dodd-Frank provided for certain offsets to gain enough votes to pass. For example, it ended the TARP program (negating about $400 billion in spending) and increased premium fees into an FDIC deposit insurance fund (*CQ Almanac* 2010).

THE RESULTS OF OBAMA'S ECONOMIC POLICIES

Obama was not only able to implement large-scale policy geared toward rescuing the economy, he did so in an extraordinarily hostile political environment. Other chapters in this volume detail those struggles, but here it is important to note that even in the face of that opposition, he was able to have significant policy impact, especially in the first two years of his administration. In this section, I examine just a few of the most telling economic indicators to see, first, how they fared during Obama's presidency, and second, how the changes over the course of his two terms compare with presidents in the post–World War II era.

What is Obama's record as he sought to try to bring the economy back from the brink? When presidents are elected, they are hired for a four-year (or eight) job. Therefore, in the rest of this chapter, I examine changes over the course of an administration rather than average levels. For example, it may be interesting to know the average unemployment rate during the administration of Bush or Clinton or Obama. But since presidents are hired to do a job, another way is to look at how the indicator we are interested in looks when the president leaves office compared to when he began. To be sure, there is likely to be variation—indicators may rise and fall over the course of four or eight years, but how did each president leave the job compared to his first day? Some presidents (such as Obama) start off in a much bigger economic hole than other presidents, and examining static levels rather than dynamic changes over the course of a presidency is likely to obfuscate the record. The key question is whether the economy is in better or worse shape at the end of a presidency than at the beginning. A quick look at the numbers indicates that the economy began its recovery more quickly than many thought possible, and looking at Obama's economic record of recovery, it is among the very best of the twelve postwar presidents.

Unemployment and Inflation

I begin with unemployment. First, recall that Campbell (2011) argues that when thinking of the economic records of presidents, presidential terms cannot be considered in isolation, starting on January 20 and ending four or eight years later. Much of the inertia in the economy builds up in the previous presidential term, and presidents may inherit a huge mess that even in the best circumstances takes time to clean up. Second, recall that in 2008, the last full year of Bush's presidency, average job losses exceeded 500,000 per month. Indeed, isolating the month before Obama's inauguration in January 2009, the economy hemorrhaged almost 800,000 jobs. If we go further back and add the losses in November plus December 2008, the total well exceeded a million jobs lost in just two months, and unemployment jumped to nearly 8 percent, an increase of nearly 3 percent in a year *before Obama ever moved into the White House*. The avalanche of job loss was at full force.

If one looks only at the average unemployment over the seven years of Obama's presidency to date, Obama's record *is* the worst of any of the post–World War II presidents. But I argue that it clouds more than it clarifies. Unemployment is hard for presidents to fix because it is a moving target. At one angle, it obviously impacts those who were laid off. But it cuts deeper because it spreads a sort of "fear factor" for those who are still employed. For them, the prospect of becoming unemployed causes many to save their money rather than spend it, thus preparing them "just in case" they too lose their job. This lack of spending contributes to the downward spiral because if potential consumers do not spend, demand goes down, profits dip, and as a result companies have to lay off more workers, more become unemployed, and the cycle continues.

But looking at the changes over the course of his term, Obama's record on unemployment is among the very best of any president. Consider the trends in Figure 9.1. The average unemployment rate was 9.3 percent in 2009 and climbed to 9.6 percent in 2010. As the effects of the stimulus began to take hold, though, the unemployment rate began to drop.

One way to compare and assess the record is to observe the unemployment rate during a presidential term, from the time a president inherits the office to when he leaves (or, in Obama's case, deep into the seventh year of his presidency, when this chapter is being written). Looking at Figure 9.1, if one transposes the trend into thinking about average changes from year to year, Obama ranks eighth of the twelve postwar presidents, ranking ahead of only Bush 43, Nixon, Bush 41, and Ford. But if we consider *absolute change*, measured as the difference from end of term (Obama's seventh year) to the beginning, Obama's record is easily *first*. To be sure, no president in the postwar era came to office with a larger inherited problem than Obama. But if one subtracts the unemployment rate at the end of term from the last year of his predecessor's term (to control for inertia), Obama's record is even better. And if we consider the average annual *percent change* in the unemployment rate, Obama is second, barely behind Bill Clinton.[7]

Another way to examine unemployment is to track the "real" unemployment rate, which accounts for the widely reported unemployment rate but adds in those workers who are marginally connected and part-time workers who want full-time employment. This number is historically about twice the average of the traditional unemployment rate and was

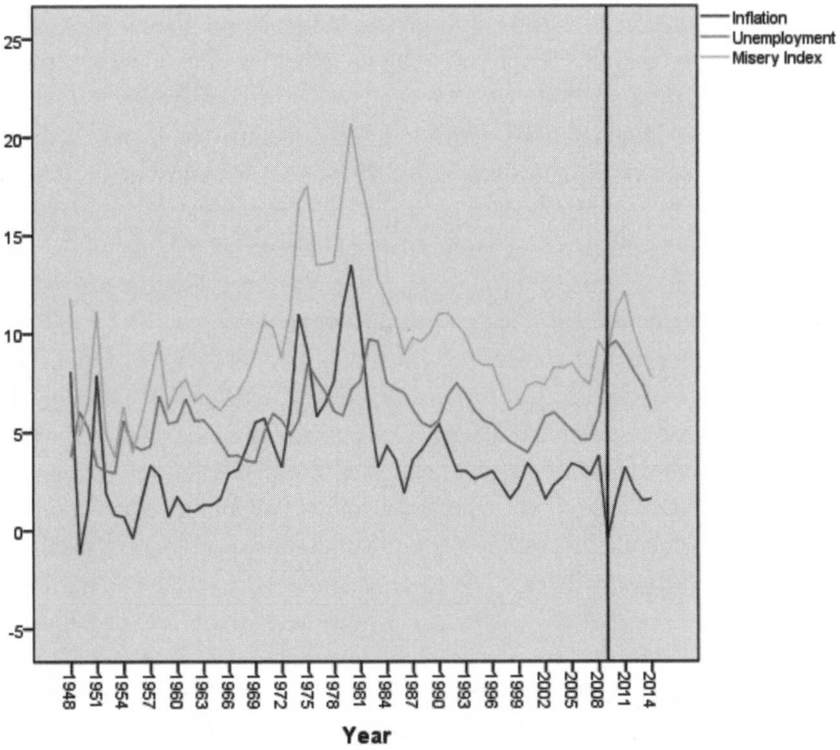

Figure 9.1. Unemployment, Inflation, and the Misery Index, Truman to Obama. Derived from Various Sources; Misery Index Calculated by Author. Vertical line denotes beginning of Obama's term.

first calculated by the Bureau of Labor Statistics in 1994. Taking this much more conservative number into account, the change during Bush's term (2002–2009) increased from 9.5 percent to 14.2 percent, an increase of 4.7 percent, and would push higher into the Obama administration. The record for Obama's first full year, reported in January 2010, saw real unemployment at 16.7 percent, but it decreased steadily to 11.3 percent in January 2015. By October 2015 it had fallen below 10 percent. While the *level* of the real unemployment rate in the seventh year of Obama's term was *slightly* higher than under Bush's last year in office, the trend *declined* dramatically under Obama (www.bls.gov/news.release/empsit.t15.htm).

Job creation showed similar improvement. The economy began to lose jobs consistently in July 2007, seventeen months before the election, and continued into Obama's first term. After the stimulus effects worked their way into the economy, job growth moved into positive territory in four of the first six months of 2010. However, jobs declined each month from June to September. But in October of 2010, the economy again added jobs and this time never looked back. By November 2015 the economy added 271,000 jobs, driving unemployment down to 5 percent. To be sure, job creation varied throughout Obama's term, but the record is clear: It has added jobs in at least sixty straight months.

Still another way to examine Obama's success is to examine his record relative to the criticisms of his opponents. In May 2012, during the heat of the presidential campaign, Republican nominee Mitt Romney made what one writer for *The Hill* called a "bold" prediction: "I can tell you that over a period of four years, by virtue of the policies that we'd put in place, we'd get the unemployment rate down to 6 percent, and perhaps a little lower" (Easley 2012). *The unemployment rate under Obama beat that mark by more than two years* as it dipped below 6 percent in September 2014 and dropped to 5 percent in October 2015. So even by the standards set by Obama's most motivated opponent, Obama's record in unemployment is impressive.

The "Misery Index"

Obama's record looks even better if we examine the so-called "misery index," which also appears in Figure 9.1. The index is a rough approximation of how "miserable" economic life is by adding indicators of various parts of the economy; the larger the number, the more misery in the economy. While there are several ways to accomplish this, the most common way is to add the unemployment rate and inflation rate together to form an index.

To be sure, inflation was never much of a problem in Obama's administration thanks to an assist by the Federal Reserve that kept interest rates at or near zero. Still, of the twelve postwar presidents, Obama's nearly two-term average (9.2) ranks seventh, just behind Bush, who ranks sixth (8.10).[8] However, if one considers the *change* in the index over the course of a term, Obama ranks *fourth*, decreasing by an average of 0.6 percent per year behind Truman, Ford, and Reagan, and just ahead of

Clinton. Bush 43 ranks eighth, with average misery increasing by an average of 0.28 points per year.

When one considers the *absolute change* in the misery index, calculated by simply subtracting the value of the index when a president assumes the presidency from the value when he (someday, she) leaves office, Obama again places *fourth*. The index in November 2015 was nearly 3.5 points lower than it was in January 2009. By way of comparison, George W. Bush ranks ninth as the index increased by more than two points in his eight years as president.

Other Indicators

Space limitations preclude the systematic consideration of other aspects of Obama's economic record, but a brief exposition of some other categories is in order. When George Bush sent troops into Afghanistan in October 2001 and Iraq in March 2003, he committed the United States to years of wartime spending, with estimates of the budgetary impact set at nearly $2 trillion, and other estimates of the "true cost" ranging as high as $6 trillion, including expected long-term effects. These commitments ballooned the deficit, and the hard choices that Obama had to make regarding the stimulus and bailouts worsened the budget situation. Joseph White, an expert on budgetary policy, was right when he argued that the contraction of slack in the budget would limit Obama's policy agenda. But when he predicted that the budget deficit would only continue to be built on "shifting sands" (White 2011, 198), he could not have foreseen the dramatic reversal in the direction of the budget deficit that was to come.

One of the issues of concern was the supposed size of the budgetary commitment that would have to go toward health care (see the O'Brien and Busch chapters in this volume). To be sure, early estimates indicated that it would place substantial pressure on the budget, but soon a series of budget analyses proved that assumption to be misguided. For example, a Congressional Budget Office (CBO) report showed that, depending on the assumptions made, repealing Obamacare would increase the budget deficit anywhere from $137 billion to $353 billion between 2016 and 2025.[9]

The budget under Obama did increase to levels not seen since World War II. But as the effects of the stimulus and bailouts began to work, unemployment decreased, and the treasury collected more revenue because people were working, earning incomes, and paying taxes. Additionally, Obama's budgets decreased spending in line with the automatic across-the-board cuts mandated by the sequester, which passed after being attached to an agreement to raise the debt limit. Because of these battles, Republicans dug in their heels, and their unwillingness to resist taking the economy to the brink led to the downgrade of the country's credit rating. But the combination of budget cuts, decreased outlays for health care in the wake of the ACA, and increased revenue from rising personal incomes and corporate profits reduced the deficit so much that by the end of 2015 it was at to its lowest level since 2007, well below its fifty-year average (Timiaros 2015). As Figure 9.2 shows, the budget deficit grew to a postwar record of more than 9 percent of GDP by the end of the Bush administration and very early in the Obama administration. But it declined throughout the Obama administration; like the absolute size of the deficit, the deficit-to-GDP ratio is at its lowest level since 2007, before the crash. What had been predicted to be an interminable period of increasing budget shortfalls turned out just the opposite, again confounding Obama's critics and even many of his supporters. The budget situation turned around more quickly than almost anyone anticipated (see Reinhart and Rogoff 2009).

Figure 9.3 displays trends in consumer confidence (sometimes referred to as "consumer sentiment") and has been collected by the University of Michigan since 1952. The index measures consumer attitudes toward the economic and business climate and is seen as a good indicator of how well the economy will progress in the near to midterm. If consumers think the economy is going to improve or remain good, they are more likely to increase their purchasing or investment activities. It is also one of the best predictors of presidential approval ratings (Erikson, MacKuen, and Stimson 2002). Consumer confidence reaches its lowest point in the last year of Carter's administration, when the nation endured persistent stagflation and high oil prices. The index hits its peak during the prolonged economic good fortune in the Clinton administration, especially in 2000, Clinton's last year in office. It dips sharply throughout Bush 43's presidency to a near record low in 2008, coinciding with the darkest days of the economic crisis. During Bush's eight years the decline in confidence averaged 3.6 percent annually and registered 25.5 points lower than when he took office. This is the worst record of the six presi-

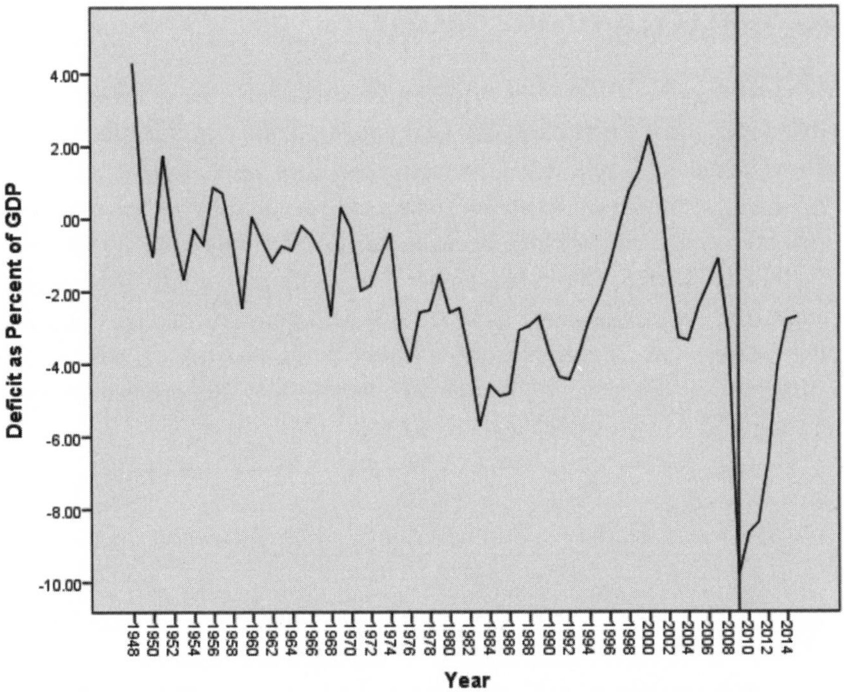

Figure 9.2. Budget deficits as percent of the sxize of the economy: Truman to Obama. Negative numbers indicate deficits; positive numbers indicate surplus. Source: https://research.stlouisfed.org/fred2/series/FYFSGDA188S.

dencies represented (as well as the worst of all eleven covered by the index but not shown here). During the first part of Obama's term, the index increases slightly but dips in August 2011, when the debt ceiling crisis was in full throttle. Since then, it has been on an upward trajectory. The average increases at 0.4 percent annually, and in absolute terms the index registered at nearly thirty points higher in May 2015 than when he took office. Both of these place Obama highest among the presidencies since Eisenhower, and as of this writing consumers are much more optimistic about the state of the economy than they have been in a very long time.

A MIXED BAG: THE STOCK MARKET, ECONOMIC INEQUALITY, AND GDP GROWTH

When George W. Bush took office in January 2001, the stock market's Dow Jones index registered just a bit above 15,000. By the time he left office in January 2009, it had lost nearly half its value, falling to 7,949. As of this writing, the DJA has increased in value by more than 115 percent and has consistently been in the 17,000 range and flirted with 18,000 late in 2015. But in November 2015, with job growth consistently robust, the Federal Reserve signaled it would consider raising the near-zero interest rate slightly in order to begin the process of staving off inflation so as to continue the recovery. Predictably, the markets reacted and adjusted downward to closer to 17,500.

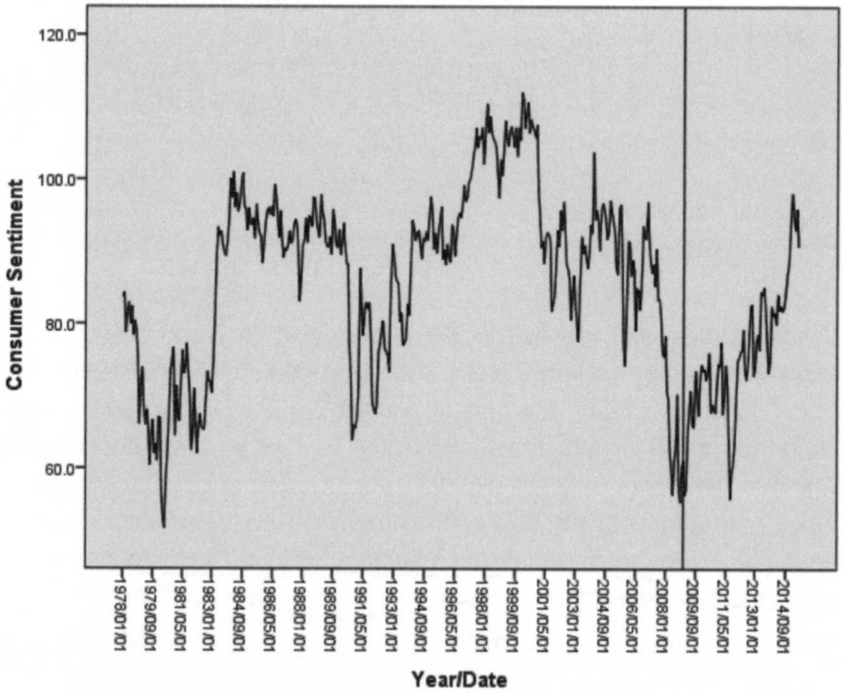

Figure 9.3. Index of consumer sentiment, Carter to Obama. Vertical line denotes beginning of Obama's administration. Chart reflects data through May 2015, the last reading available as of this writing. Source: University of Michigan Consumer Sentiment, available at https://research.stlouisfed.org/fred2/series/UMCSENT.

Obama was the first president to explicitly make reducing economic inequality a major priority (Weatherford 2012). The Gini index is a measure of inequality and ranges from zero (complete equality) to one (total inequality). The United States has a long history of increasing inequality, and the Gini index continued that trend under Obama's watch. But in some ways, he was a victim of his own success. There are at least two reasons for increased inequality. One, as just discussed, is the enormous recovery in the stock market. Much of those increases translate into "capital gains," which go into retirement accounts and dividend income to the wealthiest Americans. Additionally, these dividends are taxed at much lower rates than wage or salaried incomes.

The second reason for growth in inequality is the Fed's actions (or lack of action), which kept interest rates at or near zero for much of the crisis. This provided incentives for borrowing and spending, but it also provided disincentives for saving or investing because the yields were likely to be low. Again, the net result was to further increase the gap.

There is no denying that economic growth was sluggish during Obama's presidency. Still, real GDP (adjusted for inflation) grew every year except 2009, when the economy was in free-fall. GDP dipped almost 2.8 percent overall, and per capita GDP decreased more than 3.6 percent. But as the effects of the economic policies took hold, growth started to turn around, albeit more slowly than everyone, including the president, hoped. Still, grow it did. Real GDP increased an average of 1.45 percent over the course of his term, though that dismal number includes the massive downturn in 2009. If one excludes that year, average growth rose to 2.16 percent, eclipsing Bush 43's average of 2.11 percent. And if one looks only at 2014 and 2015, the economy showed unmistakable signs of life, growing at about 2.6 percent, approaching the postwar presidential average of 3.3 percent, but still not growing as quickly as Obama had hoped.

CONCLUSION

Recessions, particularly those that are deep and rooted in housing crises, tend to be long-term affairs that do not really begin to turn around for six to eight years. While the economy is still in recovery mode, there have been huge reversals in most sectors during President Obama's term in office.

With two exceptions, all relevant economic indicators showed dramatic turnarounds in a positive direction and did so much more quickly than many predicted. The budget deficit, unemployment, inflation, the stock market, job creation, the misery index (which combines inflation and unemployment), and many others not considered here (e.g., housing starts, durable goods, efforts to close the trade imbalance) showed robust progress. To be sure, if one examines the Obama administration only in terms of levels (e.g., average unemployment), his record does not fare as well as many other presidents. But I argue that is not the appropriate benchmark by which to evaluate his record. Presidents are elected to do a four- or eight-year job, so analysts should examine the administration's record in a dynamic way, examining movement and change in the affected areas. By virtually any metric, the economy had fallen into a "big hole" when Obama moved into the White House. But by those same metrics, the economy had either climbed out of the hole (stock market, job creation, budget deficit) or at minimum had made great progress moving back from the brink. While there is always room for improvement, the success of the Obama administration in dealing with the crisis marks his as a successful economic legacy.

NOTES

1. This is usually referred to as the "expectations gap," meaning that the public expects presidents to do things that are often well outside their ability to influence because of constitutional, statutory, and/or historical circumstances. For an overview, see Simon (2009).

2. What presidents do with regard to the economy is more than politics, of course. They are hired to try to provide peace and prosperity and, the expectations gap notwithstanding, much of what presidents do has at least some implication for the state of the economy. It is difficult to discuss the economy in isolation because so much of what constitutes public policy has deep implications for the economic health of the country. Immigration, energy, the environment, health care, education, foreign policy, trade, internal improvements, and many others all touch on the economy, even if economic issues are not their primary concern.

3. The following descriptions rely on the summary in the *CQ Almanac* (2009a and 2009b).

4. Gilmour analyzed several examples where this kind of tradeoff was considered throughout twentieth-century American politics and argues that politicians should be more accepting of something rather than nothing. Doing so provides constituencies with some relief, though perhaps not all of what politicians would like. See Gilmour 1995.

5. The following is based on timelines provided by Woodyard (2013) and Reuters (2011).

6. Much of the following description relies on *CQ Almanac* (2010).

7. Space precludes presenting these records in tabular form. Results are available from the author.

8. The lowest average belongs to Eisenhower (6.27), followed by Johnson (6.79), while the worst record belongs to Carter (16.26), who ranks just below Reagan (12.19).

9. It bears noting that one of the most strident criticisms of Obamacare was that it would be a "job killer." However, just the opposite was true as the full implementation of Obamacare occurred at precisely the same time that the economy was adding millions of jobs.

WORKS CITED

ABC News/*Washington Post*. 2010a. ABC News/*Washington Post* Poll, April 2010 [survey question]. USABCWP.042610.R02E. ABC News/*Washington Post* [producer]. Storrs, CT: Roper Center for Public Opinion Research, iPOLL [distributor]. Accessed October 16, 2015.

ABC News/*Washington Post*. 2010b. ABC News/*Washington Post* Poll, July 2010 [survey question]. USABCWP.071310.R02H. ABC News/*Washington Post* [producer]. Storrs, CT: Roper Center for Public Opinion Research, iPOLL [distributor]. Accessed October 16,2015.

Brown, Aaron. 2011. "Silent Cal at the Hull Rust Mine." http://minnesotabrown.com/2011/08/silent-cal-at-the-hull-rust-mine.html. Accessed November 7, 2015.

Burtless, Michael. 2014. "The Stimulus Program Was a Smashing Success: It Erased Most Middle Class Income Losses in the Recession." Brookings Institution Opinion, November 25, 2014. www.brookings.edu/research/opinions/2014/11/25-stimulus-program-success-burtless.Accessed October 4, 2015.

Campbell, James E. 2011. "The Economic Records of the Presidents: Party Differences and Inherited Economic Conditions." *The Forum: A Journal of Applied Research in Contemporary Politics*, v.9, n.1, article 7 (April): 1–29.

Cooper, Michael. 2008. "McCain on U.S. Economy: From 'Strong' to 'Total Crisis' in 36 Hours." *New York Times*. www.nytimes.com/2008/09/17/world/americas/17iht-mccain.4.16251777.html. Accessed October 3, 2015.

Congressional Quarterly Almanac. 2009a. "Stimulus Enacted to Pump Economy with $575.3 Billion in New Spending." Washington, DC: Congressional Quarterly. pp. 7-3 to 7.7.

Congressional Quarterly Almanac. 2009b. "Details of the Economic Stimulus Law." Washington, DC: Congressional Quarterly. pp. 7-7 to 7.9.

Congressional Quarterly Almanac. 2010. "Historic Financial Overhaul Creates Bureau, Expands Oversight of Banks." Washington, DC: Congressional Quarterly. pp. 3-3 to 3-9.

Congressional Quarterly Almanac. 2010b. "Details of Financial Regulation Bill." Washington, DC: Congressional Quarterly. pp. 3-10 to 3-18.

Easley, Jonathan. 2012. "Romney Vows to Lower Unemployment Rate to 6 Percent by End of First Term." May 23. http://thehill.com/blogs/blog-briefing-room/news/229137-romney-promises-to-lower-unemployment-to-6-percent-in-first-term. Accessed November 21, 2015.

Erikson, Robert S., Michael B. MacKuen, and James A. Stimson. 2002. *The Macro Polity*. New York: Cambridge University Press.

Federal Reserve. 2015. Federal Surplus or Deficit [-] as Percent of Gross Domestic Product. https://research.stlouisfed.org/fred2/series/FYFSGDA188S. Accessed November 18, 2015.

Gilmour, John B. 1995. *Strategic Disagreement: Stalemate in American Politics*. Pittsburgh, PA: University of Pittsburgh Press.

Lauter, David. 2014. "Five Years Later, White House and Critics Fight over Stimulus Law." *Los Angeles Times*, February 17, 2014. http://articles.latimes.com/2014/feb/17/news/la-pn-obama-stimulus-law-20140217. Accessed October 4, 2015.

Mak, Tim. 2011. "Clinton: Stimulus Wasn't Big Enough" *Politico*, June 29. www.politico.com/story/2011/06/clinton-stimulus-wasnt-big-enough-058006. Accessed October 4, 2015.

Matthews, Dylan. 2011. "Did the Stimulus Work? A Review of the Nine Best Studies on the Subject." *Washington Post*, August 24. www.washingtonpost.com/blogs/ezra-klein/post/did-the-stimulus-work-a-review-of-the-nine-best-studies-on-the-subject/2011/08/16/gIQAThbibJ_blog.html. Accessed October 4, 2015.

Pethokoukis, James. 2013. "Is This the Chart that Shows the Obama Stimulus Actually Worked? Former White House Economist Says It Is." www.aei.org/publication/is-this-the-chart-that-shows-the-obama-stimulus-actually-worked-former-white-house-economist-says-it-is/. Accessed October 4, 2015.

Reuters. 2011. "Chrysler Set to Repay $7.5 Billion U.S., Canada Loans." www.reuters.com/article/2011/05/24/chrysler-idUSN2417980220110524. Accessed October 16, 2015.

Reinhart, Carmen M., and Kenneth S. Rogoff. 2009. *This Time Is Different: Eight Centuries of Financial Folly*. Princeton, NJ: Princeton University Press.

Simon, Dennis M. 2009. "Public Expectations of the President." In *The Oxford Handbook of the American Presidency*, ed. George C. Edwards III and William G. Howell. Oxford: Oxford University Press.

Timiaros, Nick. 2015. "U.S. Posts Smallest Annual Budget Deficit Since 2007." *Wall Street Journal*, October 15. www.wsj.com/articles/u-s-posts-smallest-annual-budget-deficit-since-2007-1444937616. Accessed November 6, 2015.

USA Today. Gallup/USA Today Poll, June 2010 [survey question]. USGALLUP.10JN11.R18A.Gallup Organization [producer]. Storrs, CT: Roper Center for Public Opinion Research, iPOLL [distributor]. Accessed October 16, 2015.

Weatherford, M. Stephen. 2012. "Economic Crisis and Political Change: A New New Deal?" In *The Obama Presidency: Appraisals and Prospects*, ed. Bert A. Rockman, Andrew Rudalevige, and Colin Campbell. Washington, DC: CQ Press/Sage.

White, Joseph. 2011. "From Ambition to Desperation on the Budget." In *Obama in Office*., ed. James A. Thurber. Boulder, CO: Paradigm Press.

Wood, B. Dan. 2007. *The Politics of Economic Leadership: The Causes and Consequences of Presidential Rhetoric*. Princeton, NJ: Princeton University Press.

Woodyard, Chris. 2013. "GM Bailout Played Out over Five Years." *USA Today*, December 9. www.usatoday.com/story/money/cars/2013/12/09/gm-bailout-timeline/3929953/. Accessed October 16, 2015.

10

ECONOMIC STAGNATION IN THE OBAMA PRESIDENCY

Raymond Tatalovich, Loyola University Chicago

The reelection of Barack Obama in 2012 has shaken one of the most universally held precepts in modern political science. There is virtually a consensus among public opinion analysts and scholars of election studies that the economy is an important, perhaps the most salient, influence on domestic politics, absent any turbulent national crisis like war or 9/11. One review of nearly four hundred empirical studies concluded that the economy is a significant predictor of voter choice (Lewis-Beck and Stegmaier 2007, 518–37). There are articles on the longitudinal impact of economic variables on presidential voting (Erikson 1989, Fair 1988) and studies focusing on specific elections. In 1992, for example, unemployment was the key factor in the reelection defeat of President George H. W. Bush whereas inflation was a nonissue (Clarke, Rapkin, and Stewart 1994). Statistical models designed to predict the outcome of presidential elections invariably include key economic variables (Lewis-Beck and Rice 1992). In 2008, however, the unexpected Wall Street financial meltdown in late September was a "game changer" that augmented the size of Obama's popular vote over John McCain (Campbell 2009). There is also evidence that highly salient economic conditions like unemployment and inflation influence presidential popularity (Chappell 1990, Ostrom and Simon 1985, MacKuen 1983).

Thus, the argument that bad economic times hurt while good economic times help the incumbent or government-of-the-day, in parliamentary systems, has virtually reached the level of a truism. And this truism should have applied to the presidential election of 2012, *if* voter choice was based solely on the strength of the economic fundamentals (Lewis-Beck and Tien 2012, Hibbs 2012). But for 2012, public perceptions of the economy were more favorable toward Obama than the objective economic conditions (Erikson and Wlezien 2012), though other salient factors (incumbency) further complicated the statistical task of forecasting the presidential election outcome (Campbell 2012).

ECONOMIC STAGNATION

A review of the key economic indicators for every presidential term beginning with Harry Truman in 1948–1952 through 2014 shows that the first Obama term had the worst overall economic performance of any previous president of either political party (see Table 10.1). I coauthored such a ranking for all those presidents through George W. Bush (Dolan, Frendreis, and Tatalovich 2009, 690) based on the four-year averaged unemployment rate, percentage growth of real gross domestic product (GDP), inflation as measured by the Consumer Price Index, productivity, and the international balance on current account (goods, services, and financial transactions) as a percentage of total US GDP. For this purpose, the first three economic indicators were updated based on statistics in the *Economic Report of the President* (2015, Tables B-1, B-10, B-11, and B-16); the international statistics were derived from the US Department of Commerce, Bureau of Economic Analysis (2015, Table 1.1); and productivity was supplied by the US Bureau of Labor Statistics (2015). In any extended historical statistical series, it is not unusual for recent statistics to be revised based on the latest updated information. But any updating did not affect the specific or overall ranking previously reported by Dolan, Frendreis, and Tatalovich (2009, 690) for each president, so we simply integrated Obama's rank on each indicator within those rankings and derived an overall rank for his 2009–2012 term. Higher ranks indicate lower unemployment and inflation, higher growth and productivity, and a less negative or a positive balance on current account between the United States and other nations.

President Obama inherited the Great Recession, which began in December of 2007, but the economy was further devastated by the financial "crisis" that began in September 2008 when the Wall Street firm of Leh-

Table 10.1. Comparing the Economy under Obama and His Predecesors (N=16) (all numbers in percent)

Years	Unemployment	Inflation	Economic Growth	Productivity	Current Account Balance
1949-2008*	5.6	3.7	3.4	2.2	-1.18
Republicans*	5.9	3.7	2.8	2.1	-1.56
Democrats*	5.2	3.8	4.3	2.4	-0.60
2009-2012	9.0 (16)	2.2 (4)	0.9 (16)	1.9 (10)	-2.86
2013**	7.4	1.5	2.2	0.0	-2.25
2014**	6.2	0.8	2.4	0.7	-2.24

*Averages based on 15 presidential terms during 1949-2008, including 9 Republican and 6 Democratic presidential terms. **Comparisons based on the previous year, not the previous presidential term.

man Brothers went bankrupt. In October of 2007 the Dow Jones Industrial Average (DJIA) peaked at 14,164.53, but after Lehman's bankruptcy on September 15, 2008, the DJIA ended the month below 11,000. The DJIA did not reach 11,000 again until April 12, 2010, but since then has gradually surged to a new high of 18,312 on May 19, 2015, before settling back into the high 16,000s by the end of August 2015. If the US economy had mirrored the stock market performance, by now President Obama would be glowing with pride over his economic stewardship. But the problem is that the economy remains sluggish and growth is uneven across economic sectors, which more than raises questions about the competence of President Obama as an economic steward of prosperity.

The National Bureau of Economic Research (NBER) tracks the ups and downs of the business cycle. One indicator of recession is when the gross domestic product (GDP), which measures the value of the total output of goods and services for the American economy, declines for two consecutive quarters. The Great Recession "technically" ended in June of 2009 and, according to the NBER, its eighteen-month duration surpassed all previous post–World War II recessions: 2001 (eight months); 1990–1991 (eight months); 1981–1982 (sixteen months); 1980 (six months); 1973–1975 (sixteen months); 1969–1970 (eleven months); 1960–1961 (ten months); 1957–1958 (eight months); 1953–1954 (ten months); 1948–1949 (eleven months); 1945 (eight months). For all twelve postwar recessions, the average duration was 10.8 months, so the Great Recession deserves its name.

Best known to most people are economic growth, unemployment, and inflation, which are readily publicized as a simple percentages. Real GDP measures the total size of the domestic economy after controlling for inflation, and its growth during 2009–2012 (at 0.9 percent) was the worst record of economic growth recorded in the postwar era. The negative growth rate in real GDP for 2009 (at –2.8 percent) shows the impact of the Great Recession, but the economic expansion that followed was not robust by historic standards. The pattern of modest real GDP growth experienced in 2010 (2.5 percent), 2011 (1.6 percent), and 2012 (2.3 percent) continued into 2013 and 2014. Economic growth through twenty-three quarters of the Obama recovery was 13.3 percent compared to an average 26.7 percent at this point for ten previous postwar recessions (*Investor's Business Daily* 2015), which is why so many economists referred to the "jobless recovery" from the Great Recession.

The average unemployment rate during Obama's first term was 9 percent, again the worst record of joblessness except for the Great Depression in the 1930s. One year after the Great Recession ended, the unemployment rate was 9.5 percent, as compared to the lower rates one year following the recessions of 2001–2002 (6.0 percent), 1990–1991 (7.4 percent), and 1981–1982 (8.3 percent). Although the 1981–1982 economic contraction was the worst since the 1930s, with the jobless rate above 10 percent from September 1981 through June of 1982, eventually unemployment fell to 8.3 percent by December 1983 and 7.3 percent one year later. The problem is that the 9+ percent jobless rates have lasted thirty months, from April 2009 through September 2011, the worst performance in the postwar era, and then unemployment remained above 8 percent until September of 2012, roughly one month before the presidential election.

Even worse, it is now recognized that the unemployment rate badly underestimated the true level of joblessness caused by the Great Recession. So many individuals have stopped looking for a job that the size of the workforce has shrunk, which artificially lowered the jobless rate for those still in the workforce. The size of the workforce is technically the civilian "labor force participation rate," which declined to 62.9 percent in 2014 (the lowest level since 1977) as compared to 66.9 percent in 2007 (US Bureau of Labor Statistics 2015, Table B-11). The fact that people cannot find jobs is also reflected in the long-term (twenty-seven-plus weeks) unemployment rate, which spiked to a post-Depression high of 4.4 percent in 2010 and did not significantly decline until the end of 2013. Today long-term unemployment remains higher than what was experienced during the double-dip recessions of the 1980s (Norris 2015).

Many economists still subscribe to a variation of the theory underlying the Phillips Curve, which posits a short-term trade-off between unemployment and inflation: higher joblessness with lower inflation, lower joblessness with higher inflation. The record of Obama's first term gives support to that theory, since the Consumer Price Index recorded the fourth-lowest rate of inflation since 1948, and even less inflation in the years since. The absence of inflationary pressures allowed the Federal Reserve Board to inaugurate, and remain committed to, its monetary policy of "quantitative easing," which yielded historic low interest rates. But it remains an open question whether President Obama deserves much credit for the conduct of monetary policy because the Fed operates independently from White House dictates, although historically monetary policy has been usually compatible with fiscal policy and is not easily manipulated for partisan purposes (Kettl 1986, Woolley 1984, Mayer 1990). More to the point, it was Fed chairman Ben Bernanke, whom President Bush appointed in 2006, who steered monetary policy during the global financial crisis that aggravated the Great Recession. After his first term ended, Bernanke was so highly respected that the prospects of a political backlash and turmoil in the financial markets gave President Obama little choice but to reappoint Bernanke to a second term in 2010. Only with the appointment of Janet Yellen in January of 2014 did Obama have his own appointee at the helm of the Federal Reserve Board. But Yellen continued the Bernanke policies, though there were the beginnings of debate within the Fed about how soon to end the low interest rates in the face of signs that inflationary pressures may be returning.

The balance on current account measures the dollar outflows versus inflows between the United States and other countries that result from international trade, foreign aid, US armed forces stationed abroad, and other factors like financial transactions by multinational corporations. Chronic and substantial imbalances over time can lead to distortions in the domestic economy. Trade is a major component, for example, and dependence on costly imports that are essential to the economy (like oil) may fuel inflationary pressures at home. From 1948 through most of the

1970s, a positive current account balance (meaning that foreign countries owed the United States more than we owed them) was the norm, with rare exceptions, but since 1977 the current account balance has been negative for all but three years, and those negative imbalances have grown larger over time. By winding down the Afghanistan and Iraq wars, Obama reduced the imbalance on current account but, nonetheless, the negative current account balance for 2009–2012 ranked the fourteenth worst among sixteen presidential terms.

Finally, productivity measures the real gross domestic product "output per hour of all persons" in the nonfarm business sector. Since increased productivity means that an economic sector can produce more goods and services for the same, or less, allocation of resources, higher productivity means that the wages and salaries of workers can be raised without affecting profits or putting upward pressure on prices. But low or negligible increases in productivity restrains raises in wages and salaries, and the average yearly increase in productivity during Obama's first term was the tenth lowest since Harry S. Truman, and productivity increases have fallen to even lower levels in the years since. Stagnation in the level of productivity is one, though not the only, reason why personal income in the United States also has stagnated under President Obama.

INCOME STAGNATION

A final indicator that has both economic and social implications is growth in personal income and the degree of income inequality. A wider distribution of income generates more aggregate demand that fuels economic growth and sustains a middle class that supports democratic politics. Serious income inequality, as exists in too many developing economies, can give rise to protest movements and even political revolution. In the United States every recession forces more people into the ranks of the poor, and the Great Recession has had an especially bad impact on the poverty rate. The percentage of people below the federal poverty line has been measured yearly by the US Census Bureau (2015, Table 2) beginning in 1959. For this statistical series, the four-year average percentage rate of persons under poverty was calculated for each presidential term, giving us fourteen terms through 2012. The poverty rate during the last two years of the second Eisenhower term (22.3 percent) and the shared

Kennedy-Johnson term of 1961–1964 (20.4 percent) ranked fourteenth and thirteenth respectively. But the one-in-five Americans in poverty at that time lived during an era before President Lyndon Johnson declared his War on Poverty in 1964. Once federal antipoverty programs were launched, the poverty rate fell to its lowest level during the Carter administration (11.6 percent) but rose to 14.9 percent during Obama's first term, the eleventh-worst record since we began calculating poverty rates. In fact, poverty reached 15 percent during 2010, 2011, and 2012 before dropping slightly to 14.5 percent in 2013.

The increase in poverty was a leading indicator that income inequality across America had also gotten worse during the Great Recession. The standard measure of income inequality is the Gini coefficient, which ranges from a value of 0 (perfect equality of income) to 1 (perfect inequality of income). These are hypotheticals since perfect inequality of income would mean that one person has all the income and everybody else in a society has none. Nonetheless, the conventional wisdom is that income inequality has worsened in the United States over the past several decades, and this statistical series confirms that fact. The Gini coefficient for each year beginning in 1967 was calculated by the US Census Bureau (2015, Table A-2). For this statistical series, the four-year average Gini coefficient was calculated for each presidential term, giving us twelve terms through 2012. The most equal distribution of household income occurred during the last two years of the Johnson administration in 1967–1968 (.392), with the second-best Gini coefficient occurring during the first Nixon term (.396). Income inequality increased over every subsequent presidential term and reached its worse level under President Obama in 2009–2012 (.473) and in 2013 (.476).

Both the poverty rate and the degree of income inequality are affected by the number of households or individuals located at the extremes of the income distribution (meaning the low and high income earners), so those indicators of wealth do not measure the economic health of the American middle class. There has been much commentary in recent years about the erosion of the middle class in the United States, and this aspect is best illustrated by looking at the "real" (controlling for inflation) median household income over time. However, since both the real and nominal values for median household income usually increase over time, a more precise measure would be the percentage change in the real median household income from presidential term to term. This was calculated for the period of 1967 to 2003, also from data provided by the U.S. Census Bureau (2015, Table A-2). The best improvement in real median family income, from the prior administration, occurred in the first Clinton term (+9.2 percent), while the Obama term recorded the worst decline (–5.9 percent) among the twelve terms analyzed. In fact, this four-year averaging masks the steady deterioration in family incomes that followed in the wake of the Great Recession. In 2007, before the Wall Street financial crisis hit, real median household income reached an all-time high of $56,436 under George W. Bush. The economic and financial crisis reduced median incomes to $54,423 in 2008, Bush's last year in office, which roughly stabilized at $54,059 during Obama's first year but then continued falling to $51,759 in 2012, to rebound only slightly in 2013 (to $51,939). By any conventional standard, therefore, the Great Recession has had a devastating impact on the economic well-being of Americans, and obviously the Obama administration did little to remedy the situation.

FISCAL MALFEASANCE

The United States got a wake-up call about the serious consequences of national indebtedness when the "sovereign debt crisis" swept across Europe. It was precipitated when the credit-rating agencies (Standard & Poor's, Moody's) in 2010 downgraded the bonds issued by Greece (later also Spain and Portugal), requiring them to pay creditors more interest payments in order to secure loans. The "crisis" resulted because the expenditures of those and other European nations have long exceeded their revenues, and close attention was focused on the PIIGS nations (Portugal, Ireland, Italy, Greece, and Spain). The problem of deficits and debt also surfaced as a compelling political problem for the United States. In mid-2010 the Congressional Budget Office reported that the federal debt rose from 36 percent of GDP in 2007 to 62 percent in 2010 and could reach 90 percent of GDP by 2020 (Congressional Budget Office 2010). The politics of debt only worsened after the Republicans won control of the House of Representatives in November 2010 because the Obama administration, the Senate Democrats, and the House Republicans were now at loggerheads about how to cut spending, or raise taxes, or even whether to allow more borrowing. In early December 2010 the bipartisan National Commission on Fiscal Responsibility issued its final report, but only eleven of its eighteen members endorsed its plan to slash deficits by nearly four trillion over the next decade, reduce the national debt to 41 percent of GDP in twenty-five years, and balance the budget by 2035 (Dennis and Montgomery 2010). Its report had to be endorsed by fourteen members to force Congress to consider its recommendations, but its highly publicized findings served as an early warning alert about the imminent fiscal crisis.

Congress sets a statutory "debt ceiling" on how much money the U.S. government can borrow, and the Treasury Department said that default was a serious risk by early August 2011. As that deadline approached, President Obama gave a prime-time television speech on July 25, urging Congress to raise the debt ceiling and indirectly blaming President Bush for the runaway spending. As President Obama stated, "For the last decade, we have spent more money than we take in. In the year 2000, the government had a budget surplus. But instead of using it to pay off our debt, the money was spent on trillions of dollars in new tax cuts, while two wars and an expensive prescription drug program were simply added to our nation's credit card." Although Obama again tried to shift blame onto his predecessor, his allegations beg the question of whether Barack Obama was any less responsible than George W. Bush in bringing about this latest fiscal crisis.

To evaluate Obama relative to Bush and his predecessors, therefore, I ranked all presidents since Harry Truman on three criteria: (1) the size of their deficits in current dollars (not holding inflation constant) as a percentage of GDP, (2) the end-of-term publicly held debt as a percentage of GDP, and (3) the four-year increase in the publicly held debt as a percentage of GDP (*Economic Report of the President* 2015, Tables B-19 and B-20). A higher ranking signifies a smaller deficit or debt-to-GDP ratio. Including both Obama terms will mean that seventeen presidential terms are being compared here. The historic record (*Economic Report of the President* 2015, Table B-19) shows that expenditures by the US government regularly exceeded its revenues, and the pace of indebtedness has increased. Since 1948, balanced budgets occurred three times each under Truman and Eisenhower, and once under Johnson before a string of deficits did not end until surpluses were recorded four times under Clinton (1998 to 2001). Since then deficits have resulted every year, but compared to the historical record, President Obama is in a league of his own (see Table 10.2).

Looking back, the publicly held federal debt comprised 60.1 percent of GDP at the end of President Truman's second term in 1952. However, that mountain of debt was not caused by Truman's extravagance, since the four-year surplus averaged 1.5 percent of GPD during 1949–1952, but resulted from the accumulation of massive government deficits to fund World War II. Yet that record has been easily eclipsed by President Obama, whose four-year deficits averaged $1.273 trillion each year during his first term. As a percentage of GDP, those deficits were the highest on record, and they nearly doubled the size of the national debt held publicly at the end of 2012, also the worst performance in modern fiscal history. On August 5, 2011, President Obama again made fiscal history, but the wrong kind. The unprecedented scale of US indebtedness caused Standard and Poor's to lower the credit rating of Treasury bonds from the risk-free AAA to AA-plus, the first downgrade of US securities in history (Appelbaum and Dash 2011).

Deficits occur when expenditures exceed revenues, and the accumulation of deficits over time is the national debt. One measure of the fiscal integrity of a nation is its debt-to-GDP ratio, or the size of total national debt relative to the total size of a nation's economy. The national debt becomes "unsustainable" when its size begins to equal, or exceed, the total value of goods and services produced by the economy (or GDP). At the end of Obama's first term, the publicly held national debt represented 70 percent and, based on estimates for 2015 and 2016, the debt-to-GDP ratio will increase to 75 percent at the end of his second term. But the

Table 10.2. How Obama's Fiscal Performance Compares with his Predecessors (N=17) (all numbers in percent)

	Average Deficit		
Year	% of GDP*	% of GDP*	Four-Year Increase
1949-2008	1.73**	38.6**	27**
Republicans	2.25**	38.0**	35**
Democrats	0.95**	39.5**	14**
2009-2112	8.5 (17)	70.4 (16)	94 (17)
2013-2016**	3.2 (13)	75.0 (17)	25 (9)

*End of term publicly held federal debt. **Estimates for 2015 and 2016 are used in these calculations.

story of fiscal malfeasance does not end there, according to Federal Reserve Board Chairman Janet Yellen, an Obama appointee whom the Senate confirmed in January 2014. In testimony before the Joint Economic Committee of Congress in early May 2014, Yellen made reference to the updated Congressional Budget Office (CBO) long-term budget projections. Those ten-year CBO budget projections estimated that the federal government will produce $7.618 trillion in deficits from 2015 through 2024. The publicly held federal debt would be four times larger in 2024 than it was at the end of 2007. A question from Senator Dan Coats (R-IN) led Yellen to conclude, "I guess one recommendation that I would give you is that long-term budget deficits, we can see in, for example, CBO's very long-term projections, that they remain," said Yellen. "There is more work to do to put fiscal policy on a sustainable course. . . . [with] a combination of demographics, the structure of entitlement programs, and historic trends in health-care costs, we can see that over the long-term deficits will rise to unsustainable levels relative to the economy" (Jeffrey 2014).

PUBLIC PERCEPTIONS

We began with a question: How could President Obama get reelected based on the worst economic record since World War II? One consideration is that Americans do not necessarily blame a new president for the economic problems inherited from the previous administration. Although 1982 was the worst economic downturn to date, more Americans held Jimmy Carter to blame than newly elected President Reagan (Peffley and Williams 1985, Schneider 1982). And a Gallup Poll taken in December of 2001 found that newly elected President George W. Bush was given "a great deal of blame" by only 7 percent of respondents and "some blame" by 37 percent compared to the 24 percent who attributed to Bush "not much blame" and another 28 percent who attributed to him "no blame at all for the country's current economic recession" (Roper Center for Public Opinion Research 2015). When a slightly different version of this Gallup Poll was asked seven times during the Obama tenure, however, many more Americans generally *did* blame Bush for the economic problems facing the nation, a public perception fueled by Obama's rhetoric that cast blame on his predecessor for virtually every problem that Obama faced after 2008. The Gallup Poll question asked: "Thinking about the economic problems currently facing the United States, how much do you blame . . . George W. Bush for these—a great deal, a moderate amount, not much, or not at all?" (Roper Center for Public Opinion Research 2015). If we add together the percentages that chose "a great deal" and "a moderate amount" compared to the percentages that chose "not much" and "not at all" for each poll, the total percentage blaming Bush ranged from 68 percent (in June 2012) to 80 percent (in July 2009) while the total percentage who held Bush almost blameless ranged from 20 percent (in July 2009) to 31 percent (in June 2012).

Clearly Obama was able to shift much of the responsibility for the Great Recession onto the Bush administration, a strategy that proved electorally effective. The American National Election Study for 2012 asked two related questions: "How much is President Obama [or "former President Bush"] to blame for the poor economy?" Those who blamed Bush "a great deal" or "a lot" tended to vote for Obama by margins of 91.9 percent and 74.6 percent respectively, whereas the respondents who blamed Obama "a great deal" or "a lot" voted for Romney by 97.1 percent and 91.9 percent margins. But those numbers translated into more votes for Obama in 2012, since many more respondents blamed Bush rather than Obama for the poor economy. Overall 46.1 percent said that George W. Bush deserved "a great deal" or "a lot" of the blame for the poor economy as compared to the 29.4 percent who blamed Obama more harshly (American National Election Study 2014).

Nonetheless, the American people were not especially happy with Obama's economic stewardship. In point of fact, overall, Barack Obama is on track to being one of the least popular post–World War II presidents. But his general popularity has always been higher than how public opinion has judged his performance in specific policy areas, including the economy. Figure 10.1 shows the trend lines from February 2009 through early August 2015 for the percentage approving or disapproving how Obama was "handling his job as president" (The American Presidency Project 2015) versus the percentage approving or disapproving his "handling the economy" (PollingReport 2015).

Except for the first three polls taken during his "honeymoon" period, when asked whether they approved or disapproved "of the way Barack Obama is handling the economy," more Americans were disapproving in every subsequent Gallup Poll taken through August 2015. Indeed, an

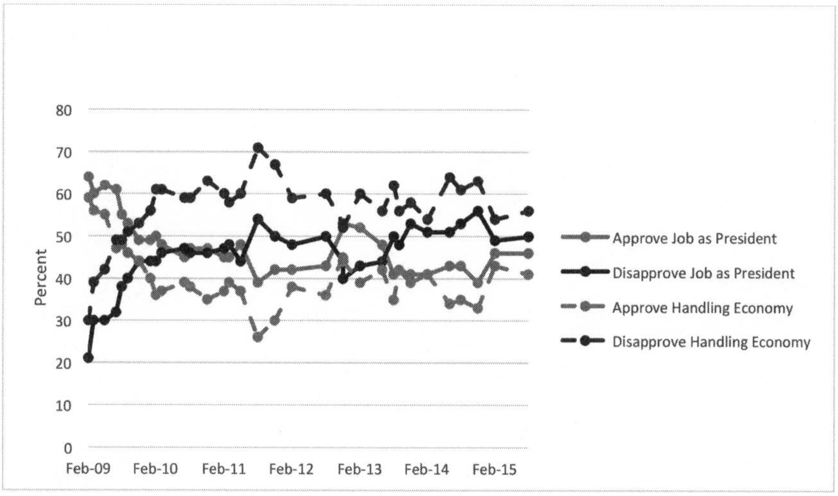

Figure 10.1. Gallup Polls on Obama Popularity Compared to Obama Economic Stewardship

absolute majority disapproved of his economic stewardship beginning in September of 2009 and, although there were brief periods during his tenure when Obama's general popularity garnered majority approval, nonetheless the majority still disapproved of his economic performance.

This assessment is also reflected in sixteen Pew Research Center surveys that asked this question: "Since taking office, have Barack Obama's economic policies made economic conditions better, worse, or not had an effect so far?" Below (see Table 10.3) are the percentages recorded in those polls from 2009 to mid-2015. The modal response in most of the surveys, except those after 2012, was that President Obama's economic policies had no effect whatsoever on economic conditions. A minority believed his policies had a more positive than negative impact during 2009, his first year, but then a larger minority believed that his policies made economic conditions "worse" during the period 2010 through 2013.

The problem with measuring the "popularity" of any president is that people judge the incumbent by different standards, including charisma, personal attributes like race, the times, and crisis management (like 9/11), as well as performance in office. Gallup Polls have never tried to dissect the popularity score in terms of those ingredients, but Gallup has added a "favorability" measure to its polling inventory. According to Gallup,

Table 10.3. Pew Research Center Survey on Obama's Economic Stewardship

Date	*Better %*	*Worse %*	*No Effect so Far* %*
March 2009	14	15	68
April 2009	26	17	53
June 2009	26	16	53
July 2009	24	21	49
October 2009	31	20	46
December 2009	30	24	42
February 2010	24	27	45
June 2010	23	29	38
September 2010	27	32	38
January 2011	28	31	37
June 2011	27	34	35
October 2011	20	38	38
February 2012	33	35	26
June 2013	35	35	31
January 2015	38	28	31

*Respondents who volunteered "too soon; early to tell" (no more than 6 percent in any poll) were added to those who chose the "not had an effect so far" response.

"presidents' favorable ratings typically are higher than their job approval ratings" and, for Obama, only thrice since 2009 has his favorable ratings dropped below 50 percent (Jones 2015). In sum, the fact that Obama's "favorability" ratings were higher than his approval rating while his economic stewardship was judged to be much worse than his overall performance, and even worse than his leadership of foreign affairs (Jones 2015), suggests that Americans held especially critical opinions of his economic policies and concluded that his was a record of failed leadership.

FAILED POLICY: ECONOMIC STIMULUS

Even before Obama was inaugurated, in December 2008 Larry Summers, the incoming director of the National Economic Council (NEC), wrote a memo to the president-elect. "The economic outlook is grim and deteriorating rapidly," it said, but Summers also warned Obama that the federal government was spending well beyond its means. "Since January 2007 the medium-term budget deficit has deteriorated by about $250 billion annually," the memo said. "If your campaign promises were enacted then, based on accurate scoring, the deficit would rise by another $100 billion annually. The consequence would be the largest run-up in the debt since World War II" (Lizza 2012). Thus, the new Obama administration was trapped on the "horns of a dilemma" between the need for fiscal discipline to restrain federal spending but also the need to confront economic recession with massive stimulus spending. That tension divided Obama's key economic advisers for the next two years (Lizza 2012).

A year later Obama's advisors met to ponder how to address the deep recession. Council of Economic Advisers (CEA) Chairman Christina Romer bluntly declared: "Well, Mr. President, this is your 'holy-shit moment.' It's worse than we thought" (Lizza 2009). Now the emerging consensus was that a stimulus package was needed; the only debate was on its size. Romer ran computer simulations of the probable impact of different-size stimulus packages, and her analysis indicated that the optimal fiscal stimulus should be more than $1.2 trillion (Lizza 2009). "The Job Impact of the American Recovery and Reinvestment Plan" was a report drafted by Romer in collaboration with economist Jared Bernstein. It argued that a massive economic stimulus package would keep unemployment under 8 percent, but, without it, unemployment would rise to 9 percent in 2010. However, Obama's economic team agreed that Congress would resist enacting a $1.2 trillion stimulus package, so an economic stimulus plan of that size was not even proposed (Lizza 2012). "An excessive recovery package could spook markets or the public and be counterproductive," wrote Summers (Lizza 2012).

Eventually NEC Director Summers persuaded his colleagues that a larger-size stimulus was needed (Heilemann 2009), and ultimately the Democratic-controlled Congress approved $787 billion. "People can quibble on the details," said CEA member Austan Goolsbee. "Republicans say that it should have had even more tax cuts. Others say that it should have had more infrastructure spending. But what's not under dispute is that in the first four weeks of the presidency, we passed the biggest stimulus package in American history" (Heilemann 2009). The 1,073 page American Recovery and Reinvestment Act of 2009 (ARRA) passed the House of Representatives on a 246–183 vote, with not one Republican voting yes; it was approved by the Senate on a 61–37 vote with only three Republicans voting with the majority. Congressional Republicans charged that the stimulus package was badly designed to fuel economic recovery, was a spending bonanza by Democrats on their favorite constituencies, and would saddle future generations with massive debt. "Yesterday the Senate cast one of the most expensive votes in history," said Senator Mitch McConnell (R-KY), the Senate Minority Leader. "Americans are wondering how we're going to pay for all this" (Herszenhorn and Hulse 2009).

The outrage among Republicans, conservative pundits, and the public at large might never have materialized had that massive expenditure helped bring down the unemployment rate. It did not. President Obama signed the stimulus legislation in February, but four months later unemployment was 9.4 percent, a twenty-five-year high, when the economic models derived by White House economists had promised an 8 percent unemployment rate. "At the time, our forecast seemed reasonable," observed Jared Bernstein. "Now, looking back, it was clearly too optimistic" (Blackledge and Apuzzo 2009). What followed was a highly publicized debate in the mass media, with Democratic-aligned economists defending the stimulus and Republican-leaning economists on the offensive. The Democratic argument was that the stimulus prevented the Great Recession from deteriorating into another depression, and the Obama administration alleged that the $787 billion "saved" jobs that otherwise would have been lost to the economic downturn.

Princeton economist Alan S. Blinder and Mark Zandi, chief economist with Moody's Analytics, authored a highly publicized study defending the Obama administration (Blinder and Zandi 2010). They concluded that "its effects on real GDP, jobs, and inflation are huge, and probably averted what could have been called Great Depression 2.0. For example, we estimate that, without the government's response, GDP in 2010 would be about 11.5 percent lower, payroll employment would be less by some 8 1/2 million jobs, and the nation would now be experiencing deflation" (Blinder and Zandi 2010).

But Lawrence B. Lindsey, director of the National Economic Council under President George W. Bush, strongly took issue with their economic diagnosis. Lindsey (2010) argued that the Blinder/Zandi simulation model was similar to the economic model generated by Romer/Bernstein in early 2009 when they advocated a massive stimulus package. Although the Romer/Bernstein model was criticized because it predicted that unemployment would peak below 8 percent in the middle of 2009 and decline to 7.5 percent by the end of 2010, its defenders argued that Romer and Bernstein had underestimated the severity of the Great Recession. That was true, according to Lindsey, who then compared the actual unemployment rate against three variations of the Romer/Bernstein economic simulation model: their original 2009 forecast beginning with a 7.5 percent unemployment rate; a second forecast beginning with a higher 8.2 percent unemployment rate (the actual rate in February 2009); and a third forecast beginning with a much higher 9.3 percent unemployment rate. Long-term, the predicted unemployment rates based on the 7.5 percent and 8.2 percent jobless rates were lower than the actual unemployment rate, whereas the forecast based on the 9.3 percent unemployment rate showed "the actual performance of the economy is almost exactly what Romer and Bernstein said would happen if we had done nothing, rather than passing the $800 billion package." In other words, the stimulus had no effect on joblessness.

In retrospect, while Obama's economic advisers were not blameless, their assumptions did not dovetail with the unique economic problems they faced. The Great Recession was not the ordinary garden variety of economic contraction that is caused periodically by the business cycle. During the nineteenth century and earlier, a financial panic was often the precursor to an economic depression, but recovery from that kind of economic contraction was slower and more sluggish. Reinhart and Rogoff (2009) reviewed this historical record and documented how recoveries after the bursting of financial bubbles were not V-shaped, with a decisive economic recovery, but U-shaped, where the recovery stage could take five or six years.

Another criticism was that infrastructure and public works projects cannot be implemented in the short-term. The claim by the Obama administration that a multitude of "shovel-ready" projects could be launched was pure propaganda. "I think we can get a lot of work done fast," said president-elect Obama in December of 2008 after meeting with governors. "All of them have projects that are shovel-ready, that are going to require us to get the money out the door." But that was not exactly true, as President Obama admitted in an ill-timed interview two weeks before the disastrous 2010 midterm elections. "But the problem is," said President Obama, "is that spending it out takes a long time, because there's really nothing—there's no such thing as shovel-ready projects" (Shear 2010). After its enactment, economic columnist Robert Samuelson called the stimulus package "a colossal waste" because "partisan politics ran roughshod over pragmatic economic policy." His primary concern is that too little money is spent in the short term, particularly on infrastructure (Samuelson 2009). Nearly two years later the *Economist* editorialized that "infrastructure may have been doomed to mediocrity from the start" because "even on the broadest definition of the term, infrastructure got $150 billion, under a fifth of the total" and, moreover, "hopes for an immediate jolt of activity were misplaced" since by October 2009 "even the fastest [highway and transit] programmes . . . had seen work begin on just $14.3 billion-worth of projects" (*Economist* 2010).

The other big point of contention about the $787 billion stimulus (which actually grew to $862 billion) focused on the arcane economic concept of a "multiplier" effect. In his October 2010 interview, President Obama said that for every dollar spent on infrastructure, "you get a dollar and a half in stimulus because there are ripple effects from building roads or bridges or sewer lines" (Shear 2010). What President Obama said was precisely what the original Romer/Bernstein economic simulation model had assumed, namely that the "multiplier" was 1.5 insofar as each $1 in federal spending would yield an additional $1.50 in private spending. Hard to believe, argued Harvard economist Robert J. Barro, who studied the "multiplier" effects that resulted from the massive defense spending (which equaled 44 percent of GDP) in 1943–1944 at the height of World War II. He found the wartime "multiplier" to be 0.8, and the addition of huge federal expenditures during World War I, the Korean War, and the Vietnam War only confirm its validity. If anything, Barro (2009) believed that "the war-based multiplier of 0.8 substantially overstates the multiplier that applies to peacetime government purchases."

In his February 2010 Budget Message to Congress, President Obama requested another $266 billion in "temporary recovery measures," but Congress failed to act, unable to block a GOP filibuster in the Senate. Now there was growing concern about deficit spending, given the projected $1.4 trillion budget deficit for FY09, and polls also showed that the public did not think the first $787 billion stimulus package worked. To encourage Congress to act, Vice President Joe Biden and President Obama kicked off a six-week campaign in June (so-called "Recovery Summer") to defend the stimulus and publicize the "shovel-ready" construction jobs. In Columbus, Ohio, President Obama reminded the crowd that a year ago "America was losing 700,000 jobs per month" and "we knew if we failed to act, then things were only going to get much worse" (Montgomery 2010). Republicans were not convinced, and House Minority Leader John A. Boehner (R-OH) sent President Obama a letter signed by one hundred economists explaining that 95 percent of the jobs created in May were temporary employees hired by the US Census (Montgomery 2010).

The promised "Recovery Summer" never materialized. What did materialize were triple-digit deficits of unprecedented size, and from that perspective the economic stimulus was another disaster. Its $862 billion price tag coupled with the $700 billion in financial bailouts (not to mention the $1 trillion health-care legislation) yielded a FY09 federal budget deficit that was 12 percent of GDP. The previous postwar high deficit resulted from President Reagan's 1983 budget, but it only equaled 6 percent of GDP. Beyond its failure to reduce unemployment, the economic stimulus now showcased the problem of deficits and the national debt as salient issues in the public mind. A June 2010 *Wall Street Journal*/NBC News survey asked people which statement reflected their views: (1) The president and Congress should worry more about boosting the economy even if it means bigger deficits; or (2) The president and Congress should worry more about keeping the deficit down even if it means the economy will take longer to recover. The latter was chosen by 63 percent of respondents (Hilsenrath 2010).

ECONOMIC PANDERING: TRADE POLICY

President Franklin D. Roosevelt persuaded Congress to enact the Reciprocal Trade Agreements Act of 1938. It began the modern era of "free trade" by authorizing the president to negotiate a lowering of tariffs with other countries. Economists generally agree that the severity of the Great Depression was worsened by the "protectionist" trade policies of the United States at that time (notably the Smoot-Hawley Tariff of 1930). Since then, every president of both parties has embraced free trade, including Democrats John F. Kennedy and Bill Clinton. But not Obama, whose pandering to organized labor and environmentalists sacrificed a long-standing policy that enjoyed broad support from business, economists, and the public.

It was President George H. W. Bush who signed the North American Free Trade Agreement (NAFTA) with Canada and Mexico, but Clinton had to lobby the Congress to approve NAFTA (with mainly Republican votes since most Democrats were opposed). NAFTA was arguably the pivotal event that fractured the long-standing bipartisan consensus favoring free trade (Destler 2005, 255). Unions representing the manufacturing sector were always opposed, believing that free-trade policies "shipped jobs" overseas to low-wage-paying nations, and environmental activists believed that less-developed countries would tolerate very lax environmental standards in order to attract more industry. Even before he challenged Hillary Clinton for the 2008 Democratic presidential nomination, Obama pandered to labor and environmentalists by criticizing free-trade agreements, including NAFTA, and promising to renegotiate them in order to upgrade environmental protections and labor rights.

Soon after taking office the Obama administration escalated a long-standing dispute with Mexico over NAFTA. In March 2009 President Obama signed an appropriations bill that included a prohibition of any funds from continuing a two-year-old pilot program that allowed some Mexican trucks to operate in the United States. The Teamsters Union had that provision included, arguing that Mexican trucks do not meet US safety standards. NAFTA mandated that Mexican truckers could begin operating near the US-Mexican border in 1995 and throughout the United States by 2000, but this dispute continued for many years until countries agreed to the pilot program in 2007. After Congress ended the pilot program, Mexico began slapping tariffs on US agricultural and manufactured goods. Although the 2010 appropriations bill was enacted without any prohibition on the pilot trucking program, this trade dispute remained deadlocked (Mitchell and Kiernan 2010) and was not resolved until July of 2011, when the United States and Mexico forged an agreement to allow long-haul Mexican trucks into the United States so long as they met heightened safety regulations. In exchange, Mexico began lifting their tariffs on several US agricultural goods. However, the Teamsters Union remained opposed to opening the United States to Mexican long-distance trucking.

The second administration of President George W. Bush had negotiated several free-trade agreements (FTA), including those with Peru, Panama, Columbia, and South Korea in 2007, but only the Peru deal was approved by the Democratic-controlled Congress before Bush's term ended. Congressional Democrats reneged on the other three, and President Obama took no action until October 2011, when the three pending free-trade agreements easily passed the House, now under Republican control as a result of the midterm elections, and a Senate with six more Republican Senators (Appelbaum and Steinhauer 2011). All three FTAs took effect in March of 2012.

Immediately after the 2010 midterm elections, Obama visited Seoul, South Korea, for the G-20 summit, which was scheduled to address a multitude of problems including trade. Obama had promised to renegotiate the FTA with South Korea and sign it at the G-20 summit, but US trade negotiators failed to get Korean concessions on automobiles despite Obama's hope that an agreement could be submitted to Congress. The South Korean deal "largely replicates" previous trade pacts "which cost the U.S. more than one million jobs," alleged the AFL-CIO (Youngman 2010). Soon after his return home, however, President Obama announced success in finalizing that trade pact, the largest since NAFTA. Perhaps the 2010 midterm elections coupled with the Republican takeover of the Senate majority in 2014 influenced Obama to rethink his strident opposition to free trade, either because he no longer needed to appease Congressional Democrats or because he began to assess his own historical legacy. Whatever the reason, Obama signaled his change of heart in the 2014 State of the Union Message to Congress. He argued that "when 98 percent of our exporters are small businesses, new trade partnerships with Europe and the Asia-Pacific will help them create more jobs. We need to work together on tools like bipartisan trade promotion authority to protect our workers, protect our environment, and open new markets to new goods stamped 'Made in the USA.' China and Europe aren't standing on the sidelines. Neither should we." So-called trade promotion authority, more commonly known as "fast track" trade authority, is an expedited legislative procedure that allows Congress to approve or disapprove but not to amend trade agreements negotiated by the president. The Trans-Pacific Partnership (TPP) involved twelve Latin American and Asian nations, and Obama's endorsement of the Trans-Pacific Partnership prompted an editorial from David E. Bonior (2014), former Michigan Representative and House Democratic Whip, who voted against NAFTA in 1993 and now argued that the TPP is no better.

Bonior wrote that Obama cannot "battle the plague of income inequality" because NAFTA resulted in "downward pressure on middle-class wages as manufacturing workers are forced to compete with imports made by poorly paid workers abroad." Since Bonior had been a strong union ally in Congress, his opposition would prove prophetic in this latest trade battle. In early June 2015 the House of Representatives defeated legislation to provide assistance to workers dislocated by any free-trade agreements. A vote on this package had to pass before the House could proceed with the vote on renewing "fast track" authority for Obama to complete negotiations on TPP. But the majority of House Democrats, including Minority Leader Nancy Pelosi, and some dissident Republicans joined forces to defeat the bill. Later in June, however, President Obama and Republican congressional leaders did prevail by separating "fast track" authority and worker dislocation assistance into two bills, and both easily passed the House and Senate. It was a victory for big business, agricultural interests, Hollywood, and Silicon Valley and a major defeat "for environmental groups, liberal activists, some Tea Party conservatives and, most of all, organized labor, which spent millions of dollars and used enormous organizational muscle pressuring lawmakers and trying to kill the trade measure" (Weisman 2015).

President Obama gave us the highest unemployment rate and the lowest rate of economic growth since the 1930s, also the largest deficits and national debt since World War II. Poverty has increased to levels not seen since 1967; median family income has stagnated; and income inequality has grown. The Great Recession was worse than usual, but Obama's economic stewardship was marked by failed policies that pandered to favored Democratic constituencies. The byline from the 1992 election was "it's the economy, stupid," but for 2012 it should be "identity trumps economics" because by no objective economic standard should Obama have been reelected.

WORKS CITED

American National Election Study. 2014. "User's Guide and Codebook for the ANES 2012 Time Series Study." Ann Arbor, MI, and Palo Alto, CA: University of Michigan and Stanford University. Pages 331–34. www.electionstudies.org/studypages/anes_timeseries_2012/anes_timeseries_2012_userguidecodebook.pdf. Accessed October 10.

American Presidency Project. 2015. www.presidency.ucsb.edu/data/popularity.php. Accessed August 29.

Appelbaum, Binyamin, and Eric Dash. 2011. "U.S. Debt Rating Is Cut by Agency, Citing More Risk." *New York Times*, August 6.

Appelbaum, Binyamin, and Jennifer Steinhauer. 2011. "Congress Ends 5-Year Standoff on Trade Deals in Rare Accord." *New York Times*, October 12.

Barro, Robert J. 2009. "Government Spending Is No Free Lunch: Now the Democrats Are Peddling Voodoo Economics." *Wall Street Journal*, January 22.

Blackledge, Brett J., and Matt Apuzzo. 2009. "Obama Repackages Stimulus Plans with Old Promises." Breitbart, June 8. www.breitbart.com/article.php?id=D98MPHJ80&show_article=1. Accessed June 9, 2009.

Blinder, Alan S., and Mark Zandi. 2010. "How the Great Recession Was Brought to an End." Unpublished Manuscript, July 27.

Bonior, David E. 2014. "Obama's Free-Trade Conundrum." *New York Times*, January 29.

Campbell, James E. 2009. "The 2008 Campaign and the Forecasts Derailed." *PS: Political Science & Politics*. 42 (1): 19–20.

Campbell, James E. 2012. "Forecasting the 2012 American National Elections." *PS: Political Science & Politics*. 45 (4): 610–13.

Chappell, Jr. Henry W. 1990. "Economic Performance, Voting, and Political Support: A Unified Approach." *Review of Economics and Statistics* 72: 313–20.

Clarke, Harold D., Jonathan Rapkin, and Marianne C. Stewart. 1994. "A President Out of Work: A Note on the Political Economy of Presidential Approval in the Bush Years." *British Journal of Political Science* 24: 535–48.

Congressional Budget Office. 2010. *Economic and Budget Issue Brief*: "Federal Debt and the Risk of a Fiscal Crisis." July 27.

Dennis, Brady, and Lori Montgomery. 2010. "Deficit Plan Wins 11 of 18 Votes; More than Expected, but Not Enough to Force Action." *Washington Post*, December 3.

Destler, I. M. 2005. *American Trade Politics*, 4th edition. Washington, DC: Institute for International Economics.

Dolan, Chris, John Frendreis, and Raymond Tatalovich. 2009. "A Presidential Economic Scorecard: Performance and Perception." *PS: Political Science & Politics* 42: 689–94.

Economic Report of the President 2015. Washington, DC: U.S. Government Printing Office 2015.

The Economist. 2010. "False Expectations: The Historic Infrastructure Investment That Wasn't." October 21.

Erikson, Robert. 1989. "Economic Conditions and Presidential Voting." *American Political Science Review* 83: 568–73.

Erikson, Robert S., and Christopher Wlezien. 2012. "The Objective and Subjective Economy and the Presidential Vote." *PS: Political Science & Politics* 45 (4): 620–24.

Fair, Ray C. 1988. "The Effect of Economic Events on Votes for President: 1984 Update." *Political Behavior* 10: 168–79.

Heilemann, John. 2009. "Inside Obama's Economic Brain Trust: It's Not Pretty at This Moment." *New York Magazine*, March 22.

Herszenhorn, David M., and Carl Hulse. 2009. "House and Senate in Deal for $789 Billion Stimulus." *New York Times*, February 12.

Hibbs, Douglas A. 2012. "Obama's Reelection Prospects under 'Bread and Peace' Voting in the 2012 US Presidential Election." *PS: Political Science & Politics*. 45 (4): 635–39.

Hilsenrath, Jon. 2010. "Course of Economy Hinges on Fight Over Stimulus." *Wall Street Journal*, July 26.

Investor's Business Daily. 2015. "As Obama's Economy Falls, White House Excuses Boom." May 29.

Jeffrey, Terence P. 2014. "Fed Chair: 'Deficits Will Rise to Unsustainable Levels.'" CNSNews.com. www.cnsnews.com/news/article/terence-p-jeffrey/fed-chair-deficits-will-rise-unsustainable-levels. Accessed August 24.

Jones, Jeffrey M. 2015. "Obama Approval on Issues, Favorable Rating Up." Gallup, February 18. www.gallup.com. Accessed August 28.

Kettl, Donald F. 1986. *Leadership at the Fed*. New Haven, CT: Yale University Press.

Lewis-Beck, Michael S., and Tom W. Rice. 1992. *Forecasting Elections*. Washington, DC: Congressional Quarterly Press.
Lewis-Beck, Michael S., and Mary Stegmaier. 2007. "Economic Models of the Vote." In *The Oxford Handbook of Political Behavior*, ed. Russell Dalton and Hans-Dieter Klingemann, 518–37. Oxford: Oxford University Press.
Lewis-Beck, Michael S., and Charles Tien. 2012. "Election Forecasting for Turbulent Times." PS: *Political Science & Politics* 45 (4): 625–29.
Lindsey, Lawrence B. 2010. "Did the Stimulus Stimulate?" *The Weekly Standard*, August 16.
Lizza, Ryan. 2009. "Inside the Crisis: Larry Summers and the White House Economic Team." *New Yorker* 85 (32): 80–95.
Lizza, Ryan. 2012. "The Obama Memos." *New Yorker* 87 (46): 36–49.
MacKuen, Michael B. 1983. "Political Drama, Economic Conditions, and the Dynamics of Presidential Popularity." *American Journal of Political* Science 27: 165–92.
Mayer, Thomas, editor. 1990. *The Political Economy of American Monetary Policy*. Cambridge, UK: Cambridge University Press.
Mitchell, Josh, and Paul Kiernan. 2010. "Mexico Adds Tariffs in Trucking Dispute." *Wall Street Journal*, August 17.
Montgomery, Lori. 2010. "Election-Year Deficit Fears Stall Obama Stimulus Plan." *Washington Post*, June 19.
Norris, Floyd. 2015. "A Drop in the Long-Term Unemployed." *New York Times*, July 26.
Ostrom, Charles W., and Dennis M. Simon. 1985. "Promise and Performance: A Dynamic Model of Presidential Popularity." *American Political Science Review* 79: 334–58.
Peffley, M., and J. T. Williams. 1985. "Attributing Presidential Responsibility for National Economic Problems." *American Politics Research* 13: 393–425.
PollingReport. 2015. http://pollingreport.com/obama_ad.htm. Accessed August 29.
Reinhart, Carmen M., and Kenneth S. Rogoff. 2009. *This Time Is Different: Eight Centuries of Financial Folly*. Princeton, NJ: Princeton University Press.
Roper Center for Public Opinion Research. 2015. www.ropercenter.uconn.edu.flagship. Accessed August 24.
Samuelson, Robert. 2009. "Obama's Stimulus: A Colossal Waste?" *Washington Post*, February 23.
Schneider, W. 1982. "Reaganomics Was on the Voters' Minds, but Their Verdict Was Far from Clear." *National Journal* 6: 1892–893.
Shear, Michael D. 2010. "Obama Lesson: 'Shovel Ready' Not So Ready." *New York Times*, October 15.
US Bureau of Labor Statistics. 2015. http://www.bls.gov. Accessed August 22.
US Census Bureau. 2015. http://wwwcensus.gov. Accessed August 22.
US Department of Commerce, Bureau of Economic Analysis. 2015. http://www.bea.gov. Accessed August 22.
Weisman, Jonathan. 2015. "Trade Authority Bill Wins Final Approval in Senate." *New York Times*, June 24.
Woolley, John T. 1984. *Monetary Politics: The Federal Reserve and the Politics of Monetary Policy*. Cambridge, UK: Cambridge University Press.
Youngman, Sam. 2010. "Rough Road Ahead for Obama, Unions as Compromises Loom." *The Hill*, November 13.

INDEX

ABOUT THE CONTRIBUTORS

Alan I. Abramowitz is the Alben W. Barkley Professor of Political Science at Emory University in Atlanta, Georgia. He received his BA from the University of Rochester in 1969 and his PhD from Stanford University in 1976. Dr. Abramowitz has authored or coauthored six books, dozens of contributions to edited volumes, and more than fifty articles in political science journals dealing with political parties, elections, and voting behavior in the United States. He is also one of the nation's leading election forecasters—his Time for Change Model has correctly predicted the popular-vote winner in every presidential election since 1988, including the 2012 election. Dr. Abramowitz's most recent book, *The Polarized Public: Why American Government Is So Dysfunctional*, examines the causes and consequences of growing partisan polarization among political leaders and ordinary Americans.

Andrew E. Busch is Crown Professor of Government and George R. Roberts Fellow at Claremont McKenna College, where he teaches courses on American government and politics and serves as director of the Rose Institute of State and Local Government. Busch has authored or coauthored more than a dozen books on American politics, including most recently *Truman's Triumphs: The 1948 Election and the Making of Postwar America* and *After Hope and Change: The 2012 Elections and American Politics*, along with more than thirty articles and chapters. He received his BA from the University of Colorado and MA and PhD from the University of Virginia.

Peter Juul is a policy analyst at the Center for American Progress, where he works on Middle East policy and space exploration. A graduate of Carleton College and Georgetown University, his work has appeared in *Aviation Week & Space Technology*, the *Wall Street Journal*, and *Newsweek.*

Lawrence Korb is a Senior Fellow in national security at the Center for American Progress. He has also been a fellow at the American Enterprise Institute, the Brookings Institution, and the Council on Foreign Relations, and has been on the faculty of several universities. He served on active duty for four years as a naval flight officer and retired from the naval reserve with the rank of captain. From 1981 until 1985, he was an assistant secretary of defense.

William G. Mayer is a professor of political science at Northeastern University in Boston. He is the author or co-author of ten books, including The Front-Loading Problem in Presidential Nominations and The Swing Voter in American Politics. He has written numerous articles on such topics as voting, public opinion, media and politics, and the presidential nomination process. Most importantly, he is married to Amy Logan and is the father of Natalie and Thomas.

Ruth O'Brien is a professor of political science at the Graduate Center at the City University of New York. Her publications as author include *Out of Many, One: Obama and the Third American Political Tradition* (2013), *Bodies in Revolt: Gender, Disability, and a Workplace Ethic of Care* (2005), *Crippled Justice: The History of Modern Disability Policy in the Workplace* (2001), and *Workers' Paradox: The Republican Origins of New Deal Labor Policy, 1886–1935* (1998); as editor/coauthor, *Telling Stories Out of Court: Narratives about Women and Workplace Discrimination* (2008) and *Voices from the Edge: Narratives about the Americans with Disabilities Act* (2004). She also edits the Public Square book series for Princeton University Press and the Heretical Thought book series for Oxford University Press.

John J. Pitney Jr. is the Roy P. Crocker Professor of American Politics at Claremont McKenna College. He received his BA from Union College and his PhD in political science at Yale. He is the author of *The Art of*

Political Warfare and *The Politics of Autism* and the coauthor of several books, including *After Hope and Change: The 2012 Elections and American Politics*. In addition to his scholarly work, he has held staff positions in the US Congress and the New York State Legislature. He has written articles for many publications, including the *Washington Post*, the *Wall Street Journal*, the *Christian Science Monitor*, and *Politico*.

Danielle Pletka was a longtime US Senate Committee on Foreign Relations senior professional staff member for the Near East and South Asia. In that role, she was the point person on Middle East, Pakistan, India, and Afghanistan issues. As the senior vice president for foreign and defense policy studies at AEI, Ms. Pletka writes on national security matters with a focus on Iran, weapons proliferation, the Middle East, Syria, Israel, and democratic governance. She also studies and writes about South Asia (Pakistan, India, and Afghanistan). She is the coeditor of *Dissent and Reform in the Arab World: Empowering Democrats* (2008) and the coauthor of "Containing and Deterring a Nuclear Iran" (2011) and "Iranian Influence in the Levant, Egypt, Iraq, and Afghanistan" (2012). Her most recent study, *America vs. Iran: The Competition for the Future of the Middle East* (2014).

Daniel E. Ponder is the L.E. Meador Professor of Political Science and director of the Meador Center for Politics and Citizenship at Drury University. He earned his BS at Missouri State University and his PhD at Vanderbilt University. He is the author of *Good Advice: Information and Policy Making in the White House*, and his articles on American national institutions have appeared in journals such as *American Politics Research*, *Presidential Studies Quarterly*, *Congress and the Presidency*, *Political Science and Politics*, and *International Journal of Public Administration*. He is currently completing a book on presidential leverage.

Steven E. Schier is Dorothy H. and Edward C. Congdon Professor of Political Science at Carleton College. He is the author or editor of twenty books, including the prizewinning *Panorama of a Presidency: How George W. Bush Acquired and Spent His Political Capital* (2008). He has published several scholarly articles and review essays and is the lead author of *Presidential Elections* with David Hopkins, Nelson Polsby, and

Aaron Wildavsky, now in its fourteenth edition from Rowman & Littlefield.

Raymond Tatalovich received his PhD from the University of Chicago, where he studied under Theodore J. Lowi. His areas of specialization are public policy analysis, economic policy, and the American presidency. Among his sixteen published volumes are his coauthored *The Presidency and Political Science: Paradigms of Presidential Power from the Founding to the Present* (2014) and *The Presidency and Economic Policy* (Rowman & Littlefield, 2008).

John Kenneth White is a professor of Politics at the Catholic University of America and the author of several books on the US presidency and political parties. His latest is titled *What Happened to the Republican Party? (And What It Means for American Presidential Politics).*